LANDSCAPE IRRIGATION

LANDSCAPE IRRIGATION

Design and Management

Stephen W. Smith

Chemical and Bioresource Engineering Department
Colorado State University

Aqua Engineering, Inc.
Fort Collins, Colorado

John Wiley & Sons, Inc.
New York / Chichester / Brisbane / Toronto / Singapore / Weinheim

Library of Congress Cataloging-in-Publication Data
Smith, Stephen W., 1950–
   Landscape irrigation : design and management / Stephen W. Smith.
     p.   cm.
   Includes index.
   ISBN 0-471-03824-5 (alk. paper)
   1. Landscape irrigation.   2. Irrigation engineering.   I. Title.
SB475.82.S55   1997
635.9'187--dc20   96-8028

Printed in the United States of America

10 9 8 7 6 5 4 3 2 1

PREFACE

This book is intended to be used as a landscape irrigation textbook for junior and senior level students in landscape architecture, landscape design, and turf management curricula. It is intended for students with limited starting knowledge of landscape irrigation, but a goal is to stimulate further interest in students who have irrigation design, construction, or maintenance experience with in-depth and new subjects.

The book is also designed to be a reference for others interested in landscape irrigation, including irrigation design professionals.

The names of irrigation equipment manufacturers do not appear in this textbook. Various manufacturers provide catalogs, credible performance data for their products, and a wealth of design assistance materials, such as Hazen–Williams friction factor tables. However, an important consideration is that the student not become biased toward a manufacturer or manufacturers, at least not as a result of using this textbook. It will be desirable for students using this book to have current equipment catalogs available from the major irrigation manufacturers. Manufacturer catalogs and data can be scrutinized in parallel with reading the book and homework can be assigned that uses real manufacturer data in calculations. It is also desirable for students to hear presentations from irrigation salespeople as a part of a structured course of study.

When necessary, generic (fabricated) performance data for sprinklers and valves are used in the book. All generic performance data can be found in Appendix A.

Appendix B contains hydraulic reference data suitable for all the examples found in the text, and Appendix C contains Construction Specification Institute (CSI) style irrigation specifications, which will prove useful as an overview reference and specification starting point for students.

Special thanks go to my partners at Aqua Engineering, MaryLou M. Smith, Robert W. Beccard, and Richard L. Aust for their support

v

in writing this book. They supported the effort in a very real sense through direct monetary assistance, and they supported me through several years of distraction and effort on this project. Thanks as well to Barbara Wilson and Donna Weyer for their help with the CAD-produced graphics used throughout the book.

We all have our biases, and I certainly have mine. My primary bias is exemplified by my definition of **landscape.** A landscape is an array of various plant materials, selectively picked and appropriately placed, so as to enhance and beautify the irrigation system.

With that definition, this book is begun.

CONTENTS

LANDSCAPE IRRIGATION

Introduction

■ **The goal of today's irrigation designer is to produce a system that keeps the landscape green while conserving water and keeping costs down.**

Landscape irrigation has certainly found a place in our society. Consider the wealth of aesthetically pleasing landscapes that surround us, and the fact that most of these landscapes are irrigated in order to keep them alive or to supplement natural precipitation. Much would be lost if we could not surround ourselves with irrigated parks, open spaces, trail systems, and turfed recreational facilities. Continued wise and efficient use of our water resources will, it is hoped, enable us to maintain and expand our irrigated landscapes.

Not too many years ago, the park or golf course manager's basic goal was, simply, "Keep it green." Now the goal is, "Keep it green, and don't use too much water while doing it." Water availability, coupled with rising water costs, has definitely changed our design and water management philosophies for the better.

A quick terminology "tour" of typical landscape irrigation systems is probably a good way to start a study program in landscape irrigation.

Definitions and Terminology

An **irrigation system** is the entire pipe, valve, control, monitoring, instrumentation, water emission device (sprinklers, emitters, bubblers), and related component package used to deliver water to the landscape.

A **sprinkler** is a water emission device that throws water through the air with a predictable pattern and radius. The **effective radius of throw** is the distance a sprinkler will throw and still apply 0.1 inch in an hour at the outside extent of the radius. The effective radius of throw and other performance data are found in the manufacturer's catalog or obtained from independent test facilities such as the Center for Irrigation Technology (CIT).

Every sprinkler has a **nozzle**, which is probably the smallest orifice the water flows through in a sprinkler irrigation system. The nozzle's **effective radius** and **flow** vary with pressure at the nozzle.

With most nozzles, an increase in pressure will cause the sprinkler to throw a greater distance and to flow with more water. Some sprinklers or sprinkler nozzles can have **pressure compensating devices**, which would cause the sprinklers to operate fairly consistently, even if pressure varies, because the devices hold nozzle pressure to the desired level.

A sprinkler also has an **arc**, which is established by either the mechanical setting of the sprinkler itself, or, in the case of pop-up spray sprinklers, the nozzle pattern. Arcs are said to be **full circle** or **part circle.** Fixed arcs are available in the patterns one expects most commonly—full, half, 90 degrees ($\frac{1}{4}$ arc), 120 degrees ($\frac{1}{3}$ arc), and 270 degrees ($\frac{3}{4}$ arc).

Sprinklers, overlapping and in accepted layout patterns, apply water at a given rate called the **precipitation rate** (synonymous with the rate that rain falls), which is expressed as a depth of application in one hour or inches per hour.

Sprinklers can be matched so that a quarter-circle sprinkler applies water at the same rate as a half- or a full-circle sprinkler. Nozzle families that are matched in this way are called **matched precipitation rate** nozzles. Sprinkler nozzles are also said to be "balanced" if precipitation rates are close enough to be used together on a single lateral.

Sprinklers generally apply more water near the sprinkler and less as the distance from the sprinkler increases. A **single-leg distribution rate curve** (**DRC**) shows the laboratory results of testing sprinkler performance over the distance of throw. Single-leg DRCs are appropriate for rotor sprinklers but are generally not useful for pop-up spray sprinklers. A single-leg DRC does not correctly describe the performance of a pop-up spray sprinkler, but it appears that three-dimensional data will allow improved analysis of pop-up sprays in the future.

Overlapping sprinklers should complement each other. Statistical or **uniformity parameters** can be used to compare various sprinkler-pressure-nozzle combinations in order to pick the best combination for a given circumstance. Commonly used sprinkler uniformity parameters are **Christiansen's coefficient of uniformity (CU), distribution uniformity (DU),** and **scheduling coefficient (SC).** SC has come to be most accepted and most commonly used parameter in landscape irrigation because it is an indicator of the least-watered area that correlates well with turf quality and aesthetic appeal.

Bubblers are water emission devices that tend to bubble water directly to the ground or that throw water a short distance, on the order of one foot, before water contacts the ground surface.

Drip irrigation is commonly applied in landscape shrub beds and uses water emission devices called **emitters**, which have low flow rates, on the order of 0.5 to 2 gallons per hour. Emitters are often color-coded for flow rate and are available in single-outlet or multi-outlet models. A small-diameter polyethylene or flexible PVC hose ($\frac{1}{2}$-inch or $\frac{3}{4}$-inch) wanders throughout a shrub bed, and emitters are located on the pipe and adjacent to individual plants. Small-diameter **micro-tubing** can be used, within limits, to deliver water to a point away from the emitter and closer to the desired position required to properly irrigate the plants.

A **valve** is a control device that can be opened, either automatically or manually, thereby causing water to flow. An automated valve is often called a **remote control valve**, a **solenoid valve**, an **electric valve**, or an **automated control valve.** All of these terms are synonymous and refer to a diaphragm-controlled (hydraulically-actuated) valve that is normally closed but that can be opened by applying a 24-volt AC power source to the solenoid on the valve.

A **master valve** is a single remote control valve located at the water source. This valve provides a safety feature and is opened only when other remote control valves in the system are programmed to open. Wasted water from mainline failure can be prevented, or at least min-imized, in systems that have master valves.

A **curb stop valve** is a heavy-duty, bronze ball valve that is opened or closed by rotating the handle through 90 degrees. It is often used as the main shutoff valve for the system and is located near the street curb.

Valves are generally installed in a **valve box** to protect the valves and to make it easy to locate them over time.

An **irrigation controller** is an electric panel designed to apply 24 volts AC across a given **station** on the controller in order to open a valve or valves in a programmed sequence. The sequence and time settings are programmed by the system operator. The irrigation con-troller is powered by 110-volt AC but outputs 24-volt AC power to a **terminal strip** and, hence, to valves.

A **central control system** generally runs on a microcomputer and provides program changes and rain shutdowns from a central location using radio or telephone as a communication link. The **satellite con-troller** is the basic hardware required in the field, and at individual sites, to communicate back to the central control system.

Mainline pipe is the portion of the irrigation pipe network that is pressurized all or most of the time. The mainline is the pipe network beginning at the water source and continuing downstream but upstream of the lateral remote control valve. The pipe network downstream of the remote control valve and delivering water to water emission devices is the **lateral pipe.** The lateral pipe is pressurized only when the lateral's remote control valve is open.

Irrigation systems use both metallic and plastic pipe. **Polyethylene (PE) pipe** is flexible, black pipe that comes in rolls. **Polyvinyl chloride (PVC) pipe** is rigid, white pipe that comes in 20-foot lengths. PE pipe is connected using mechanical or threaded fittings, whereas PVC pipe is connected using glued or threaded fittings.

Mainline pipe is isolated in logical subsections by **isolation gate valves. Quick coupler valves** are often located on the mainline at points where incidental water may be needed for maintenance purposes.

Sprinklers and other water emission devices can be attached to the lateral pipe using a **swing joint**, which is a series of fittings and nipples designed to move so sprinklers can be set to grade initially and moved over time. Swing joints also protect against breakage due to heavy mowing equipment. Factory-made swing joints are called **prefabricated swing joints.**

A **filter** is a device or assembly used to prevent particulate material, such as suspended solids or organics (algae, for example), from passing. Irrigation systems may have **primary filtration** at the water source and **secondary filtration** at individual laterals in the system. Whether either or both are needed is a function of the type of irrigation, the quality of the water, and the size of sprinkler or emitter orifices.

A **pressure regulator** is a device used to reduce water pressure to a desired, lower level. A pressure regulator has a **pressure falloff curve**, which describes how much water will flow through the regulator given the size of the regulator and the difference between upstream and downstream pressure.

A **pump** is a device used to boost existing pressure in a pressurized irrigation system or to create a pressure from a surface water supply. A **booster pump** is typically a centrifugal pump used to increase pressure (not flow) to the minimum appropriate to the irrigation system.

A **fertilizer injector** is a device, possibly a small diaphragm pump or a pressure differential arrangement, which is used to inject water-soluble chemicals into irrigation water at a known rate.

A **backflow prevention device** is a mechanical assembly used to prevent potentially contaminated water from flowing out of the irrigation system and back into a potable water system due to back pressure or back siphonage.

A **water meter** is a mechanical device that uses a propeller or other means to measure the volume of water flowing through the pipe per unit of time. Instantaneous flow rates can be read, and the total volume may be recorded as well. Water meters can be read manually or remotely by irrigation control systems. Some water meters may be owned by the water purveyor to be used for billing, whereas other water meters may be owned by the project owner to be used for management of water applications.

A **point of connection (POC)** is a known point, available to the contractor, from which the irrigation system will be built. The term is contractual in many instances, as it defines the contractor's starting point and the point from which the contractor can expect a minimum available flow and pressure. A common POC with landscape irrigation systems is a cap or threaded connection immediately downstream of the project's water meter.

During the winter months in freezing climates, irrigation systems are winterized from the POC and downstream by blowing air through the system using a compressor or by draining the system using **drain valves** installed at low points. When compressed air is used, the assembly designed to facilitate attachment of the compressor hose is called a **winterization assembly.**

Pressure is the inherent force of the water created by a pump or relative vertical position below a free water surface. Pressure calculations for no-flow conditions are called **static hydraulics**, whereas calculations under flowing conditions are termed **dynamic hydraulics.**

Water is generally billed according to usage, with the local purveyor delivering water for a dollar amount per 1,000 gallons or per 100 cubic feet. Some **water rate structures** are escalating, in that the unit cost goes up for each additional unit or each additional volume threshold delivered.

Water purveyors generally have an initial charge, called a **plant investment fee**, which reflects the water customer's proportional contribution to the existing infrastructure of the delivery system.

In managing irrigation systems, it is important to know the **evapotranspiration rate**, or **ET rate**, of the plant materials to be irrigated. Evapotranspiration is the evaporation from the soil surface plus the transpiration through the plant. In research, a device and monitoring system called a **lysimeter** is used to measure the ET rate using a container closed at the bottom and with the top flush with surrounding grade and planted with turf. After rainfall and irrigation applications are accounted for, daily change in the weight of the lysimeter is directly related to daily ET.

When the evapotranspiration rate and the available flow are known, the probable length of the **peak season** irrigation cycle, or **water window**, can be predicted. The water window must, in most cases, allow for peak season ET to be met during the night and include any water restrictions (such as every-third-day requirements) and downtime for maintenance.

Terminology to Avoid and Units of Measure to Use

Some irrigation terms come from field jargon, which is generally informal and inappropriate within the design professions. "Heads" may be used in lieu of **sprinklers**, "zones" in lieu of **laterals**, "circuiting" to describe **lateral layout**, and "clock" to describe the **irrigation controller**. It is preferable to adapt appropriate terms to our vocabulary so that our presentations as irrigation designers or consultants are as articulate and professional as possible.

Common units of measure utilized in landscape irrigation are found in Table 1.1.

System Components

Figure 1.1 shows a generic overview of basic components inherent in any irrigation system.

The system begins with a water source. In the case of a potable, municipal water supply, the irrigation system is afforded an inherently pressurized supply, and a pump would be needed only if pressure was deficient and needed to be boosted. If, as in the figure, the water source is a lake, canal, or other nonpressurized source, pressure is created using a pump.

Continuing downstream in Figure 1.1, note the fertilizer injector. Water-soluble fertilizers, such as urea (nitrogen), can be successfully injected into irrigation systems. This approach is quite useful in irrigated agriculture, where there are many acres of a single crop, and fertilizer is applied specific to that crop and the measured soil fertility level. In landscapes, the plant pallet frequently consists of 10 to 20 (or more) plant varieties; every plant has a fertility requirement, probably different from every other plant. The injection of an appropriate amount of fertilizer for a whole plant pallet thus becomes more difficult, if not impossible. The fertilizer rate calculations and the management issues are not trivial. Further, some fertilizers must be side dressed adjacent to the plant in any case, because they are not water-soluble. The question, then, is: Just how useful is fertilizer injection for landscape irrigation systems? Many feel that all fertilizers should be side dressed, given the

TABLE 1.1
Common English Units of Measure in Landscape Irrigation

Parameter	Typical Math Symbol	Typical English Units	Abbreviation
Flow	Q or Q_a	Gallons per minute or gallons per hour	GPM or GPH
Velocity	V	Feet per second	FPS
Precipitation Rate	PR	Inches per hour	IPH
Pressure	P or P_1 or P_3	Pounds per square inch	PSI
Evapotranspiration	ET or ET_0	Inches per day	IPD
Water Cost	n/a	Dollars per 1,000 gallons or dollars per 100 cubic feet	\$/1000 gallons or \$/100 Ft^3

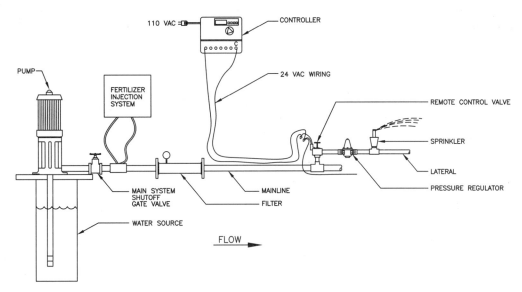

FIGURE 1.1. *A generic overview of basic components inherent in many pressurized irrigation systems. Many landscape irrigation systems use potable municipal water as a water source and a pump is not required unless pressure must be boosted.*

differing fertility requirements and the need to side dress some fertilizers in any case.

The next system component, continuing downstream in Figure 1.1, is a filter. Primary filtration with a screen or media (sand) filter is necessary with many surface water supplies and with most, or all, drip irrigation systems.

Further downstream is the lateral valve, which, in this case, is a remote control valve automated by applying 24 volts AC to the solenoid using the controller. This valve is depicted as being installed in an angle configuration. Water flows from the mainline pipe, through the valve, and then out into the lateral.

The controller is programmed electronically to open and close the valve on selected days and at selected times. Controllers need one station for each remote control valve in the system, plus extra stations for future expansion.

Downstream of the remote control valve is a pressure regulator. A pressure regulator may be required, depending on the water pressure available as compared to the water pressure required in the lateral.

Note that, as defined previously, the mainline pipe is the portion of the pipe network upstream of the remote control valve. The lateral pipe is the pipe network downstream of the remote control valve. Sprinklers, or other water emission devices, are located on the lateral pipe.

Review Questions

Describe the difference between a sprinkler arc and a sprinkler nozzle.

List the common units of measure used in landscape irrigation and provide the abbreviation.

Determine the water rate for your city and nearby cities or towns for comparison.

2

Irrigation Methods and Components

■ Ideally, an irrigation system should apply water efficiently and be easy to install, operate, repair, and maintain. There may be a number of ways to accomplish this in a given application.

There are numerous approaches to irrigating landscapes, which can be used singly, or in combination, to minimize installed cost, minimize annual water applications, or otherwise match the differences and complexity of landscapes. The ideal system applies water efficiently, is easy to repair and maintain, and is operationally simple.

This book describes several irrigation methods that are commonly used to irrigate landscapes, namely sprinkler, bubbler, and drip irrigation. Table 2.1 briefly describes and provides an overview comparison of landscape irrigation methods.

Some reasons for selecting a method, or combination of methods, for a particular project are subjective. Individual experience, manufacturer and local distributor presence, and the very arbitrary likes and dislikes of the owner or end user frequently come into play. The irrigation designer is frequently in the orchestrating position of listening, commenting, questioning, and ultimately recommending. The result of such a process is a coherent balance of the project issues.

From the strictly technical point of view, the following parameters must be understood and evaluated before appropriate irrigation methods can be ascertained:

- Soil texture and profile
- Soil infiltration rate
- Water source
- Available flow and pressure

TABLE 2.1
Comparison of Landscape Irrigation Methods

	Sprinkler Irrigration	Bubbler Irrigation	Drip Irrigation
Basic Concept	Sprinklers are patterned to fit the irregular shapes of the landscape and spaced to complement one another	Bubblers are located in planting wells or gridded in shrub beds to irrigate level basins	Emitters are located at each plant, and water drips slowly and directly to the root zone of each plant
Precipitation Rate	Medium to high	Medium to high	Very low to low
Slope Considerations	Suitable for moderate slopes	Not suitable for slopes	Suitable for many sloped situations
Unit Installed Costs	Medium to high	Medium to high	Low to medium with shrub beds, high with turf grass
Turf Application	Suitable	Not appropriate	Some line source products suitable for turf applications
Shrub Bed Application	Appropriate	Very appropriate	Very appropriate
Operating Pressure	Medium to high	Low	Very low
Water Quality Considerations	Minor concerns	Minor concerns	Filtration required, as well as periodic lateral flushing for maintenance

10

- Water quality
- Water cost
- Irrigated area
- Site grading and elevation changes over the site
- Plant material type, treatment, and placement
- Historical evapotranspiration rate and annual rainfall
- Construction budget

Ideally, a serious irrigation design effort does not really begin until each of these parameters is understood and evaluated. Data can often be obtained from other professionals working on the project, from site investigations, and from extrapolation of data or experience from other nearby sites. There is nothing wrong with making assumptions if they are clearly understood by the designer and others who will be affected by the assumptions.

Frequently, a **memorandum of design** is prepared to state factual information (such as irrigated area or soil texture), make assumptions, and submit concepts and recommendations. This approach is one of the best means of submitting ideas for comment, as the process naturally forces resolution of design issues and conflicts. Manufacturer catalog information is appropriately submitted at this time as well.

An outline example of a memorandum of design can be found in Appendix D.

Note that some of the parameters listed are a function of, or a product of, progress with landscape design. If the landscape designer and the irrigation designer are the same person, the iterations with issues occur quickly. If the landscape designer and the irrigation designer work for one firm, the process should occur expeditiously. On the other hand, if the landscape designer and the irrigation designer are not working together closely, for whatever reason, then the irrigation design is generally going to lag behind the landscape design, and time must be allowed for review and coordination.

From the mostly nontechnical point of view, the following parameters may come into play while selecting the most appropriate method:

- End user preferences, likes, and dislikes
- Designer preferences and knowledge of new technology applications, research, and product recalls or field problems
- Independent testing lab evaluation and reports
- Government-imposed regulations and laws
- Public comment and input

Cost Estimations and Cost versus Quality

Most design trades require the designer to exercise knowledge, generally through experience, of product quality versus cost. Landscape irrigation is no exception. A review of any irrigation equipment catalog will yield a full range of products. Some products are intended for residential projects and should not be used on commercial projects. Some products are designed for the extreme conditions of a sports field or golf course and are too costly for residential or commercial projects. The designer, through experience and discussions with other irrigation professionals, must select appropriate equipment for the project.

A major issue at the start of the irrigation design process is construction budget. Initial budgets clearly cannot be based on a complete design, so they are frequently based on unit irrigated areas.

Table 2.2 indicates a typical, initial cost analysis intended to provide a construction budget. In this example, the project is first broken into phases and then into irrigation approach. Specifically, the project irrigation system has drip irrigated shrub beds and sprinkler-irrigated perennial bed and turf grass.

The unit costs that one must estimate for this analysis are based on experience. From the designer's standpoint, unit costs should be conservative and influenced by judgments regarding project specifics. Rocky soil conditions, steep slopes, traffic control requirements, irrigation pipe sleeving, an onerous construction schedule, or prevailing wage rates all tend to increase the installed unit cost. Favorable soil conditions, a comfortable construction schedule, and helpful and competitive local product distributors tend to decrease installed unit costs.

With respect to sprinkler equipment, high pop-up sprinklers, stainless steel components, swing joints, and brass nozzles all increase costs.

Part-circle sprinklers increase costs as well. Typically, part-circle or full-circle sprinklers have identical installed costs, but the part-circle sprinkler irrigates only a portion of the area irrigated by a full-circle sprinkler. Hence, the unit cost for the part-circle sprinkler can be substantially higher.

TABLE 2.2
Landscape Irrigation: Opinion of Probable Construction Costs

Project Area	Landscape Treatment	Quantity	Unit Cost	Extended Cost
Phase 1	Drip irrigated shrubs	9,000 SF	$ 0.18 / SF	$ 1,620
	Pop-up Spray-irrigated turf grass	22,000 SF	0.85 / SF	18,700
Phase 2	High pop-up spray-irrigated perennials	700 SF	1.50 / SF	1,050
	Drig-irrigated shrubs	17,500 SF	0.18 / SF	3,150
	Pop-up rotor-irrigated turf grass	67,000 SF	0.35 / SF	23,450
Total Probable Cost of Landscape Irrigation				**$ 47,970**

Central control systems are usually more expensive than independent control systems, and instrumentation, such as flow meters and rain sensors, adds to construction costs.

A relatively small POC for the project increases installed unit costs because it is necessary to design the system with more laterals, and the total quantity of valves, wire, and controller stations is increased as compared to a design around a larger POC with a greater available flow.

A good practice, although not shown in Table 2.2, is to add a percentage to the total probable cost as a contingency budget for unknowns. The designer should also be alert to whether or not the irrigation construction budget is to include municipal plant investment fees, design fees, winterization the first year, startup in the first spring, one year of annual maintenance, or irrigation sleeving.

It should be noted that the accuracy of cost estimates can be improved dramatically once the irrigation system design is completed. Computer-aided drafting (CAD), in particular, affords the ability to very quickly, and as an afterthought to the design process, produce a quantity for all the assemblies in the system. Pipe quantities for the various sizes of pipe can also be produced easily. Any aspect of the design that is represented by a symbol can be counted and reported using CAD. Then, a unit cost can be attached to each assembly and each foot of pipe, the quantities and unit costs can be extended, and a probable total cost computed.

Case Studies   Consider a landfill closure and revegetation project with 30-degree slopes, low soil infiltration rates, a highly compacted subsoil, and a requirement that there be no excavation or trenching. *A solution is*: very low precipitation rate sprinklers installed on pipe networks supported by a concrete and metal superstructure to hold pipes above grade. A central control system is used to schedule irrigations precisely in accordance with recent ET rates. Sprinkler run times are short, with repeats added to avoid overland flow of water. Sensors allow for rain and high wind shutdowns. An on-site weather station allows for precise monitoring of day-to-day ET rate changes.

Consider a revegetation project needed to reestablish native plants (no turf). *A solution is*: an automated drip irrigation system. A temporary (three- to five-year life) drip irrigation system is installed on the soil surface using UV (sunlight) radiation-resistant pipes "stapled" to the earth with steel stakes. Products are selected to have a functional five-year life, but high quality is not necessary because of the short useful life of the system. The surface pipe network and other components are to be salvaged and sold, reused, or discarded after establishment. Subsurface pipe networks are to be abandoned.

Consider a prestigious office building with a high-quality turf, tree, and shrub landscape surrounding. *A solution is*: an automated combination sprinkler and drip irrigation system. Rotor sprinklers are used on large turf areas, pop-up spray sprinklers on small turf areas, high pop-up spray sprinklers on perennials (for foliage washing benefits), and drip emitters on shrub beds. Sensors allow for automatic rain, high wind, and low temperature shutdowns. High-quality, proven products are selected with design-stage input from maintenance personnel. A handheld remote control device is added to the controller so that maintenance personnel can quickly "walk through" the system looking for problems.

Consider an urban streetscape with trees in tree pits surrounded by concrete, but with metal grates covering the pit in which each tree grows. *A solution is*: an automated bubbler irrigation system. Two bubblers are located in each tree pit, with the bubblers protected from vandalism by the tree grate. The tree pit forms a level basin, so the bubblers, in their most basic form, allow the basin to quickly fill with water. (In effect, this system is a surface or flood irrigation system similar to that is used in agriculture.) Most bubblers make noise, so maintenance personnel can hear the bubblers functioning and probably see water, after or during irrigation, beneath the tree grate.

Consider a theme park with a plant pallet of more than 500 differing varieties of trees and shrubs and a requirement that irrigation cannot occur when (1) there is a fire to fight or (2) people are visiting the park. *A solution is*: an automated combination sprinkler/drip/bubbler irrigation system. Sprinklers or drip emitters or bubblers are used to discretely and precisely irrigate differentiating landscape treatments with attention to detail. Sprinklers are carefully placed or screened to prevent them from being seen. A normally closed master valve ensures that the mainline cannot flow even if a lateral valve is opened. Pressure sensors are used to cause an alarm condition if low pressure occurs (presuming a firefighting need) and landscape irrigation is terminated. Further, an alarm condition is created if flow meters indicate any flowing water during nonirrigation time periods.

Consider a sports complex with soccer, football, baseball, and softball fields having a soil that is highly amended with sand. *A solution is*: an automated sprinkler irrigation system. The sprinklers have a very low profile at the surface and rubber covers to prevent injury. Further, each sprinkler is installed on a swing joint to allow the sprinkler assembly to be pushed down in the soil by mowing equipment or athletes, thereby prevent broken pipe or injuries.

Note that in each case, the project description says "*a solution is*." Any of these projects could have other, quite suitable, irrigation solutions. As with other design disciplines, the solution is the *culmination of a process* by a designer or design team. Another designer or design team could, and will, take a different approach and still have an equally viable solution.

Dr. Jack Keller[1], a respected irrigation engineer and educator once said:

> To me irrigation system design is a game like putting a puzzle together. The purpose of the system design is to develop assemblages of individual components that will fit together to make a workable and optimized irrigation system for specific site. . . . The irrigation designers art is to know the systems which are appropriate for a given site and the order in which selected components fit together to make a system. This takes experience and a multi-disciplinary approach since there are numerous system variations to select from and the site includes both the natural and social sciences. . . . I cannot give my students a blueprint for the design process; but I can give suggestions that are helpful in the search for an image of the system and the engineering solution for achieving it. The solutions are all quite simple—after we have arrived at them.

It is helpful to now consider several major components of most landscape irrigation systems such as backflow devices and valves. Further, the water source itself is an important factor in appropriate design and equipment specification.

Backflow Prevention

Backflow prevention, cross connection, degree of hazard, contamination, liability, and public health. What do all these terms have in common? Landscape irrigation with potable water.

Most landscape irrigation projects in the United States use potable, municipal water supplies. This is good, because potable water is readily available to most projects through the water utilities infrastructure, which is financed, constructed, and maintained by others. The project owner simply pays the initial fee, often called the plant investment fee, and subsequently pays for the water used on a volume basis. Clean, pressurized water is provided to the project and that water is usually available on demand, day or night, summer or dead of winter.

There is at least one catch. The water user is generally required to install, maintain, and periodically test a device, called a **backflow prevention device**, which is designed to prevent any contaminated, and therefore nonpotable, water from flowing backward into the potable water system.

But does water flow backward? When a valve is opened in a pressurized system, water flows through the valve and "forward." So, why the concern?

---

1. Dr. Jack Keller is a Professor of Agricultural and Irrigation Engineering at Utah State University in Logan, Utah. The quote is from a speech entitled "Irrigating for Rainbows" and presented at the Sixty-first Honor Lecture in the Sciences at Utah State.

The problem is that certain circumstances, intentional or accidental, permanent or temporary, can cause water to flow backward. For example, a break in the delivery system can cause water that is downstream of the break to flow backward and toward the break. If pressure drops in the delivery system, contaminated water that is at a higher level than another outlet in the system can flow to the lower outlet.

If contaminated water does enter the potable system, the problem may be mostly aesthetic or it can actually endanger human life. Because landscape irrigation water can be mixed or injected with chemicals, such as fertilizers, herbicides, pesticides, or fungicides, landscape irrigation is considered to be a high hazard because these chemicals pose a health hazard to humans.

Definitions

By definition, **backflow** is the undesirable reversal of the direction of flow of water or other substances into the distribution pipes of the potable water supply from any source or sources caused by backpressure and/or backsiphonage. **Backpressure** is backflow caused by a pump, elevated tank, boiler, or pressure "head" in pipe, or any means that could create greater pressure within a piping system than that which exists within the potable water supply. **Backsiphonage** is the reverse flow of water, mixtures, or substances into the distribution pipes of a potable water supply system caused by negative or subatmospheric pressure in the potable water supply.

A **backflow prevention device** is equipment or means designed to prevent backflow created by backpressure, backsiphonage, or backpressure and backsiphonage acting together.

Devices

Backflow prevention, under high hazard circumstances, may be accomplished with any of the following methods:

- An air gap
- A reduced pressure principle backflow prevention assembly
- A pressure vacuum breaker backflow prevention assembly
- An atmospheric vacuum breaker backflow prevention assembly

Each approach has specific applications, criteria, and requirements.

An **air gap**, as shown in Figure 2.1, is an unobstructed vertical distance of twice the diameter of the supply pipe between the lowest portion of the supply pipe and the overflow rim of the container or vessel. Clearly, this approach is very simple and low-cost. However inexpensive and effective it may be, a distinct disadvantage with the air gap is that all inherent pressure from the supply system is lost and a pump must be used to recover the pressure needed for landscape irrigation.

The **reduced pressure principle device**, or RP device, as shown in Figure 2.2, is composed of two internally loaded check valves with

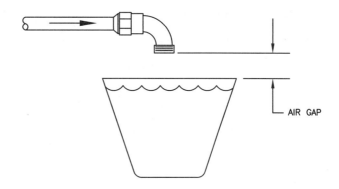

FIGURE 2.1. *An air gap is one of the least expensive and most effective means of preventing backflow. However, any inherent pressure available for the irrigation system is lost with this approach.*

AIR GAP

a mechanically independent, pressure-dependent relief valve between and below the check valves. The differential pressure relief valve is designed to maintain a pressure between the check valves of at least two pounds per square inch (PSI) lower than the upstream supply pressure. The RP device is intended to protect against either backpressure or backsiphonage. The device can be installed below sprinklers or other water emission devices, but the device must be installed above grade, or otherwise with suitable positive drainage, so that the relief valve is never submerged.

A **pressure vacuum breaker device**, or PVB device, is shown in Figure 2.3. It consists of an internally loaded check valve and a loaded air inlet opening between two resilient-seated shutoff valves and test cocks. The device is not intended to respond to backpressure and must therefore be located at least one foot above all sprinklers or other water emission devices.

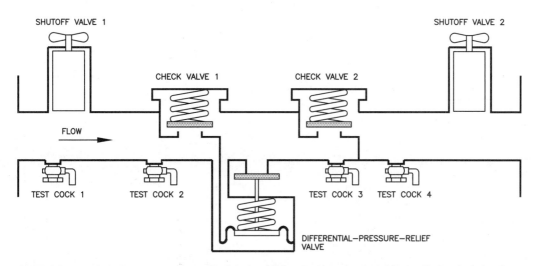

FIGURE 2.2. *A reduced pressure (RP) principle backflow device uses two internally loaded check valves with a mechanically independent, pressure-dependent relief valve between and below the check valves.*

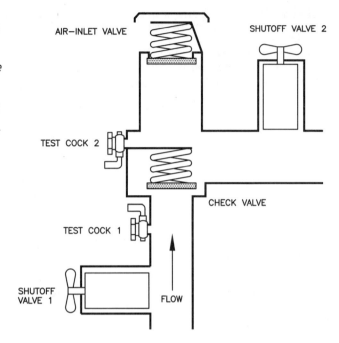

FIGURE 2.3. *A pressure vacuum breaker (PVB) is relatively low-cost, as compared to a reduced pressure principle device, but a properly installed device must be installed one foot above the highest water emission point in the system. A PVB consists of an internally loaded check valve and a loaded air inlet opening between two resilient-seated shutoff valves and test cocks.*

An **atmospheric vacuum breaker device**, or AVB device, is shown in Figure 2.4. It is composed of a float–operated air inlet valve, which admits air whenever the pressure in the unit drops to zero. The device is not intended to be pressurized continuously, so there can be no downstream valve of any type that would keep the unit under continuous pressure. In landscape irrigation, this requirement translates to one device for each lateral in the system, so although one device is rather inexpensive, the total system cost can easily be high. When used,

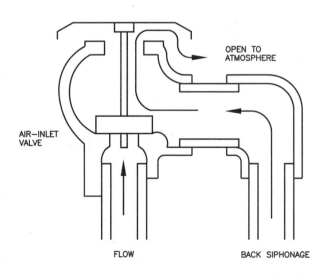

FIGURE 2.4. *An atmospheric vacuum breaker (AVB) device is composed of a float-operated air inlet valve, which admits air whenever the pressure in the unit drops to zero. An AVB cannot be pressurized continuously, so, although it is inexpensive one must be installed on every lateral in an automated system, and it is difficult to aesthetically hide so many backflow devices in the landscape.*

the device must be installed six inches above all sprinklers or other water emission devices.

As to equipment cost, the RP device is the most costly but also the most flexible in application. The PVB device is substantially lower in cost than the RP device, but must be installed at the high point in the irrigation system. And the AVB is the least expensive of these three devices, but one must be installed on every lateral in the system and the device must be six inches above grade. Because of the constraints noted, the AVB is seldom used with landscape irrigation systems.

Further, there are pressure loss differences to consider with these devices. An RP device experiences the highest pressure loss because of the manner in which the device functions. Most RP backflow devices have a loss of approximately 12 PSI. All other devices have a lesser loss, which is associated with the flow through the device. The pressure loss is higher at high flow rates and lower with low flow rates.

In the past, another device, called a double check valve backflow prevention assembly, was used in landscape irrigation. This device is not suitable for high hazard conditions so it is not discussed here, as it is inappropriate for landscape irrigation.

Selection of the appropriate backflow prevention device often takes some contemplative effort to make the best choice. For example, a designer might initially elect to use an RP device, but later choose to use a PVB in order to minimize pressure losses in the system and avoid a booster pump. Experience with the devices and iterations with alternatives for real projects are invaluable with the decision process.

The Cold Climate Situation

A dilemma exists for cold climate situations, where freezing temperatures mandate that the backflow prevention device be protected. The device must be insulated or heated, or the water removed from the device, during winter months. Ideally, the backflow device is winterized with compressed air at the same time the entire irrigation system is winterized. This means that a connection point must be provided upstream of the backflow device so that air can be passed through the device to remove water or otherwise drain the device. But this upstream connection is, in fact, another cross connection—specifically, an unprotected cross connection. This dilemma is dealt with in different ways in different locales.

One practical approach is to allow a small-diameter (say, $\frac{1}{4}$-inch) connection just downstream of the main shutoff valve for the irrigation system. This connection should be installed in a valve box and marked with its purpose. Once a year, an air compressor hose is connected and the water blown out of the device. It is preferable that tools be required to make the connection, as opposed to equipping the winterization point with a quick coupler valve. A quick coupler might be too easily used for other, contrary purposes.

For small pipe systems of less than two inches, an alternative is to use a **stop and waste valve.** A stop and waste valve allows downstream water to drain out through a small port in the side of the valve when the valve is closed. Note that the waste port is also, technically, an unprotected cross connection. A gravel sump should be provided in sufficient size to receive all the drain water. As a practical example of a stop and waste valve used as a primary shutoff valve and a backflow prevention assembly, see Figures 2.5 and 2.6.

Figure 2.5 shows a **stop and waste valve assembly**, which consists of the valve itself, typically located below the frost line, and an access sleeve, which itself is accessed via a valve box. A **valve key**, approximately eight feet long, is used to open or close the valve by rotating the handle 90 degrees. Gravel must be used to form a sump around the stop and waste valve, and is also used for cosmetic appearances in the valve box. Bricks add stability to the valve box assembly. Note that the pipe in this part of the irrigation system is often copper.

The **backflow prevention assembly**, which is downstream of the stop and waste valve assembly, is shown in Figure 2.6. The concrete pad and enclosure noted in the figure are optional. The concrete pad adds stability to the assembly as a whole, while the enclosure helps prevent vandalism.

This particular assembly shows a flow meter installed on the vertically rising, upstream pipe coming to the backflow device. A growing number of control systems are capable of taking pulses from a flow meter as an input. A flow meter is generally located a minimum of 10 pipe diameters upstream and 5 pipe diameters downstream of a fitting or any other component that would cause flow turbulence. Each water

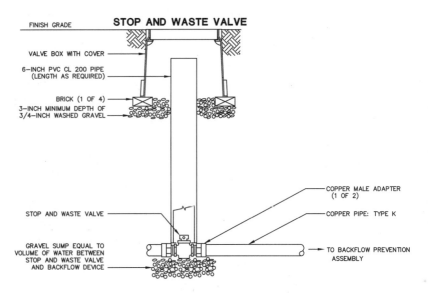

FIGURE 2.5. *A stope and waste valve allows water in the downstream pipe to drain through a small port on the side of the valve when the valve is closed. These valves are frequently used as the primary shutoff valve for the system. Many systems are winterized at the end of the season from the stop and waste valve and on downstream.*

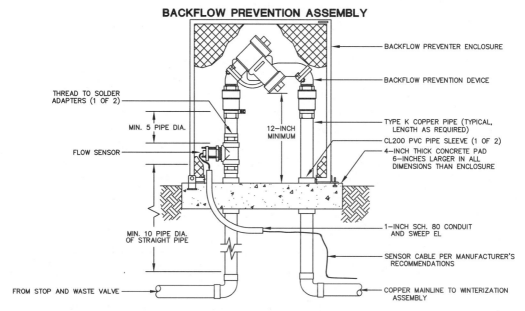

BACKFLOW PREVENTION ASSEMBLY

FIGURE 2.6. *A backflow prevention assembly is generally installed above grade. The assembly can be protected by an enclosure and a concrete pad. This assembly indicates a flow meter on the vertically rising portion of the upstream pipe. The flow sensor provides instantaneous and totalized flow readings back to the control system for management purposes.*

meter manufacturer will have specifications that apply specifically to its equipment regarding turbulence, installation practices, wiring, outputs, and related items. The manufacturer's specific recommendations and requirements should be researched and adopted in the design.

The backflow prevention assembly may be the only irrigation component other than the controller that is above ground. Most or all of the pipe, valves, sprinklers, and other components and devices are at grade or below grade. Early or late in the irrigation season, ambient temperatures can drop below freezing. The equipment in the ground is fine because, presumably, the ground is not frozen and a short-term drop in ambient temperature is not sufficient to freeze equipment that is protected and insulated by the soil. The backflow prevention assembly, however, is exposed and subject to freezing. There are several solutions, including: (1) draining the system down when freezing temperatures are anticipated so that there is no water standing in the backflow prevention assembly, (2) insulating the backflow prevention assembly against short-term cold, and (3) heating the enclosure. The third option is the most expensive, and also requires that 110 VAC power be available, but this solution is also the most flexible.

Governing Authorities

Who are the authorities that are developing and enforcing the ordinances, manuals, and review procedures on backflow prevention in landscape irrigation? At the state level, the state health department probably has a manual. Municipalities may simply require that local landscape irrigation projects adhere to the state health department's manual. Alternatively, the municipality may have its own manuals, ordinances, and procedures to provide direction and enforcement. In either case, most municipalities use building inspectors to watch for correct procedures, equipment, and applications.

Approval of devices and applications is provided by a 46-year-old organization called the Foundation for Cross-Connection Control and Hydraulic Research (FCCC&HR) at the University of Southern California. This noteworthy organization tests, evaluates, and approves devices for use. Most governing authorities require that the backflow device be approved by FCCC&HR.

The Future

The landscape irrigation industry can expect to see increasing emphasis on backflow prevention and cross connection control in the future, especially with regard to enforcement. Many irrigators, such as school districts and parks departments, are already taking steps to replace backflow prevention devices that have been incorrectly placed or applied in the past.

Testing will continue to be an issue. How municipalities will implement (and enforce) annual testing is a concern to yet be resolved.

Water Source Alternatives

Only 1 percent of the world's water is fresh. Ninety-nine percent of the fresh water is underground. As it becomes more expensive to develop and deliver groundwater supplies, treat and deliver surface water, desalt sea water, and so on, the conservation and efficient use of all available water resources becomes increasingly important. Effluent or wastewater supplies are often "there for the taking," and more golf courses and other large landscape projects are looking closely at reclaimed water with envy, not trepidation.

The use of reclaimed effluent will increasingly be a viable approach for mitigating or, in some cases, solving water shortages. Reclaimed effluent is undoubtedly here to stay. Therefore, those of us in the landscape irrigation industry need to learn to properly use and manage reclaimed municipal effluent.

Why Consider Recycled or Reclaimed Effluent Water?

The various circumstances surrounding reclaimed water are as numerous as there are state governments and administrating agencies. Each project probably has a new set of constraints and variables to be addressed.

In general, effluent sources are considered and evaluated because:

- They are probably less expensive.
- They may not be subject to the rigorous restrictions placed on potable supplies during a drought.
- The use of reclaimed effluent may be mandated by government entities.
- The use of effluent is generally viewed as an environmentally sound practice.
- Potable sources may be limited in quantity, restricted in practice, or increasing in cost.

As to cost, potable supplies in some areas are being charged on an **escalating rate structure.** This means that the last unit of water used is higher in cost than the first unit. The water users with the highest annual volume requirements then have the higher bills and the most incentive to look hard at alternatives to potable water.

Changing from Potable to Effluent Water

There may be very little involved in making the change from, say, potable water to reclaimed effluent. The newer irrigation systems may already have the sprinklers, valves, and other components that are suitable for effluent. Otherwise, consideration must be given to changing equipment, and this need often dictates a general upgrade in the irrigation system. Most irrigation systems constructed 15 or more years ago need to be upgraded because they are beyond their useful life expectancy.

If the irrigation equipment is suitable, and if the flow and pressure from the effluent source are equal to or greater than the flow and pressure from the existing source, the physical switch can be as simple as disconnecting from one source and connecting to the other.

Any cross-connection between the previous water supply and the effluent water supply must be corrected. A physical disconnect must be made and maintained. If an existing tap is to be abandoned, some water purveyors will require that the tap be cut and plugged at the point where it connects to the purveyor's distribution system.

One complication can be the primary delivery system—the pipe system delivering water to the project. Although it may be more common in the future, very few locales currently have both potable and effluent delivery systems. The end user may be responsible for providing or extending the effluent delivery system to the project.

Permitting should not be overlooked. Depending on the project and the locale, state or local agencies will have application, permit, and annual reporting requirements that must be met.

Water Quality

Certain water quality measurements, available from the effluent provider or made by a commercial laboratory, are needed to determine the suitability of any water for irrigation. These measurements include:

- Electrical conductivity (Ec_w) in dS/m or mmhos/cm (numerically equivalent units)
- Total dissolved solids (TDS) in mg/L
- Cations and anions in mg/L
  - Sodium (Na^{2-})
  - Calcium (Ca^{2+})
  - Magnesium (Mg^{2+})
  - Chloride (Cl^-)
  - Carbonate (CO_3^{2-})
  - Bicarbonate (HCO_3^-)
  - Sulfate (SO_4^{2-})
- pH
- Boron in mg/L

Additional parameters must be evaluated to determine the suitability of reclaimed municipal wastewater for irrigation:

- Nutrients:
  - Nitrate-nitrogen (NO_3-N)
  - Ammonia-nitrogen (NH_3-N)
  - Organic-nitrogen (Org-N)
  - Potassium (K)
  - Total nitrogen (N)
  - Ortho-phosphate-phosphorus (PO_4-P)
  - Total Phosphorus (P)
- Residual chlorine (Cl_2 in mg/L)
- Trace elements

The **sodium absorption ratio** (SAR) must be calculated to fully analyze and understand a water sample. SAR is an indicator of the probable influence the sodium ion has on soil properties.

The project consultants, as well as the irrigation manager, need to be familiar, or become familiar, with water quality parameters and their importance. Some change in effluent water quality during the year and/or over the lifetime of the project can be expected, so vigilance is also necessary.

Irrigation Equipment

The differences between irrigation components that are suitable for only potable water versus effluent water are not particularly dramatic. Contamination-proof valves are desirable and possibly necessary. High-grade plastic is probably preferable to metal, unless the metal is epoxy-coated. Larger nozzles are preferable to small nozzles when the water source contains suspended solids.

The requirements for pumps, filters, pressure relief valves, control components, and related items are generally identical, regardless of the water source. High quality with all these components is necessary.

Some administrative agencies now require the use of color-coded components (valve box lids, pipe, quick coupler covers) in irrigation systems using effluent water. Purple is the required color. Additionally, valve boxes may need an advisory stamped into the lid, and warning tape may be required in the trench above pipe networks.

Many new irrigation systems are designed and built with the appropriate components to cover the contingency or the eventuality that effluent will become the water source in the future. This makes particularly good sense when the cost differences between equipment suitable for effluent and equipment that is risky or marginal for effluent usage.

Irrigation System Hydraulics for Changeovers

If the future flow and pressure from the effluent source are not equal to those from the previous source, then piping changes may be necessary. Some irrigation systems use loops within the mainline. The best way to understand complex loops is to model them using a hydraulic modeling program. The model can then be used to better understand the sensitivity of the existing pipe network to changes in the available flow and pressure from the source.

When the available flow from the effluent is greater than the previous available flow, it is common to find that replacement of some portion of the existing mainline with a larger pipe size is desirable.

A Successful Case Study in a Golf Course Project

A new reclaimed water irrigation system was designed and constructed for the Ken McDonald Golf Course, a 130-acre municipal golf course in Tempe, Arizona. The new irrigation system was designed using the latest water management and energy conservation technology available. To facilitate the use, function, and efficiency of the many water management components installed, initial software programming, scheduling, and pump sequencing were provided by the design engineers. A weather station was included to meet the exact daily water requirement for the turf based on the modified Penman equation (see Chapter 9) for ET_0 (reference evapotranspiration).

The design effort at the golf course included three separate irrigation systems. A potable water irrigation system was designed adjacent to residential backyards to create a buffer zone from the golf course's reclaimed-water irrigation system. A bubbler irrigation system was designed to provide separate control and management for all trees on the golf course. The main golf course system was designed with almost 2,000 valve-in-head sprinklers and 56 satellite controllers. A hydraulic model was used to optimize the mainline pipe size and provide uniform mainline operating pressure. Low-pressure, large-radius sprinkler nozzles were selected to provide a large droplet size, minimizing wind drift and evaporation, and to reduce energy requirements at the pump stations.

The main golf course system was designed with valve-in-head sprinklers, with each sprinkler controlled by a separate valve. The buffer zone (potable water) system was designed as a "block type" control system that uses matched precipitation rate sprinklers grouped on a common valve. All the sprinklers were designed and placed to allow precise, uniform application of the irrigation water requirement. Valve control zones were grouped by precipitation rate, but in addition, each zone was also grouped based on exposure, location type (i.e., greens, tees, fairways), and slope.

The complete golf course irrigation design includes 1,055 separate valve control zones. Each valve-in-head sprinkler is equipped with a pressure regulating valve to assure operation at the design pressure of 60 PSI. The sprinkler precipitation rate was calculated for each of the 1,055 valve control zones based on irrigated areas and flow rates. After construction were completed, the precipitation rate data were updated based on the as-built information furnished by the irrigation contractor.

Initial control system programming was provided for each of the 1,055 control zones to apply the peak season irrigation water requirement within a nine-hour (nighttime) irrigation window. An on-site weather station allows for the global adjustment of water applications based on the specific daily ET requirement. The software also allows each control zone to be fine-tuned for soil type, exposure, slope, turf condition, and so on without overwatering or underwatering any adjacent areas.

During the construction, the design engineers worked with the irrigation contractor to ensure that the irrigation installation met the intent of the design. The contractor assisted the designer with the staking and placement of individual sprinklers on the golf course. Weekly meetings were held with the owner, the engineer, and contractor to ensure good communication and minimize construction problems.

The Future

Reclaimed municipal effluent is no panacea because of unique operational constraints, design constraints, and new management criteria imposed on irrigation managers; but, given rising potable water costs and other benefits, effluent water is definitely a viable irrigation alternative.

Economic Life of an Irrigation System

Any equipment or system is subject to obsolescence. Irrigation systems are most commonly thought to have an **economic life** of 10 years, but the **useful life** may be much longer. The primary system components that contribute to obsolescence are control components and water emission devices.

As an example, sprinkler manufacturers work toward better nozzles with improved performance. Improved performance probably means that a reduction in water applications is possible because application efficiency is improved. Reduced water applications implies water savings. Water savings can pay for the cost of improvements. A public agency often looks at a 10-year payback of an investment as being acceptable.

Control systems offer some of the best opportunity for quick capital payback. Adding a low-cost rain sensor to a controller may pay for itself when the first significant rainfall occurs after the sensor is installed.

The useful life of an irrigation system can be extended for so long that it becomes problematic to the owner, and even to the public. An old, inefficient system may apply water so poorly and require so much additional water application that waterborne herbicides and pesticides can be washed into an ecosystem.

It is clear that the liability to the owner of an outdated, inefficient irrigation system can become an issue.

Valves and Valve Assemblies

Valves offer the primary means of hydraulic control in irrigation systems. They are used manually to close off the entire system or some portion of the system. They are used automatically, and operated from the programmed controller, to allow fully automated irrigation.

Consider valves from the start or POC of the irrigation system, working downstream along the mainline.

The first valve may actually be the **water purveyor's valve**; it may require a special valve box key or valve key to fit and operate the valve itself. This valve is equipped in this way so that unauthorized persons cannot open or close it. Typically, this valve is used only by the water purveyor when service is required within its system or when the water bill has not been paid by the customer.

The next valve downstream is generally the **primary shutoff valve** for the entire system. A curb stop ball valve is generally used. It may be a stop and waste valve as depicted in Figure 2.5 and as described previously. This valve, being below the frost line, is the valve that would be closed throughout the winter months when the irrigation system is winterized and not in use.

The next valve downstream may be a part of the backflow prevention assembly. Some backflow devices require upstream and downstream valves, adjacent to the device itself, for testing purposes. This valve can also be used to shut off the irrigation system for maintenance and, being above grade, it is easily accessed if the backflow assembly is not in an enclosure.

Isolation gate valves, such as that depicted in Figure 2.7, are generally the next valves in the system. It is not necessary that irrigation

FIGURE 2.7. *An isolation gate valve is used on the irrigation system mainline to isolate portions of the irrigation system for maintenance purposes. Some irrigation systems do not need or warrant isolation gate valves. If used, the number and placement are subjective. Normally, the valve is sized identically with the mainline pipe on which it is located.*

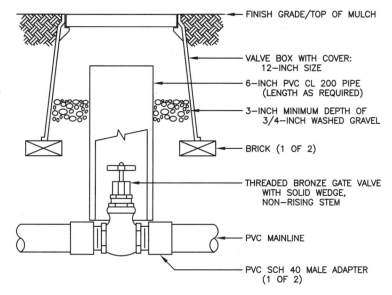

FINISH GRADE/TOP OF MULCH

VALVE BOX WITH COVER: 12-INCH SIZE

6-INCH PVC CL 200 PIPE (LENGTH AS REQUIRED)

3-INCH MINIMUM DEPTH OF 3/4-INCH WASHED GRAVEL

BRICK (1 OF 2)

THREADED BRONZE GATE VALVE WITH SOLID WEDGE, NON-RISING STEM

PVC MAINLINE

PVC SCH 40 MALE ADAPTER (1 OF 2)

systems have isolation gate valves, but larger systems have them so that some portion of the irrigation mainline can be closed off for maintenance purposes. These valves are most often manually actuated. Good-quality valves that seal tightly and do not experience water "flow by" or leakage are important.

Figure 2.8 shows a depiction of a large irrigation system having a POC and five isolation gate valves on the mainline pipe. Any of the five valves in this example affords the opportunity to isolate a substantial portion of the irrigation system.

The question of how many isolation gate valves to use is a judgment on the part of the irrigation designer and, preferably, the manager or operator. The tradeoffs in the decision are cost versus maintenance flexibility. Some smaller irrigation systems may have only two isolation gate valves, one for each plus-or-minus "half" of the system.

Continuing downstream on the mainline, the next valve frequently encountered is the **quick coupler valve.** Quick coupler valves are manually actuated and suitable for incidental water demands around the site. In a way, quick couplers are a "tap" into the mainline. Exact placement is, again, a subjective decision on the part of the design or maintenance person. These valves can be added or removed over time. Basically, the quick coupler valve is situated at any convenient location along the mainline where incidental water may be required or desired.

Figure 2.9 shows a quick coupler valve on a swing joint and inside a valve box. The valve box is optional; some would prefer that the top of the quick coupler be installed at or somewhat above grade with no valve box. A stake is often used to stabilize the quick coupler and prevent the assembly from becoming canted from hoses being pulled.

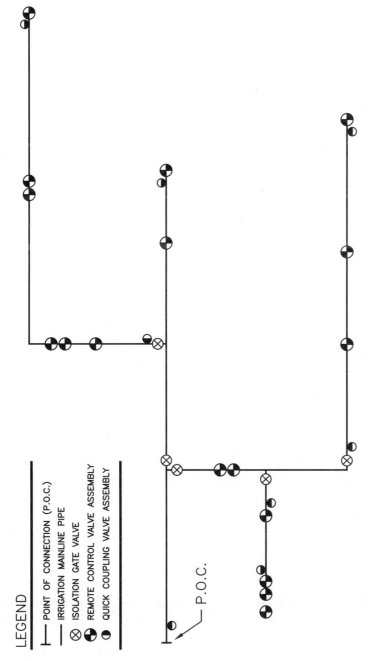

LEGEND

— POINT OF CONNECTION (P.O.C.)

— IRRIGATION MAINLINE PIPE

⊗ ISOLATION GATE VALVE

REMOTE CONTROL VALVE ASSEMBLY

QUICK COUPLING VALVE ASSEMBLY

P.O.C.

FIGURE 2.8. A mainline routing concept, which shows several different types of valves, including isolation gate valves, quick coupler valves, and remote control valves.

FIGURE 2.9. *A quick coupler valve assembly. It is good practice to provide a swing joint with a quick coupler. A swing joint allows the entire assembly to be set to grade at the time of construction and to be moved up or down over time. This assembly is shown to be stabilized with a stake secured with gear clamps.*

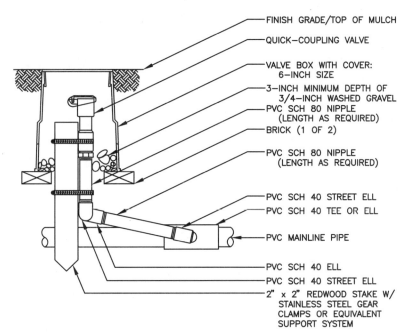

FINISH GRADE/TOP OF MULCH

QUICK–COUPLING VALVE

VALVE BOX WITH COVER: 6–INCH SIZE

3–INCH MINIMUM DEPTH OF 3/4–INCH WASHED GRAVEL

PVC SCH 80 NIPPLE (LENGTH AS REQUIRED)

BRICK (1 OF 2)

PVC SCH 80 NIPPLE (LENGTH AS REQUIRED)

PVC SCH 40 STREET ELL

PVC SCH 40 TEE OR ELL

PVC MAINLINE PIPE

PVC SCH 40 ELL

PVC SCH 40 STREET ELL

2" x 2" REDWOOD STAKE W/ STAINLESS STEEL GEAR CLAMPS OR EQUIVALENT SUPPORT SYSTEM

Quick couplers come in $\frac{3}{4}$-inch, 1-inch, and $1\frac{1}{2}$-inch sizes and are available with different colored covers to indicate potable versus effluent water. Covers can have a lock if desired. Both quick couplers and quick coupler keys are manufactured of metallic materials.

It is good to locate quick couplers near other equipment and valve boxes or near physical features of the site that allow the valves to be found easily. Figure 2.8 depicts quick coupler valves on the irrigation system mainline at points throughout a site. Maintenance personnel may opt for a criterion that dictates a maximum distance between quick couplers; two 50-foot hose lengths or 100 feet, for example, would ensure that exceptionally long hose lengths are not required.

A key is used to open a quick coupler valve. The key usually has a swivel on the top so that hose can be directed in a 360-degree arc around the valve and not kink in the process. A manual valve on the key itself is desirable to allow for on–off operation without removing the key and for controlling flow.

Quick couplers are often used near ball field infields to add water to the infield soil before play. They are often found near sidewalks or entryways to allow for washing of hard surfaces. Quick couplers may also be placed near perennial plantings to provide for incidental washing or watering of plants. Quick couplers have also been used to provide short-term water for establishment of dry land grasses or native plant materials. The quick couplers can be salvaged and used elsewhere when the buried pipe is abandoned in place.

The next, most important valve in the system, and necessary valve in almost all irrigation systems is the **lateral valve**, which is also called a **remote control valve** when the system is automated. A remote control valve is depicted in Figure 2.10. Remote control valves are also referred to as **solenoid valves** and **automated electric valves**—all three terms are synonymous.

Some features of the remote control valve assembly are important. The valve itself, as shown in the figure, can be installed in either a "globe" or "angle" configuration. The figure shows the globe configuration, with a plug used on the bottom inlet, of the valve. Alternatively, the plug can be situated in the other inlet, and the nipple rising vertically from the mainline can be threaded directly into the bottom inlet of the valve.

Note the hydraulic performance data for a remote control valve in Appendix A. The loss in PSI can be determined by selecting the flow rate through the valve and reading the loss data in the correct valve size column. For example, a 1-inch valve flowing at 20 GPM has a pressure loss of 2.5 PSI.

For a given size valve, the manufacturer infers a maximum or minimum flow rate when loss data are discontinued. In the 1-inch valve, a flow of 75 or 100 or greater GPM would not be desirable. Similarly, a flow of one GPM is too little.

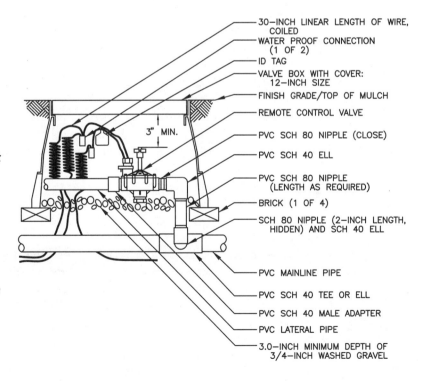

FIGURE 2.10. A remote control valve assembly. Some solenoid valves are manufactured so that they can be installed in either a globe or an angle configuration. There is less pressure loss through the valve when the angle configuration is utilized. All connections between the valve and the 24 VAC wiring should be completed with waterproof wire connectors.

30-INCH LINEAR LENGTH OF WIRE, COILED
WATER PROOF CONNECTION (1 OF 2)
ID TAG
VALVE BOX WITH COVER: 12-INCH SIZE
FINISH GRADE/TOP OF MULCH
REMOTE CONTROL VALVE
PVC SCH 80 NIPPLE (CLOSE)
PVC SCH 40 ELL
PVC SCH 80 NIPPLE (LENGTH AS REQUIRED)
BRICK (1 OF 4)
SCH 80 NIPPLE (2-INCH LENGTH, HIDDEN) AND SCH 40 ELL
PVC MAINLINE PIPE
PVC SCH 40 TEE OR ELL
PVC SCH 40 MALE ADAPTER
PVC LATERAL PIPE
3.0-INCH MINIMUM DEPTH OF 3/4-INCH WASHED GRAVEL
3" MIN.

The pressure loss data found in any irrigation equipment manufacturer's catalog are provided for fully open valves. The pressure loss increases as the flow control on the valve is closed.

Refer again to the remote control valve performance data in Appendix A. Assume that a lateral has a flow rate of 15 GPM. Fifteen GPM is not shown in the left column, but 10 GPM and 20 GPM are. A **straight-line interpolation** can provide the required data as follows:

$$20 \text{ GPM} - 10 \text{ GPM} = 10 \text{ GPM}$$

$$2.5 \text{ PSI} - 2.2 \text{ PSI} = 0.3 \text{ PSI}$$

$$\frac{0.3}{10} = \frac{X}{5}$$

$$X = \frac{0.3(5)}{10} = \frac{1.5}{10} = 0.15 \text{ PSI}$$

$$2.2 \text{ PSI} + 0.15 \text{ PSI} = 2.35 \text{ PSI}$$

So, the approximate pressure loss for a 15 GPM flow rate is 2.35 PSI.

Some remote control valves can be installed in either a globe or an angle configuration. In a globe configuration, the inlet and outlet are more or less in line with one another. In an angle configuration, the inlet is on the bottom of the valve and the outlet is on the side. Some valves offer either configuration, and a plug is installed in the inlet that is not used. Angle configurations experience less pressure loss due to the less turbulent way water passes through the valve.

All remote control valves should allow for flow control by virtue of the valve handle depicted on the top of the valve. Although some low-cost remote control valves are manufactured without a flow control, they should be avoided. Flow control allows for fine tuning of the lateral operating pressure by using the flow control to create additional pressure loss across the valve. There is no easier or less expensive way to provide this flexibility.

Some maintenance people prefer that the remote control valve have unions, both upstream and downstream, to assist in valve removal. Further, some prefer a manually actuated valve at each solenoid valve to avoid pressuring down the mainline for valve repair or replacement. Both of these features in the assembly are nice for purely maintenance purposes, but both add substantially to cost.

Gravel is placed under and around the valve for both practical and aesthetic purposes. When some valves are opened manually, using the manual bleed on the top of the valve, water flows through a port on the side of the valve and out into the valve box. Gravel provides a sump for the water. Gravel also provides a neat, finished appearance to the overall valve assembly.

From the electrical perspective, note that the wires are connected by a waterproof connector and coiled to allow for wire expansion and maintenance. When excess wire is used in this way, the top of the valve, or bonnet, can be removed for maintenance without affecting the wire or the valve's solenoid.

Remote control valves are located throughout an irrigated site near the laterals associated with the valve. It may be desirable to group two or three remote control valves together for ease in finding the valves or, potentially, to group multiple valves in one valve box. A disadvantage of grouping multiple valves in a single valve box is that maintenance problems can be exacerbated if the valves are physically too close to allow comfortable room to work.

Remote control valves, as well as other valves, should never be located in low spots, in the landscape. Valve leakage, valve sticking, and mainline failure all result in excess water flowing to low spots, and valve boxes filled with water or even covered by standing water add substantially to maintenance problems.

What if a remote control valve, even when installed in a valve box, disappears into the landscape over time? There are several ways to locate lost, buried equipment. One is to refer to the irrigation as-built or record drawings, where equipment can be located with two measurements from fixed locations on the site. This assumes that the as-built drawing was, in fact, produced and can be found. The second way is to put an electronic signal on the control wire going to the valve, and then track the route of the wire to the valve where it terminates.

Review Questions

Determine the probable pressure loss through a $1\frac{1}{2}$-inch remote control valve flowing at 60 GPM. Use the generic performance data in Appendix A.

Familiarize yourself with the drawing of a site and conceptualize the irrigation approach for the various areas considering the size and shape of the area as well as planting treatment.

List the backflow prevention devices that are suitable for high-hazard situations and contrast the differences in installation approach, pressure loss, and cost.

3

Design Techniques and Drawing Presentation

■ **Coherent, well-executed construction documents are essential to a successful project. Computer-aided design is a valuable tool for producing these documents.**

However skilled the designer, an irrigation design is not finished until it is coherently presented as a construction document. The ultimate test of the construction document package comes during the bidding process—the number and nature of questions from bidders will be indicative of the quality of the irrigation design, as well as the quality of the presentation. The designer's knowledge and experience, including an understanding of symbols and presentation techniques, whether hand-drawn or produced by computer-aided drafting (CAD), all come into play.

Common Symbols

Figure 3.1 shows symbols that are commonly used in landscape irrigation design to depict system components. Note that most symbols represent an *assembly*. For example, a sprinkler symbol is, in fact, an assembly consisting of the fitting or fittings between the lateral pipe and the sprinkler, in addition to the sprinkler itself. Likewise, a valve assembly includes the valve box, gravel, wire connectors, and all the required fittings, in addition to the valve. Some of the detail inherent in the assembly occurs in the horizontal plane and some in the vertical plane.

A symbol is used in lieu of attempting to show all the subtlety of the assembly because it is not possible to show all the detail, given typical drawing scales. Scales of 1 inch = 10, 20, 30, 40, or 50 feet are common. A sprinkler rotor symbol is often depicted as a measurable

LEGEND

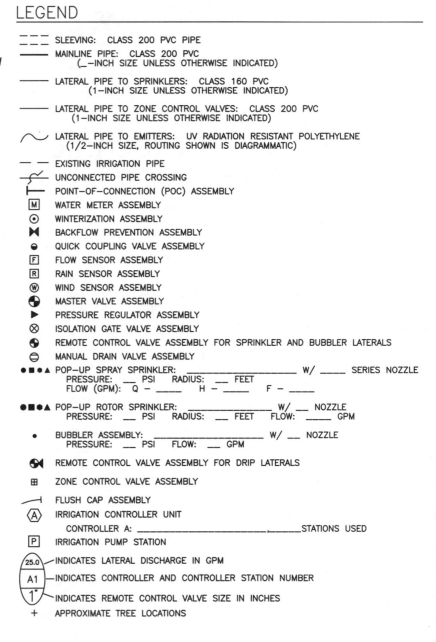

0.075 inch in diameter on a design drawing. At 20-scale, the rotor symbol is therefore 0.10 times 20, or 2 feet, as a scaled dimension. At 50-scale, the rotor symbol measures 10 feet as a scaled dimension. Clearly, there are limitations as to how much detail can be practically shown on the design drawing when the symbol is so "large" on a scaled drawing. So, the symbol, the legend callout, and the installation detail, taken together, provide the irrigation contractor with a clear picture of an assembly.

The symbols in Figure 3.1 are representative, as there is no widely accepted standard for landscape irrigation symbols. Symbolism varies somewhat depending on the region of the country. Symbolism also varies from firm to firm. Some irrigation designers have endeavored to standardize symbols, within their design team. Some groups, particularly government groups such as state highway departments, have endeavored to standardize symbols and they require design consultants to adhere to specific symbolism and other drawing standards. Professional organizations, such as the American Society of Irrigation Consultants, have developed landscape irrigation standards, which include symbol standards. However, no one firm or government group or professional organization has ever successfully implemented irrigation symbol standards and subsequently seen them widely accepted. The American Society of Agricultural Engineers is developing standard symbols for landscape irrigation; this standard, once completed, has a good chance of gaining wide acceptance.

On occasion, a disservice is done to the project owner when different designers, working on different phases of a project, use differing symbols. Can you imagine the frustration and consternation of maintenance personnel when they use design drawings from different phases of the project and must adapt to different legend symbols, each describing the same sprinkler or valve?

The irrigation designer must assign a unique symbol for each unique component in the irrigation system, define the component in a legend, and preferably tie, and cross-reference, the symbol back to an installation detail. The scaled drawings show the layout of components. The legend names the symbol. And the installation detail shows all the minor nuances and subtleties of the assembly.

Some of the best, and most readable, designs are created when the installation detail includes the symbol or symbols that the detail represents as part of the detail title. Figure 3.2 shows an example of an installation detail title block that includes legend symbols.

Pipe is generally represented by a line. **Line weight**, meaning the actual width of the line, should be varied for the mainline versus the lateral. The mainline is shown in a heavier weight so that it "stands off

FIGURE 3.2. *An example of an installation detail title block, which includes symbols for reference. Including symbols on the installation detail helps tie the detail and the legend together for the reader.*

the page" when one views the completed design. Practically, this is accomplished with drafting pens of differing weights or with differing line types with computer-aided drafting.

With symbolism and line weights, there is a definite need for some artistic input from the designer. A broad-brush or overview look at the irrigation design allows one to quickly pick up key features of the system, including the POC, the controller, the mainline pipe network, and the remote control valves, including the valve designators.

Dashed lines are generally used to represent existing pipe. The second phase of a project might show the new pipe and equipment as solid line work, while existing information, including pipe installed in a previous phase, is shown as dashed.

In Figure 3.1, the topmost symbol for sleeving is shown as dashed. A **sleeve**, in landscape irrigation, is a pipe through which another pipe passes. Generally, a sleeve is installed on a project before the hard surface (sidewalks, asphalt, and the like) is installed. Thus, sleeve installation often occurs before the balance of irrigation construction and is existing, and therefore dashed, in the symbol when the irrigation system is built. Additionally, irrigation sleeving is often installed by a contractor other than the irrigation contractor. The general contractor is often responsible for the installation of sleeves for all the various trades (electrical, plumbing, signage, and so on) working on the project.

Some peculiarities of other irrigation symbols should be noted as follows:

- An unconnected pipe crossing is depicted with a half circle positioned where one pipe crosses another *but is not connected.* Many times, lateral pipes must cross other lateral pipes or mainlines. This symbol indicates there is no physical connection between the two pipes; they simply cross one another graphically on the drawing and physically in the ground.
- A master valve assembly is typically depicted using the same symbol as a lateral remote control valve, but larger. Often, the valve used for a master valve is identical to the lateral valve, except the assembly is probably different. A master valve is typically installed on the mainline in an in-line configuration and without a service tee.
- A remote control valve assembly for sprinklers or bubblers is identical to a remote control valve assembly for drip irrigation, except that a triangle symbol is added. The blackened-in triangle depicts the pressure regulator, which is a likely part of the drip lateral valve assembly. (A blackened-in triangle may be used for a stand-alone, in-line pressure regulator as well.)
- The valve designator is a very important part of the design drawing, as it imparts a great deal of important information, including information used for system management. Designator symbols are an

example of a symbol that is quite different in various parts of the country. Whatever the presentation style, the designator is intended to show the lateral flow rate, the valve size, and, most importantly, the controller and controller station.

The valve designator is often one of the last symbols to be added to the drawing. The designator is placed as close as possible to the valve represented, but not so close or "tight" with other symbols to confuse or crowd the drawing. The designator can be placed to the side and an arrow used to point to the appropriate valve. It is good practice to insert or draft in the designator but leave the controller and station slot blank, to be completed later. Generally, **valve sequencing**, or numbering of the valves in a logical fashion, is one of the last tasks to be completed in an irrigation design.

The controller and station portion of the valve designator indicates the controller to which that valve is wired and, more specifically, the controller station that is utilized. Many projects require only one controller, but others have two or more. Common practice is to name the first controller "A" and additional controllers as "B," "C," and so on.

When multiple valves are wired to one controller station, as will be described in Chapter 8, it is best to indicate this on the design drawings. For example, it can be confusing when two "A2" valves are found on the drawings. One way to deal with this problem is to use subscripts and designate one valve as $A2_1$ and the other as $A2_2$. This approach clearly indicates that both valves are wired to station 2 on controller A, but each valve still has a unique character.

The symbol at the bottom of Figure 3.1 is often used as an approximate tree location. It is not necessary to show tree locations on the irrigation design, but this symbol reminds and helps the designer and irrigation contractor to consider trees in sprinkler placement and pipe routing.

Other symbols shown in Figure 3.1, and not verbally described here, are assumed to be self-explanatory as to purpose, except for sprinkler symbols, which deserve special consideration.

Sprinkler Symbols

Figure 3.3 indicates common sprinkler symbols consisting of a blackened-in circle, square, hexagon, or triangle. The same shapes can again be used, but left open, to provide additional symbols. Also, these common shapes can be used to represent pop-up spray sprinklers when they are 0.10 inch in diameter but rotor sprinklers when they are 0.15 inch in diameter. The irrigation designer's objective is simply to pick readable symbols that are unique for each sprinkler and nozzle combination used in the design.

Further, if it is necessary or desirable to indicate the sprinkler's arc on the design drawing, then some indication of arc must also be found

FIGURE 3.3. *Sprinkler symbol possibilities. A single symbol will typically represent a specific sprinkler model, operating pressure, and nozzle. The legend should fully describe the sprinkler, including nozzle designation, pressure, and flow. The lower grid depicts suitable symbols to use when arcs must be indicated.*

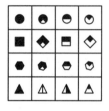

TYPICAL SPRINKLER SYMBOLS WITHOUT ARC DEPICTION

TYPICAL SPRINKLER SYMBOLS WITH ARC DEPICTION

with the sprinkler symbol. Figure 3.3 shows a family of potential sprinkler symbols. The top part of the figure shows how the circle, square, hexagon, or triangle can each be blackened in, or not, and contain a slash through the symbol, or not. Sixteen suitable and readable symbols are thus created with these graphic techniques. If arcs must be indicated, then symbols must be selected that lend themselves to depicting the arc as shown in the lower part of Figure 3.3. Also, remember that simply using different sizes for these symbols to depict pop-up sprays versus pop-up rotors will double the number of easy-to-read symbols available for use.

If a sprinkler symbol with no arc indicated is located in a 90-degree corner created between a driveway and a sidewalk, then it should be obvious that the sprinkler arc needs to also be 90 degrees. Sprinklers in open turf areas clearly need to be full-circle arcs. Many designers have used this approach historically and done so successfully. But, an important change that pushes us toward arc depiction has occurred in recent years. There are two primary reasons for this. First, the liability-conscious designer may wish to provide as much detail as possible in order to mitigate liabilities. In other words, if a 90-degree arc is desired, then clearly call out the arc as being 90 degrees. Secondly, if the design is created using computer-aided drafting techniques, and if the CAD system is used to accomplish hydraulic calculations, then the arc must be depicted and "tied" to a flow rate in the database for the appropriate arc to be used.

Symbols, if measured to scale on the drawing, are depicted as being quite large. This alone reinforces the fact that the irrigation design is diagrammatic, and skill and experience in the field are necessary to properly read, understand, and translate the design into practice. With sprinkler staking in the field, full-circle sprinklers must be located, more or less, near the center of the symbol, while part-circle sprinklers need to be located more or less at the edge of the symbol and against the boundary of the sidewalk or other structure.

Drawing Notes   Drawing notes are an important communication tool. The general description, as the name implies, provides a concise overview description of the system. Water source, irrigation design intent, winterization approach, and type of irrigation are the usual topics covered in a general description.

A typical general description might say:

> A fully automated combination sprinkler and drip irrigation system will irrigate turf areas and tree, shrub, and ground cover planting areas. Pop-up spray and rotor sprinklers will irrigate turf areas. Single- and multiple-outlet drip emitters will irrigate plant material in planting beds.
>
> Municipal (potable) water will be used for irrigation. The point of connection (POC) is immediately downstream of the irrigation water meter installed by others.
>
> The irrigation control system uses an existing central control system and is compatible with control satellites to be installed under this contract.
>
> Quick coupling valves have been provided throughout the site for incidental watering. Winterization is accomplished using compressed air applied from a winterization assembly near the POC.

Flag notes are a good method for communication of details, design intent, or nuances of component placement. Flag notes are numbered and may point to a specific area or symbol on the drawing. As an example, a flag note may be written to call for the addition of extra wires to strategic points on the project. Such a flag note might say:

> Install two #14 AWG UF wires from controller "A" to each of the remote control valve assemblies indicated for use as spare wires in case of control wire failure or valve additions.

Many projects consist of more than one drawing. Typically, the general description should appear on the first drawing sheet in the package. The legend should appear on the first sheet and, should there be adequate drawing space, on every sheet in the package. General notes and flag notes should appear on the first drawing sheet or on some other sheet or sheets with adequate space.

"White space," or open areas between various layout or note components of the drawings, is desirable. It is best to not crowd the design sheets, even if additional sheets must be added to the drawing package.

A complete package of irrigation construction documents is generally organized as shown in Figure 3.4. A cover sheet is optional. The installation details, if presented on drawing sheets, are generally found at the end of the package. Alternatively, installation details can be included in an $8\frac{1}{2}'' \times 11''$ format following the specifications.

An irrigation construction document package is not complete without written specifications. An example of irrigation specifications, in

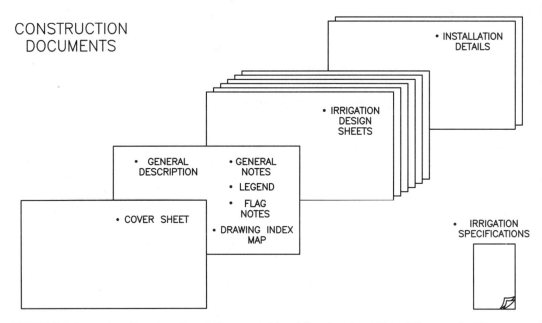

CONSTRUCTION
DOCUMENTS

• INSTALLATION
  DETAILS

• IRRIGATION
  DESIGN
  SHEETS

• GENERAL
  DESCRIPTION

• GENERAL
  NOTES

• LEGEND

• FLAG
  NOTES

• COVER SHEET

• DRAWING INDEX
  MAP

• IRRIGATION
  SPECIFICATIONS

FIGURE 3.4. *A construction drawing package consists of the drawing set and the specifications. Installation details can be presented on drawing sheets or as sheets appended to the specifications. General description, legend, general notes, and other elements of the drawings that help the reader become oriented quickly should be found on the cover sheet or immediately following the cover sheet.*

the format recommended by the Construction Specifications Institute (CSI), is found in Appendix C. CSI-style specifications for landscape irrigation are given section number 02810. All CSI specifications are broken into three parts: General, Materials, and Execution. There is a one-on-one relationship between the materials section and the execution section. If a materal is described in Part 2, the use or installation of the material is described in Part 3.

The Irrigation Design Process

Little has been written about the irrigation design process per se. Yet, it is very important for a designer to maintain an overview of the process, continuously evaluating the place in the big picture and always remembering critical assumptions that have been made as the design develops. Early assumptions materially influence the design, and changed assumptions during the design process can have major significance, depending on when they occur.

Consider a scenario where the irrigation designer has picked a sprinkler spacing for the project but has not yet determined the available pressure at the POC. Assume the sprinkler needs to operate at 60 PSI and that many design hours have gone into detailed sprinkler layout based on this assumption. Now, after sprinkler layout is completed under the 60 PSI assumption, it is determined that the static pressure at the POC is only 55 PSI. As you will soon learn, it is impossible to deliver 60 PSI to the sprinkler without having a substantially higher pressure at the POC. A different sprinkler or sprinkler nozzle that would function at a lower pressure could be used, but this means the effective radius of the sprinkler is less. More important to the irrigation designer, it means that much of the sprinkler layout work is no longer valid and must be redone. Unnecessary iterations can be avoided by understanding the irrigation design process.

The irrigation design process is depicted in a flow chart format in Figure 3.5. Note that one of the first activities in the flow chart, immediately following site evaluation, is to determine available flow and pressure. Sprinkler layout follows available pressure determination for the reasons implied in the design scenario.

It is good to note the design tasks where iterations are appropriate. For example, it is appropriate to iterate with sprinkler layout on the smaller discrete areas of the site. Certain sprinkler and nozzle combinations are going to work best given the irregular shape involved and the actual dimensions. Iterations are the best way to determine a good sprinkler and nozzle for an area. Iterations can be accomplished expeditiously using design techniques that allow a quick solution. Some designers will overlay portions of the landscape with tissue paper and then make rough marks on the tissue to depict sprinklers. The finalized layout can then be transferred to the drawing.

Likewise, iterations can be helpful as the mainline routing is conceptualized. After sprinkler layout is completed, many designers will quickly and roughly sketch in pipe routing to get a feel for the project and pipe routing approaches that may be employed.

There is no "best" or "perfect" landscape irrigation system design. Two very skilled individuals will design two very different irrigation systems for the same project, and both systems will be quite functional. Sprinkler layout and pipe routing are two of the areas in which significant differences between designs can appear.

A Practical Design Example

Some of the skills needed by an irrigation designer can only be developed by practice. Consider the project area depicted in Figure 3.6. Sprinklers have been laid out in acceptable patterns that consider the maximum sprinkler spacing and the irregular shape of the landscape. (Chapter 4 presents more details and specifics regarding sprinkler layout criteria.) The legend describes the sprinklers as full- and part-circle rotary sprinklers with a 14.8 GPM flow rate. For reasons that will be described further in Chapter 4, it is necessary to design laterals with all

ITERATE AT DESIGNER DISCRETION TO OPTIMIZE COST AND/OR APPLICATION EFFICIENCY

DATA BASE

DATA BASE UPDATES

USER UPDATES

IRRIGATION EQUIPMENT DATA BASE

DRAWING/USER SPECIFIC DATA BASE

ACCESS AS NECESSARY

ITERATE AS NECESSARY

ACCESS AS NECESSARY

ACCESS AS NECESSARY

ACCESS AS NECESSARY

ITERATE AS NECESSARY

DIGITAL TERRAIN MODEL (DTM)

INPUT CONTOURS

CREATE DTM

ACCESS AS NECESSARY

ACCESS AS NECESSARY

ITERATE AS NECESSARY

ITERATE AS NECESSARY

START

DETERMINE REFERENCE EVAPOTRANSPIRATION RATE CURVE FOR AREA

EVALUATE SITE CONDITIONS & CONSTRAINTS

ESTABLISH DESIGN CRITERIA

DETERMINE AVAILABLE FLOW & PRESSURE

SELECT APPROPRIATE SPRINKLER, VALVE, & OTHER EQUIPMENT

DETERMINE CONTROL CONCEPT

SPRINKLER LAYOUT

EVALUATE LAYOUT

CONCEPTUAL LATERAL ROUTING (FLOW)

CONCEPTUAL MAINLINE ROUTING

DETERMINE VALVE LOCATIONS

FINALIZE PIPE LAYOUT

SIZE VALVES & OTHER COMPONENTS

SIZE LATERAL PIPE AND EVALUATE LATERAL HYDRAULICS

SIZE MAINLINE AND EVALUATE MAINLINE HYDRAULICS

MODEL COMPLEX DISTRIBUTION SYSTEMS USING COMPUTER SIMULATIONS

SELECT PUMP & FILTRATION SYSTEM IF REQUIRED

DETAILED EVALUATION & REPORT OF "WORST CASE" HYDRAULICS

SIZE CONTROL & POWER WIRING

DRAFT CONSTRUCTION SPECIFICATIONS AND INSTALLATION DETAILS

FINALIZE CONSTRUCTION SPECIFICATIONS AND INSTALLATION DETAILS

QUANTITY TAKEOFFS BY SYMBOL

PROJECT PROBABLE CONSTRUCTION COSTS

EVALUATE SYSTEM OPERATION UNDER PEAK DEMAND CONDITIONS

PROJECT ANNUAL WATER AND POWER COSTS

DETERMINE PERIODIC OPERATING SCHEDULES FOR ENTIRE SEASON

CREATE DATA INPUT REPORT

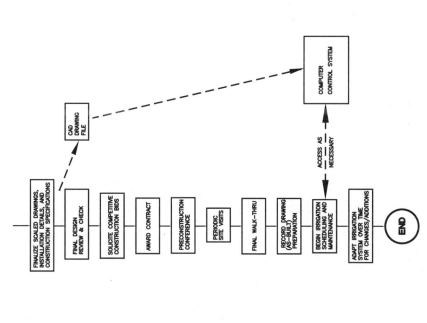

IRRIGATION SYSTEM DESIGN PROCESS

FINALIZE SCALED DRAWINGS, INSTALLATION DETAILS, AND CONSTRUCTION SPECIFICATIONS

CAD DRAWING FILE

FINAL DESIGN REVIEW & CHECK

SOLICITE COMPETITIVE CONSTRUCTION BIDS

AWARD CONTRACT

PRECONSTRUCTION CONFERENCE

PERIODIC SITE VISITS

FINAL WALK-THRU

RECORD DRAWING (AS-BUILT) PREPARATION

BEGIN IRRIGATION SCHEDULING AND MAINTENANCE

ACCESS AS NECESSARY

COMPUTER CONTROL SYSTEM

ADAPT IRRIGATION SYSTEM OVER TIME FOR CHANGES/ADDITIONS

END

FIGURE 3.5. *The irrigation design process. Certain aspects of the irrigation design process must occur before other processes start. The available flow and pressure at the POC should be known before an appropriate sprinkler, pressure, and nozzle can be selected and sprinkler layout completed.*

FIGURE 3.6.
*Laterals can be
"clouded" as a
means of quickly
grouping
sprinklers on a
lateral to
ascertain logical
lateral patterns.*

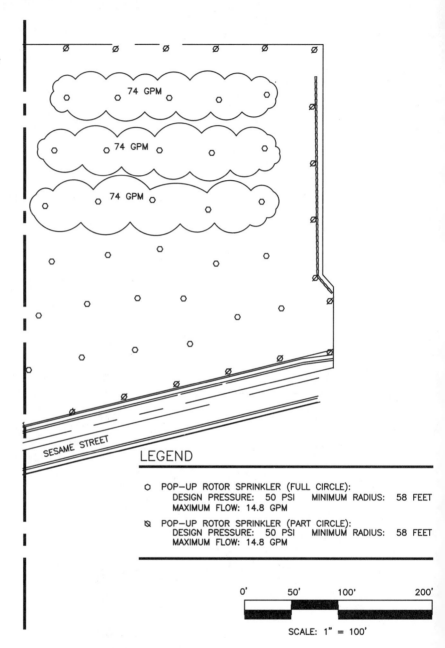

the full-circle sprinklers together and all the part-circle sprinklers together.

A good practice is to "cloud" selected sprinklers together on a lateral. In this example, five sprinklers are conceptualized to be grouped together on a single lateral. Five sprinklers, each having a flow rate of 14.8 GPM, implies that the lateral flow rate will be 5 times 14.8 GPM, or 74 GPM. A cloud is sketched in around the group of five sprinklers conceptualized to be on a single lateral, and the flow rate is noted inside the cloud. The entire project, or large portions of the project, can be clouded in this way to assist the designer and move along through the design process. A good designer can conceptualize the entire project in this way, get an overview quickly, and determine if the key assumptions and the strategy for irrigating the site are valid.

It is important to not agonize too long over sprinkler layout or pipe routing. It is best to sketch, cloud, or otherwise simply get thoughts down on paper in order to then contemplate and evaluate the idea. This process can be done quickly, and iterations should follow. Several sketches can be compared to help determine a sound approach. The best aspects from several different sketches can often lead the designer to a finalized layout.

Sketching techniques can help an irrigation designer to complete a conceptual design of the entire irrigation system. This is a good way to evaluate alternatives and avoid time consuming pitfalls.

When lateral pipe routing begins to firm up, it may be helpful to sketch in lateral pipe routing as is depicted in Figure 3.7. Simply sketch a pencil line from one sprinkler to the next.

A next step would be to sketch in mainline pipe and even consider remote control valve locations. Figures 3.8 and 3.9 show progress with the design in this respect. Although the line work in these textbook figures is formal in nature, remember that every aspect of the system depicted can still be sketched.

Note that the legend in Figures 3.8 and 3.9 is growing in detail along with the design. Many designers will develop the legend in parallel with the layout drawing, thereby making it easier to finalize the legend later. Now, the "pipe hop" symbol for an unconnected pipe crossing has been added to show where pipes cross graphically but are not actually connected.

The point of connection, or POC, is clearly delineated in Figure 3.9. By making the POC letters bold and larger than other text, the reader's eye is quickly drawn to a vital piece of information—the starting point of the mainline pipe system and the connection to the water source.

As can be seen in Figures 3.8 and 3.9, remote control valves are positioned along the mainline at convenient locations and close to the lateral. Some designers will group valves in pairs, or even locate three valves together. The best approach is often determined through discussions with the end user. Likewise, the locations picked for quick couplers, and even the quantity of quick couplers, are often quite arbitrary and an afterthought to other design processes.

The next major phase of the design process is to determine and show valve sequencing and pipe sizes. Pipe sizing (lateral hydraulics) is covered in detail in Chapter 6. Valve sequencing, the assignment of

FIGURE 3.7. *Lines depicting lateral pipe can be sketched in to indicate laterals.*

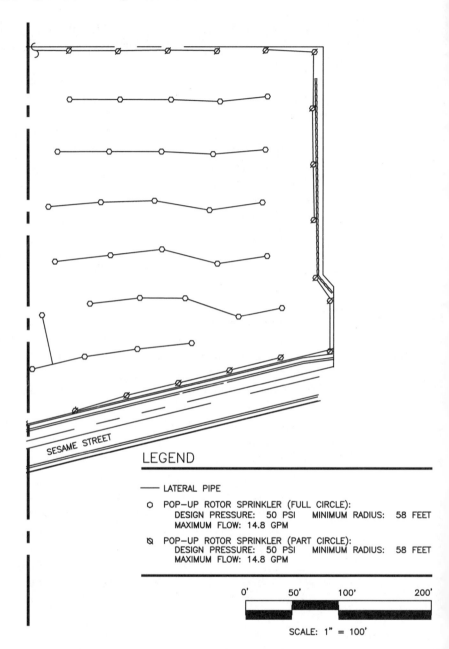

LEGEND

—— LATERAL PIPE

○ POP–UP ROTOR SPRINKLER (FULL CIRCLE):
    DESIGN PRESSURE: 50 PSI   MINIMUM RADIUS: 58 FEET
    MAXIMUM FLOW: 14.8 GPM

◙ POP–UP ROTOR SPRINKLER (PART CIRCLE):
    DESIGN PRESSURE: 50 PSI   MINIMUM RADIUS: 58 FEET
    MAXIMUM FLOW: 14.8 GPM

0'   50'   100'   200'

SCALE: 1" = 100'

controllers and controller station numbers, is generally started at a logical point—for example, the POC—and valves are numbered sequentially downstream from that point. Submains are generally sequentially numbered as well, starting from the point where they begin off the primary mainline and proceeding downstream. Review the valve sequencing shown in Figures 3.10 and 3.11. In this case, sequencing was

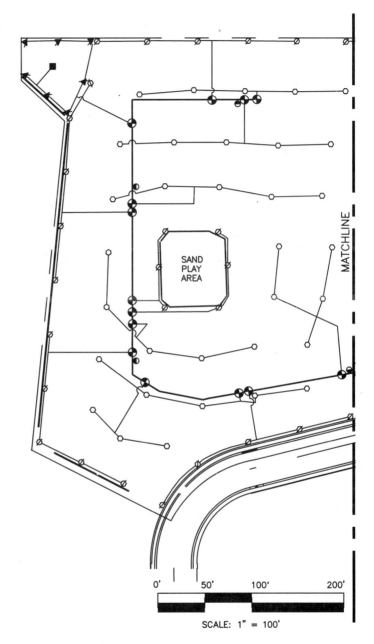

FIGURES 3.8 and 3.9 (p. 50).
Continued progress with lateral layout as well as mainline routing and remote control valve locations.

MATCHLINE

SAND
PLAY
AREA

0'   50'   100'   200'

SCALE: 1" = 100'

started at the POC, and the sequential numbering continues, following the mainline, and terminating back at the POC.

The approach to valve sequencing is very arbitrary and is often changed during construction. Finalized valve sequencing would be shown on record drawings, as would any future changes to sequencing. (Valve sequencing can be changed at the controller during construction,

FIGURE 3.9.
Continued progress with lateral layout as well as mainline routing and remote control valve locations.

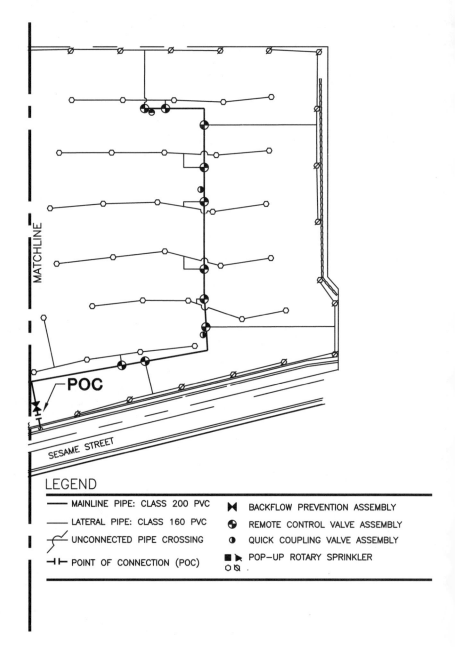

or even later, by simply moving the control wire from one post or station on the controller to another. This is described further in Chapter 8.)

As one proceeds with an irrigation design, there are several critical "node points" to be alert to. Sprinkler layout is one. Once the sprinkler layout is completed, it should not be necessary to change layout after

FIGURES 3.10 and 3.11 (p. 52). *A completed irrigation design, including pipe sizing and valve sequencing. The valve designator presents all pertinent data about the lateral that cannot otherwise be determined from the drawing, namely controller and controller station number, flow rate, and remote control valve size.*

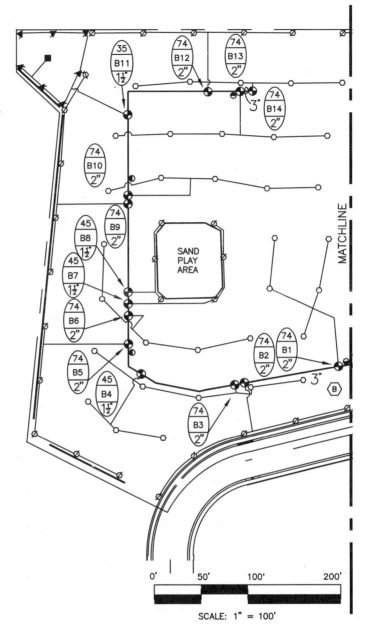

SCALE: 1" = 100'

pipe routing is done because moving sprinklers also requires the pipe routing be changed. The next step in the irrigation design process builds on the preceding steps. Another important node point in irrigation design is the completion of pipe routing, because pipe sizing (hydraulics), valve locations, and valve designators must all be changed if pipe routing changes.

FIGURE 3.11. *A completed irrigation design, including pipe sizing and valve sequencing. The valve designator presents all pertinent data about the lateral that cannot otherwise be determined from the drawing, namely controller and controller station number, flow rate, and remote control valve size.*

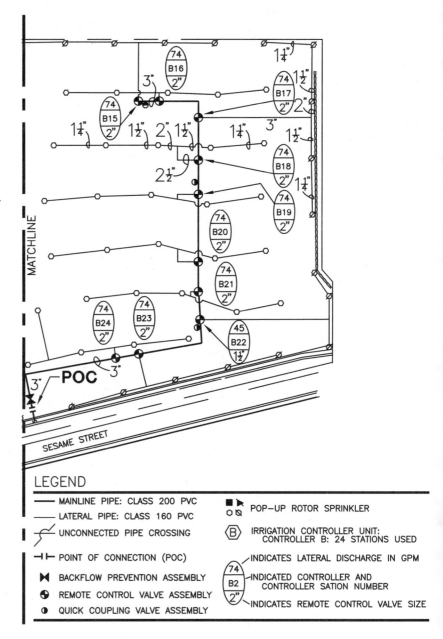

LEGEND

—— MAINLINE PIPE: CLASS 200 PVC	■ ▶ POP–UP ROTOR SPRINKLER
—— LATERAL PIPE: CLASS 160 PVC	○ ◙
⤲ UNCONNECTED PIPE CROSSING	Ⓑ IRRIGATION CONTROLLER UNIT: CONTROLLER B: 24 STATIONS USED
⊣⊢ POINT OF CONNECTION (POC)	⟋ INDICATES LATERAL DISCHARGE IN GPM
◲ BACKFLOW PREVENTION ASSEMBLY	⟋ INDICATED CONTROLLER AND CONTROLLER SATION NUMBER
✪ REMOTE CONTROL VALVE ASSEMBLY	
◐ QUICK COUPLING VALVE ASSEMBLY	⟍ INDICATES REMOTE CONTROL VALVE SIZE

The subject of iterations within the design process and moving symbols on the drawing makes one consider how a designer can improve personal efficiency, increase accuracy, and decrease the pain of iterations or changes. Computer-aided design is a very effective tool in this respect.

Computer-Aided Design and Computer-Aided Engineering

What single technology is having more impact on us than computers? Almost every newspaper and television news show contains relevant articles or segments that force us to consider the importance of computers on our lives and businesses.

In landscape and irrigation, the need for design professionals to understand and use computer-aided design (CAD) and computer-aided engineering (CAE) has almost become mandatory. Not so many years ago, the question, "Do you have a fax machine?" was frequently asked. Now, it is assumed you must have a fax machine or your business would be handicapped. This phenomenon is also occurring with CAD. The new questions asked between design firms are, "What version of AutoCAD® do you use?" or "What is your e-mail address so I can upload our latest drawing for you?"

CAD has already dramatically changed irrigation design, and more changes are coming. There is a wonderful opportunity, for those who readily embrace CAD technology, to use it to produce improved, more accurate designs and better irrigation drawings.

All aspects of the irrigation design process are enhanced, and accuracy improved, through CAD. One of the primary ways in which the design process is furthered with CAD can be noted in those portions of the flow chart where iterations can or should occur. With CAD, the designer can bring the design to a critical point, such as a completed sprinkler layout, and then decide to try an alternative sprinkler, pressure, and nozzle combination to achieve the project goals. Several iterations with alternatives can be completed quickly with CAD for the optimization of sprinkler application efficiency or minimization of construction costs.

The benefits of CAD, other than speed and accuracy, are many:

- Standardized, precise symbol presentation is feasible.
- Colors enhance overall presentation and plots.
- Drawings are more readable.
- Varying line widths improve presentation style.
- Individual drawing symbols may have numerous descriptive "attributes" or descriptive assignments.
- Layers can be used to create and present the specific drawing information desired.
- Lines and symbols can be easily edited or moved.
- Computer-aided engineering is possible.

Of these benefits, the most dramatic may be computer-aided engineering. Design processes, such as sprinkler layout and pipe hydraulics, can be accomplished faster and more accurately with CAE, leaving the designer with increased time and energy for creativity and alternative evaluation.

The CAD Process

The CAD process has notable parallels with manual drawing production methods. With manual methods, the designer starts with a base drawing sheet. With CAD, the designer starts with base line work in a computer drawing file. With manual methods, information concerning different trades is often "stacked" via a pin bar registration system so that multiple trades can use the same base information. With CAD, the information concerning different trades is contained on a layer or layers within the drawing file. Layers containing similar or related information are frequently identified with a specified color, as well as line type, for clarity.

The base drawing file is produced by "digitizing" appropriate line work or by simply receiving the drawing file from others. Base drawings can also be produced by "scanning" the hard copy of a drawing. With the scanning of a base drawing, it may be necessary to remove line work to eliminate unnecessary information. With digitizing, only the required information is input. The time required can sometimes be essentially the same in either case.

A mental shift is necessary for a person switching from manual drafting to CAD drawing production. Possibly the best biggest change is learning to deal with a computer screen instead of a drafting pen and paper. Experience with the computer, and familiarity with the new and dynamic capabilities of CAD, should help the transition.

The primary benefits of CAD use in irrigation design are as follows:

- **Layering** can be used to the designer's advantage to "build" drawings with appropriate design information. Utilities, and even the landscape design, can be seen on the monitor while the design is in progress, even if those background data are not necessary on finalized and plotted project drawings.
- **Edit / Move / Copy** commands help in creating all the irrigation-specific lines and symbols. The designer is free to quickly modify the design, and there is no reluctance to change the drawing as there would be if time-consuming erasures were required.
- **CAE** allows much of the routine and boring tasks to be done by the computer. The irrigation designer's attention and interest in the design process can be enhanced.
- Drawing **presentation** improvements are numerous. Drawings are more readable. Color plots make it easy to understand the system at a glance, with the mainline piping "standing off the page" due to color and line widths.
- **Efficiency** in making design changes is enhanced. Regardless, changes take time, and therefore cost money, and are a distraction

to the designer. Changes can be made more easily and the changes accomplished in a more gratifying way with CAD.

In addition to these benefits, there are others that come to bear even after the project is built. The irrigation contractor can produce the record drawings with CAD, future changes made to the irrigation system can be implemented and documented over time, and the CAD drawing can be mounted over the control system to assist with day-to-day management.

Some facility managers are commissioning a CAD production effort to turn their existing manually drawn irrigation designs into CAD drawings. This can be done by scanning the existing drawing or by simply digitizing the drawing—the alternatives and issues that were mentioned earlier concerning base drawing production.

Some irrigation managers have hung color-plotted CAD drawings on the wall, protected under Plexiglas® sheets, so that problems or operational issues can be noted with a grease pencil. Also, it is now possible to "capture" selected portions of the CAD drawings to use as quick reference drawings while working in other applications.

In effect, the finalized CAD drawing of the project has an ongoing life and utility of its own for the project owner or manager.

Computer Hardware and Software

Some general suggestions can be made for hardware and software, assuming that the goal is to create irrigation construction documents as scaled, final documents. With this in mind, certain computer equipment, peripherals, and software are needed:

- Pentium class or better **microcomputer** running at 90+ megahertz
- $5\frac{1}{4}$ or $3\frac{1}{2}$-inch **floppy diskette drive(s)**
- 300-megabyte **hard disk** (or larger)
- **color monitor** (a large monitor offers many benefits)
- Streaming tape or optical disk **backup system**
- **Large digitizer** (D or E size)
- **Small digitizer** (approximately 12-inch)
- **Plotter** (D or E size)
- **AutoCAD**® (most recent version)

Most CAD production people will say, appropriately from their perspective, that it is not possible to have too much memory or too much speed in the computer. Studies do show that even the short computer or disk access delays that occur during the design process become subliminally frustrating to the CAD operator working for hours at the computer.

Specific models of computers, peripherals, graphics boards, and the like should be discussed with the computer dealer from whom equipment is purchased and supported. Local support of this equipment is important because CAD software and hardware are much more demanding and technically complicated than most computer applications.

CAE in Landscape Irrigation

Many CAE applications are structured on top of the CAD software and can be used seamlessly while the designer works with CAD. All of the CAD drawing features can be used and, in addition, utilities and process that help the designer can be accessed.

Basic irrigation design capabilities with CAE are:

- **Computer-aided sprinkler layout**: Sprinklers can be automatically laid out in irregular shapes using rectangles, triangles, and distorted rectangles and triangles. The result should be a credible sprinkler layout that the designer can consider, check, modify, and improve at will. Alternative layouts can be quickly evaluated to achieve a finalized sprinkler layout.
- **Computer-aided pipe sizing**: Pipe should be sized on the basis of the hydraulic criteria; i.e., the operating pressure at the sprinkler is held within user-specified (configurable) limits.
- **Computer-aided symbol counts**: A single drawing sheet, or a whole project consisting of 20 sheets, can be analyzed and symbols and pipe lengths reported. It should be possible to edit the output at will for presentation and even import output to a spreadsheet program for expansion into a full cost analysis.
- **Specialized irrigation design menu**: A menu should allow for having all the irrigation symbols at hand for easy picking and insertion into the drawing. Symbols should automatically rotate to align properly with the pipe line work.
- **Database**: It should be possible to "map" irrigation equipment in a database to symbols so that attributes for specific equipment can be readily accessed and used.

When pipe sizing is complete, the pipe size symbol should be placed in a position that is offset from the pipe segment and between sprinklers. The designer should then be able to visually evaluate placement and move pipe sizing symbols at will. It should be possible to insert a pipe size to pipe line "pigtail," if desired, for size clarification when pipes are close.

The database should be inherently tied to many of the CAE capabilities. Imagine that the designer need not refer to a catalog for sprinkler performance data, but can simply insert a sprinkler symbol with all necessary design information "attached" as well. This capability is powerful in its own right. For example, if a given symbol represents a particular sprinkler with a particular nozzle, then each time you insert that symbol into the drawing file, flow rate, sprinkler distribution rate curve, and other essential information are known. The database should be expandable to contain other pertinent information such as cost data as well.

It is important to note that CAD and CAE are not a panacea allowing novice irrigation designers to complete complex designs. Computer-aided design requires skilled irrigation designers to utilize the tools described and ultimately complete, check, and stand behind their design.

The Future

None of us know what the future will hold in this arena, but some possibilities are:

- Improved and expanded hydraulic analysis capabilities, such as loop hydraulics
- Symbol counts that lead directly to complete material quantities suitable for order placement
- Concept irrigation designs that result quickly in material takeoffs, cost estimates, projected annual water requirements and other information so that full-fledged alternative designs can be analyzed and compared quickly
- Further analysis of irrigation system efficiencies according to the equipment selected and the design

It is safe to assume that the irrigation design process will become less laborious and, at the same time, more accurate in the future.

Review Questions

Consider and explain why it is important for the irrigation designer to know the probable static pressure at the project's POC before sprinkler layout is initiated.

Describe the information contained in the valve designator and why the information is important on a design drawing.

Consider an irregular shape from an existing area landscaped in turf grass and lay in rotor sprinklers with an effective radius of 40 feet and 60 feet, respectively.

Sprinkler Irrigation

■ Various types of sprinkler systems are available. The optimal irrigation design will usually include several different kinds of sprinklers fitted to the size and shape of the landscaped area.

Sprinkler irrigation has been a viable irrigation method for more than 60 years. The first "horizontal impact sprinkler" was invented by Orton H. Englehart. A U.S. patent for the device was issued on April 16, 1935. Sprinkler rotation was provided at that time by a spring-loaded arm striking the high-velocity flow of water coming through a nozzle. Other sprinkler drive mechanisms have come, and some have gone, since then. The term "rotor sprinkler" has come to describe a large-radius sprinkler, with any number of differing mechanical drives.

Sprinkler Types

There are two broad categories of sprinklers used in landscape irrigation: pop-up spray sprinklers and pop-up rotor sprinklers. Pop-up sprays are generally suitable for small-radius applications and small or irregular areas. Pop-up rotors are suitable for large-radius applications and larger areas.

The term "pop-up" implies, in both cases, that the top of the sprinkler is installed flush with the finished grade. When the irrigation system is not operating, only the sprinkler top can be seen from the surface. When a lateral valve opens, sprinklers on that lateral rise up for operation as the lateral pressurizes. When the lateral is fully pressurized, the sprinklers are fully popped up; sprinklers begin to function normally, rotate, and throw the distance specified.

The pop-up height is a function of manufacturer and sprinkler model. In the distant past, a two-inch pop-up height was something of a standard. Now a four-inch minimum pop-up height is much more common because recommended grass mowing heights have increased, and nozzle spray from a four-inch pop-up height is less likely to be influenced by the surrounding blades of grass.

The material cost of a single pop-up spray sprinkler is low compared to that of a pop-up rotor sprinkler. The installed unit cost of rotors, however, is lower than the installed unit cost of sprays. This is simply because a single rotor covers a dramatically bigger area than a spray sprinkler, and the associated trenching and pipe lengths are reduced. Even though lateral pipe size is greater for pipes serving rotor sprinklers, the total length of pipe can be dramatically lower. When the cost of the installed sprinklers and pipe is divided by the area of coverage, the installed unit cost of rotors is almost always less than the installed unit cost of sprays.

Sprinkler flow rates are express as gallons per minute (GPM). A frequently used mathematical symbol for flow is Q, and Q_s (pronounced "Q sub s") is often used as a symbol for sprinkler flow rate. Q_s can be measured, even under field conditions, by allowing the uninhibited sprinkler to flow into a container of known size for an appropriate time increment.

Sprinkler pressures are expressed in pounds per square inch (PSI). The operating pressure of a sprinkler is most often considered to be the pressure at the nozzle. Alternatively, the operating pressure can be noted as the pressure at the base of the sprinkler. The manufacturer should specify in its catalog where performance pressure is taken.

A device called a **pitot** (pronounced "pea-toe") **tube** can be used to measure pressure at the sprinkler nozzle under field conditions. A pitot tube is simply a small-diameter copper tube, gradually sweep-curved to 90 degrees, and attached to a pressure gauge. The tube is inserted into the flow stream coming from the nozzle, approximately at the center of the stream, and held in position while a pressure is read off the gauge.

Spray Sprinklers

Plastic pop-up spray sprinklers are very simple in mechanical action. Water pressure causes the stem of the sprinkler to pop up, overcoming the resistance of an internal spring resisting the pressure and trying to pull the stem back down. The stem seals when it reaches the full-up position. At this time, under normal conditions, the nozzle reaches full operating pressure and the sprinkler throws the specified distance and flows at the specified rate.

While the stem is rising, there may be some "flow-by" or "blow-by" of water when water flows between the sprinkler body and the stem. Various manufacturers have dealt with flow-by in different ways. Some flow-by may actually be desirable because it can force particles that are caught in the seal between the sprinkler body and the stem to be flushed out. On the other hand, if every sprinkler on the lateral is experiencing flow-by at the same time, the lateral may not be able to come up to pressure because the instantaneous flow can exceed the available flow from the system's POC.

Because of user feedback to the manufacturers, many spray sprinklers now have "zero flow-by" when the sprinkler begins to operate. In these sprinklers, a small flushing action may be allowed when the sprinkler stem is on the downstroke, after the lateral valve is closed.

One of the best ways to determine the approximate operating pressure for an installed pop-up spray sprinkler is to simply make a visual evaluation of performance. Performance specifications may indicate that a particular pop-up spray nozzle will throw 15 feet at a pressure of 30 PSI. Therefore, when a 15-foot radius is observed in the field, the operating pressure can be assumed to be approximately 30 PSI. If the same nozzle is throwing only 4 feet, then, clearly, either it is not coming up to pressure or the nozzle is clogged. If the same nozzle is throwing 17 feet and a light mist or fog is observed to be coming off the top of the pattern, the sprinkler is operating at an excessively high pressure.

"Misting" of operating pop-up spray sprinklers is not desirable and should be avoided. The easiest corrective action for misting is to turn down the flow control at the lateral valve enough to create additional pressure loss and reduce the operating pressure at the sprinkler. This is an important reason why remote control valves should always have a flow control feature.

Pop-up spray nozzles are available from most manufacturers in the nominal effective radius alternatives of 10, 12, and 15 feet. Commonly available arcs are $\frac{1}{3}$, $\frac{1}{2}$, $\frac{3}{4}$, and full. Other options in radius and odd arcs are often available, depending on the manufacturer.

Some manufacturers offer a **variable arc nozzle**, which can be adjusted in the field to odd arcs as required by landscaped areas that are not easily fitted with common arcs. The question may be asked, "Why not use adjustable nozzles throughout?" Adjustable nozzles should not be used in place of the fixed arcs because the pattern predictability for the adjustable nozzles is not as good as that for the fixed arcs.

A pop-up spray sprinkler nozzle can usually be adjusted down about 30 percent, using the nozzle's adjustment screw. So a commonly available 10-foot nozzle can be reasonably adjusted down to 7 feet. Any greater adjustment than 30 percent of the effective radius may distort the pattern and result in poor application efficiency. For this reason, and because spray nozzles are not commonly available in an effective radius of less than 10 feet, the practical minimum width of turf that can be effectively irrigated using sprinklers is considered to be 7 feet.

Some special patterns to handle narrow rectangular turf areas are available, but nozzle performance is not as predictable or as uniform as compared to quarter-, half-, or full-arc nozzles. Special pattern nozzles may be referred to as "end strip," "center strip," or "side strip" nozzles. Experience with a particular nozzle is about the only sure way to learn something about the benefits and utility of specialty nozzles. Careful application, followed by field evaluation, will give a designer a feel for specialty nozzles and a confidence for places where they can be used effectively.

Characteristics of pop-up spray sprinklers include:

- Appropriate for small radius (7 to 15 feet), small areas (generally less than 45 feet in width), and irregular or curvilinear areas.
- No mechanical action except for riser pop-up caused by pressure in the sprinkler lateral. In plastic pop-up sprays, retraction is caused by a stainless steel spring. In the older brass sprinklers, retraction is caused by the weight of the riser stem.
- Operating pressures: 15 to 45 PSI± (relatively low).
- Nozzle arcs: quarter, half, and full (abbreviated Q, H, and F); three-quarter and one-third (3Q and $\frac{1}{3}$) arcs are also possible. Specialty nozzles may be available, depending on manufacturer.
- Throw adjustment is accomplished (within limits) using a screw in the nozzle.
- Material: plastic or brass[1] or a combination thereof.
- Precipitation rates: 1 to 2.5 IPH (inches per hour) (i.e., relatively high).
- Installed unit cost: $0.30 to $1.00 (or more) per square foot.
- Recent innovations: matched precipitation rates (MPR), high pop-up models, pressure-compensating nozzles or screens, ratcheting of the stem for easy field adjustments, and check valves to prevent low-head drainage.

A classic, and suitable, application for pop-up sprays is a turfed roadway median. Consider a turf median that is a consistent 15 feet in width. The obvious solution, understanding commonly available sprinklers and throw radius, is half-circle, 15-foot pop-up spray sprinklers located next to the curb, throwing away from the curb, and complementing one another. Sprinklers on the opposite side of the strip, placed against the opposite curb, complement as well and sprinklers are typically laid out in an equilateral triangle pattern. In this application, the roadway median is "trimmed out" effectively and little water is overthrown onto the roadway under no-wind or low-wind conditions.

Some pop-up sprays allow the stem to be "ratcheted" in the field into the correct position for the sprinkler's arc. The installer screws

---

1. All-brass sprinklers were the de facto standard of the past, but brass is now uncommon due to the high reliability and low cost of plastic sprinklers.

down the desired nozzle until it is snug, probably leaving the arc pattern in an incorrect position relative to the landscape. The stem, along with the attached nozzle and arc, can then be rotated, while operating, until the correct position is found. This adjustment action makes a ratcheting sound with most sprinklers, hence the terms "ratcheting" or "ratcheted."

High pop-up spray sprinklers can be set in shrub beds with the top above grade to achieve a higher functioning position. Twelve inches is the standard pop-up height for high pop-up sprinklers, but the top of the sprinkler body may be set somewhat above grade. Consider a shrub bed with ground cover that is initially 6 inches deep, but where the ground cover can be expected to be 15 inches deep when mature. Twelve-inch pop-up sprinklers are appropriate. The top of the sprinkler can be set 4 to 6 inches above grade, still leaving enough of the sprinkler body in the ground for stability, while remaining "low profile" in the landscape. The operating sprinkler then pops up 12 inches, and the nozzle sprays at the 16- to 18-inch level above ground and over the mature plant material.

Some high pop-up spray sprinklers are manufactured with two inlets, one on the side of the sprinkler body and the other on the bottom. Irrigation contractors may prefer the side inlet because less excavation is required to connect to the lateral pipe. However, use of the side inlet may cause sprinkler winterization problems (water retained in the sprinkler body) or inadvertently bypass the sprinkler's check valve feature located in the bottom. The manufacturer's specification or sales personnel should be consulted regarding suitable applications and possible pitfalls.

Check valves may be desirable added features with pop-up sprays if there are elevation changes within the lateral. If elevation changes and there are no check valves in the sprinklers, water will drain through the sprinkler or sprinklers in the lowest part of the lateral after the lateral valve is closed. A check valve prevents this action within certain specified limits. For example, the check valve may be designed to "hold back" eight vertical feet of water in the lateral. A spring in the check valve exerts eight pounds of force to keep the valve closed. The valve opens under an elevation head (pressure) greater than eight feet and closes again at eight feet. This prevents **low head drainage** from occurring. Low head drainage, as the name implies, is water draining from the lowest sprinklers on the lateral. Such drainage is undesirable because water is wasted and excessive water can accumulate in low areas. Plant material can be lost due to excessive water or, potentially worse, a liability can be created due to excess water applied adjacent to buildings or other structure. The problem of low head drainage is compounded when the lateral operates frequently, as when an area is newly seeded or sodded or when short run times with repeats are programmed.

Some spray sprinklers can have optional **pressure compensating devices** added to the screens under the nozzles or built into the sprinklers when they are manufactured. The device, as the name implies, compensates for varying pressure within the lateral and causes the nozzle to flow at or near the nominal flow rate.

Pressure compensating devices sometimes can be retrofitted into an existing system to improve operating pressures, overall lateral hydraulics, and lateral performance. One manufacturer offers screens with a pressure compensation device built in. The original nozzle screen can be removed and replaced with a color-coded pressure compensating screen. One downside of pressure compensating screens, though, is simply that the device can not be seen until the nozzle is removed, so future maintenance becomes more difficult.

Purely from the irrigation designer's perspective, it should be noted that added features like check valves or pressure compensation devices should not be indiscriminately specified or "called out" on the drawings. The irrigation designer is the project owner's advocate. These features may look inexpensive and actually be inexpensive to manufacture, but they may be "value added" or costly features to the end user. Some features come at a high incremental cost to the end user, all the more so if the feature is unnecessary. Consider these examples: If a sprinkler lateral is properly designed, then pressures will fall within specified limits and a pressure compensation device is not required to meet the lateral design criteria. If a given lateral irrigates an area that is flat, or nearly flat, then internal check valves have no function and the added cost is entirely wasted.

Figure 4.1 shows a typical installation detail for a pop-up spray sprinkler. Spray sprinklers commonly have a $\frac{1}{2}$-inch female threaded inlet. The sprinkler can be installed on a $\frac{1}{2}$-inch **cutoff nipple**, which is a single polyethylene nipple, easily cut at $\frac{1}{2}$-inch increments to the desired length. Alternatively, the sprinkler may be installed on a **swing joint** or **swing pipe**, either of which allows for movement and sprinkler height adjustment. With swing pipe, the sprinkler can be easily set to finish grade at the time of construction. Over time, the sprinkler can be moved up or down if necessary. Swing pipe can also be cut to length in the field to carefully locate the sprinkler in a corner or adjacent to a hard surface. (Swing joints are described in greater detail for rotor sprinkler installations.)

Rotor Sprinklers

Rotor sprinklers can be further described by the mechanism that causes the sprinkler to rotate. **Impulse** or **impact sprinklers** use a spring-loaded arm that strikes the water stream coming from the nozzle to cause rotation. A **ball drive sprinkler** uses centrifugal force and the impact forces from two stainless steel balls to cause sprinkler rotation.

FIGURE 4.1. *A typical installation detail for a pop-up spray sprinkler. Spray sprinklers commonly have a $\frac{1}{2}$-inch female threaded inlet (FPT or "female pipe thread"). The sprinkler can be installed on a cutoff nipple as shown, or, alternatively, the sprinkler may be installed on a swing joint or swing pipe to allow for sprinkler height adjustment at construction and over time.*

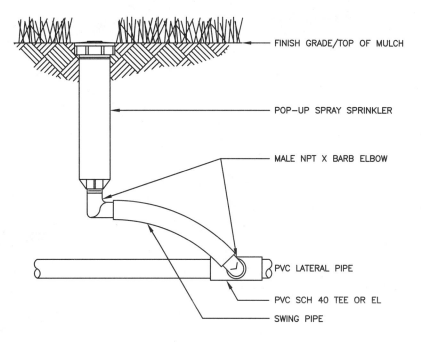

FINISH GRADE/TOP OF MULCH

POP-UP SPRAY SPRINKLER

MALE NPT X BARB ELBOW

PVC LATERAL PIPE

PVC SCH 40 TEE OR EL

SWING PIPE

Piston drive sprinklers utilize a diaphragm and piston, which together move the sprinkler a few degrees each time the piston finishes a stroke. **Gear drive sprinklers** use flowing water and a series of intricate gears (similar to an automotive transmission) for rotation.

Various drive mechanisms have differing susceptibility to poor water quality. Generally, Impact sprinklers tend to exhibit the fewest problems under marginal (dirty) water conditions, followed by piston drives, ball drives, and gear drives, respectively. Many dirty water situations will necessitate primary filtration at the water source to remove suspended solids that may cause sprinkler mechanical failure or premature wear.

Manufacturer sales engineers, as well as product end users, are an invaluable source of product performance information under adverse water conditions. Almost nothing is better than personal field experience where product selection is concerned. Further, a designer must constantly stay in tune with product announcements or industry "scuttlebutt" concerning changes or recalls. Water quality, manufacturing flaws, and incorrect installation technique are frequently reasons for product failure or factory recalls.

Characteristics of rotor sprinklers include:

- Appropriate for large-radius (30 to 90 feet) applications, large areas (generally greater than 30 feet in width), and more regular landscape areas.

FIGURE 4.2. *A rotor sprinkler installed on a swing joint, a series of elbows and nipples, designed for movement and allowance for setting the sprinkler to grade.*

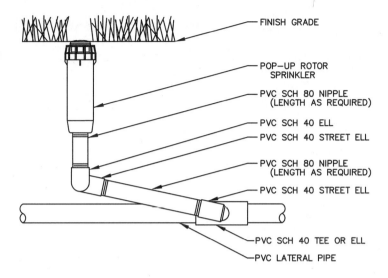

FINISH GRADE

POP–UP ROTOR SPRINKLER

PVC SCH 80 NIPPLE (LENGTH AS REQUIRED)

PVC SCH 40 ELL

PVC SCH 40 STREET ELL

PVC SCH 80 NIPPLE (LENGTH AS REQUIRED)

PVC SCH 40 STREET ELL

PVC SCH 40 TEE OR ELL

PVC LATERAL PIPE

- Flowing water and a mechanical action, working together, cause rotation.
- Operating pressures: 40 to 90 PSI± (relatively high).
- Nozzle arcs: infinite arc adjustment in many sprinklers or fixed arcs in 15-degree increments.
- Radius of throw is adjustable in some sprinklers, but not all.
- Material: plastic or brass or combinations thereof.
- Precipitation rates: 0.30 to 0.75 IPH (i.e., relatively low).
- Installed unit cost: $0.20 to $0.60 per square foot.
- Recent innovations: built-in check valves, small cross sections at the surface, rubber covers,[2] high pop-up models, color-coded nozzle sets, complete nozzle sets delivered with every sprinkler, and increasingly lower precipitation rates.

Figure 4.2 shows a rotor sprinkler installed on a **swing joint.** Factory-made swing joints are called **prefabricated swing joints.** A swing joint is a series of elbows and nipples designed for movement in setting the sprinkler to grade during construction or to facilitate sprinkler height adjustment over time. Sprinklers can be pushed down below grade by athletes, by mowing equipment, or by the buildup of turf thatch on the surface. Whatever the cause, some rather minor excavation allows the sprinkler to be raised back into position when the sprinkler is installed on a swing joint. Also, a swing joint avoids damage to the lateral pipe and tee fitting that might occur if the assembly were rigid and unmoving.

---

2. Small sprinkler profiles at the surface and rubber covers are particularly important for sports applications. Small exposure and protection of the sprinkler can mitigate potential injuries to athletes.

The material cost of swing joints assembled in the field is much lower than the cost of prefabricated swing joints, but the factory-built swing joints may be cost-effective when installation labor is included.

Pop-Up Sprays versus Pop-Up Rotors

Many small projects, and most large projects, require both pop-up spray and pop-up rotor sprinklers to address different size and shape attributes in the landscape. From the designer's standpoint, the best sprinkler, whether rotor or spray, is chosen based primarily on the dimensions of the area to be irrigated and the relative complexity of the shape. Many curvilinear shapes warrant short-radius pop-up sprays because they can be located so as to avoid overspray onto hard surfaces.

There is usually no advantage to be gained by using all rotor or all spray sprinklers; a combination of sprinkler types on a single project is almost always appropriate and desirable. The differing sprinklers are used to their best advantage at different places in the landscape. Spray sprinklers tend to increase installed costs, but they offer the only suitable alternative for small, irregular turf areas. Rotor sprinklers tend to decrease installed costs on large areas of turf. Sprays are preferred next to irregular boundaries to avoid over spray onto curvilinear boundaries. Rotors are definitely better than spray sprinklers for sports applications because fewer sprinklers translate to less potential for injury, and rotors can be fitted with rubber covers for sports applications. Rotors have lower precipitation rates than spray sprinklers and can more easily be scheduled to avoid overland flow on soils with low infiltration rates. For a given available flow, rotor sprinkler laterals cover larger areas of the landscape than spray sprinkler laterals and, consequently, fewer laterals are necessary.

Table 4.1 presents a summary comparison of the key differences between pop-up spray and pop-up rotor sprinklers.

Choosing a Manufacturer

Sometimes, the most difficult job for an irrigation designer, especially a new designer, is picking a sprinkler when the sprinkler is to be specifically called out or "proprietary" to the project. The irrigation product distributors or manufacturer sales staff can be unmerciful in their push to have their products accepted and specified. The designer's primary role is to be an advocate for the owner and make choices that are in the owner's best interest. The irrigation designer may be called on to justify the equipment selected or offer expert opinion. Experience will guide the designer toward a straightforward, honest discussion of pros and cons between alternatives. Equipment manufacturers and distributors should appreciate, understand, and acknowledge both the pluses and minuses of their equipment offerings. Salespeople who get too caught up in thinking that their product is superior in every way generally need to stand back a few paces and look again.

Occasionally, the irrigation designer's clients (often the end users or project owners) dictate preferred equipment. And well they should,

TABLE 4.1
Comparison of Pop-Up Spray and Pop-Up Rotor Sprinklers

	Pop-Up Spray Sprinklers	Pop-Up Rotor Sprinklers
General description	Manufactured of plastic or brass (more commonly plastic) or a combination such as a plastic sprinkler body with a brass nozzle; no mechanical action except for riser pop-up as effected by lateral pressure, water throw adjustment via screw-in nozzle	Manufactured of plastic, metal, or some combination of plastic and metal; mechanical action (gears, pistons, levers, centrifugal force) causes rotation, water throw adjustment possible with many models
Radius of throw	Radius of approximately 7 to 15 feet; appropriate for small dimensions (<30 feet), smaller areas, and irregular areas	Radius of approximately 30 to 90 feet; appropriate for large dimensions, larger areas, and more regular areas
Operating pressure at the sprinkler nozzle	15 to 50 PSI (relatively low)	40 to 90 PSI (relatively high)
Precipitation rate	1 to 2.5 IPH (relatively high)	0.30 to 0.75 IPH (relatively low)
Approximate installed unit cost	$0.40 to $1.00 per SF (relatively high)	$0.25 to $0.75 per SF (relatively low)
Innovations in recent years	Matched precipitation rates (MPR), high pop-up models, pressure compensating nozzles designed to achieve regulated pressures and constant sprinkler flows, check valves to minimize low sprinkler drainage	Built-in check valves to avoid low sprinkler drainage, small surface area and rubber covers for sports applications, high pop-up models, color coded nozzle sets, increasingly lower precipitation rates to match low soil infiltration rates, and distribution rate curve improvement

since they must live with the irrigation equipment that is selected. The irrigation designer, in this case, owes the client any cautionary comments if there are concerns with the client's desires. It is always best if the end user is involved, or "vested," in the decision. However the decision is made, and whatever the process, a balance of experience with the product, local representation, end user preferences, and other, often subjective, factors generally come into play.

One way to avoid a proprietary equipment specification is to simply describe the product and the product performance in the drawing legend and through the written specifications. The performance of some equipment—pop-up spray sprinklers are a good example—is fairly uniform among manufacturers. Further, for irrigation design purposes, the designer can pick a number of proprietary alternatives, then use the worst–case performance[3] to complete the hydraulic calculations. When sprinklers or other equipment are described in a nonproprietary way,

---

3. Worst–case performance for a sprinkler would be the sprinkler alternative with the highest flow rate. Worst–case performance for a valve would be the valve with the highest pressure loss.

Bob Gannon
Danny

dding process should result in the correct
s specified) at the lowest possible cost.

---

tion rate for sprinklers is the rate at which
water. The concept is similar to expressing
the units are the same, as well. Common
on rates are inches per hour (IPH).
prinklers and half-arc sprinklers are grouped
ll-arcs are grouped together on a separate
lateral because of precipitation rate differences. Partial arcs of 180 degrees and less are often mixed together on laterals for economy, even
though the precipitation rate may vary somewhat.

Some nozzle families, for some sprinklers, are developed such that
a nozzle for the quarter-arc can be picked to be approximately half the
flow rate of the half-arc, thereby keeping the precipitation rates closer.
Likewise, the half-arc nozzle will have half the flow of a full-circle arc
nozzle, and so on. Nozzle families created in this way are said to have
balanced precipitation rates.

Refer to the rotor sprinkler performance data in Appendix A. Note
that one could pick a #1 nozzle for the 90-degree arcs and a #2 nozzle
for the 180-degree arcs so that, when the two nozzles are mixed on
the same lateral, the flows are more or less proportional, or "balanced."

In recent years, many manufacturers provide **matched precipitation rate** (MPR) sprinkler nozzles. With the MPR concept, nozzles
are engineered and manufactured such that quarters, halves, and fulls all
complement one another with flow rates proportioned to the arc.
When the flow rates are proportional to the arc, precipitation rates can
be identical or nearly identical. For example, within an MPR nozzle
family, a half-arc nozzle has exactly (or very close to) one-half the flow
rate of a full. A quarter-arc nozzle has exactly one-quarter the flow rate
of a full and half the flow rate of a half-arc. Using this concept, each
sprinkler, regardless of arc, applies water at the same precipitation rate.
The matched precipitation rate concept allows the various arcs to all be
grouped together on a single lateral without concern.

Even considering the MPR nozzles, the idea of grouping similar
arcs together may still have merit. For example, in larger irrigated areas
having numerous sprinklers and requiring multiple laterals, it is still
appropriate to group quarters and halves together on a lateral and, likewise, to group fulls together. This lateral layout concept allows the
management flexibility to operate the laterals at different times of day
and for differing time increments. Why? It is desirable to avoid operating the half-circle sprinklers when wind is tending to blow water onto
hard surface, so the halves on a separate lateral can be delayed until the

least windy time period. Also, it can be argued that the turf immediately adjacent to hard surface has a higher evapotranspiration rate that turf away from hard surface; hence, a longer operating time can be programmed if the lateral layout allows this flexibility.

The precipitation rate of overlapping sprinklers, or PR, is calculated by a simple but very important, and frequently used, equation. Practicing irrigation designers use this equation frequently and often program it into their desktop computers or calculators. The **precipitation rate equation** is:

$$PR = \frac{(96.3)\ (Q_s)}{(S)\ (L)}$$

where

PR = precipitation rate in IPH

Q_s = sprinkler flow rate in GPM

S = sprinkler spacing in feet

L = lateral spacing in feet

In a square layout pattern, S equals L. Figure 4.3 shows an equilateral triangle sprinkler spacing with S and L denoted and indicating that L is a function of S. In the case of an equilateral triangle:

$$L = S\ (\sin 60°)$$

$$= S\ (0.867)$$

The 96.3 factor in the precipitation rate equation is constant and is simply a conversion factor required because of the units involved in the equation.

The sprinkler spacing, S, is generally the maximum spacing recommended by the manufacturer; however, spacing can be less than the maximum. Spacings less than maximum are necessary because of actual site dimensions force the designer to close up the spacing to fit the

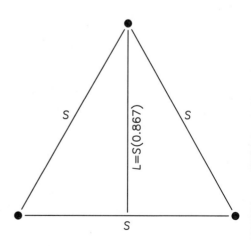

FIGURE 4.3. *An equilateral triangle sprinkler layout pattern.* S *is the sprinkler spacing.* L *is the lateral spacing.* L *is equal to* S *multiplied by the sine of 60 degrees, which is 0.867.*

project. Sprinkler spacing should not be stretched, but sprinklers can be closer together and the actual spacing within a given area can vary. The spacing does not need to be constant between sprinklers.

As an example, use this equation to calculate, and verify, the precipitation rate for sprinklers found the Appendix A, Generic Performance Data. The rotor sprinkler performance data indicate that at 60 PSI, the rotor sprinkler with #4 nozzle has an effective radius of 60 feet and a sprinkler flow rate of 16.3 GPM.

For an equilateral triangle layout pattern, Q_s equals 16.3 GPM, S equals 60 feet, L equals 60 feet times 0.867 or 52.02 feet. So, using the precipitation rate equation:

$$PR = \frac{(96.3)\ (16.3)}{(60)\ (60 \times 0.867)} = \frac{1569.69}{3121.20} = 0.50 \text{ IPH}$$

For a square layout pattern, Q_s is unchanged at 16.3 GPM, S equals 60 feet, and L equals 60 feet.

$$PR = \frac{(96.3)\ (16.3)}{(60)\ (60)} = \frac{1569.69}{3600.00} = 0.44 \text{ IPH}$$

Note that the triangular pattern PR is greater than the square pattern PR. For a given sprinkler, the equilateral layout patten PR will always be greater than the square pattern, assuming a head-to-head layout pattern in both cases. Triangular sprinkler layout patterns are preferred because triangular patterns exhibit less distortion due to wind. However, it is generally not considered good practice to force a triangular pattern into a landscape shape that is rectangular. More discussion of this subject can be found under the topic of sprinkler layout.

Some sprinkler manufacturers allow, and even recommend, that the spacing of sprinklers laid out in an equilateral triangle pattern can be increased to 60 percent of the effective diameter. For this reason, the triangular pattern precipitation rate may be reported in the catalog for a 60 percent of the maximum diameter spacing. Refer to the rotor sprinkler performance data in Appendix A and note the footnotes at the bottom of the table. If you should verify the the precipation data for the equilateral triangle layout, you must use the radius times two (the diameter) times 60 percent to obtain the numbers in the table. The first footnote states that the precipitation rates are based on half-circle (180-degree arc) operation, so the result that is obtained using the precipitation rate equation must be multiplied by two.

There are actually four ways to estimate or measure sprinkler precipitation rates. These methods are:

- Determine PR from the manufacturer's catalog data (generally presented in the catalogs only for equilateral triangles and square spacings—perfect layout shapes that are seldom actually found in a landscape situation).

- Calculate PR for the actual spacings in the design or in the field.
- Measure actual PR depths applied in the field and as accumulated in a grid of "catch cans."
- Calculate as a weighted PR for the entire lateral.

The first method is the least accurate, because the calculation is based on equilateral triangle or square patterns and it is hard to achieve perfect square or equilateral triangle layout patterns in a landscape. The actual field layout patterns do not match the specified patterns; hence, PR from the catalog is incorrect. Measurement is a desirable approach but is time-consuming and, therefore, costly. The last approach often has the most merit because it provides the best estimate from the design drawings but saves time as compared to actual measurement in the field.

When the weighted PR for the entire, as-designed or as-built, lateral is calculated, the PR equation becomes:

$$PR_L = \frac{(96.3)\ (Q_L)}{A_L}$$

where

PR_L = weighted precipitation rate of lateral in IPH

Q_L = lateral flow rate in GPM

A_L = irrigated area under the lateral in ft^2

This equation is preferred in the case of laterals that have been fully designed or built because irregular sprinkler spacings within the lateral itself are accounted for. Consider a lateral with part of the sprinklers spaced at the maximum, the effective radius from the manufacturer's catalog, but other sprinklers on the lateral spaced closer because of physical aspects of the site. In this case, the PR varies somewhat within the lateral because of spacing differences. As S becomes smaller, the calculated PR increases. By measuring the irrigated area under the lateral, this differential is accounted for, and a **weighted precipitation rate** for that lateral is calculated. The result is a better PR estimate for irrigation scheduling purposes than simply using sprinkler spacing at one arbitrary point in the lateral.

In practice, A_L is estimated by using a planimeter to determine the irrigated area, or the area under the lateral can be broken up into geometric shapes for which the area is easily determined. The areas of the respective geometric shapes are added together to get an estimate of the total area.

Why is it so important to thoroughly understand sprinkler precipitation rates? First, the PR should be known in order to avoid using sprinklers with *PR*s higher than the intake rate of the soil. Second, to correctly manage the irrigation system and schedule irrigations, the *PR* must be known to determine lateral operating time. For example, if the *PR* is 0.30 IPH and it is desirable to apply 0.60 inches of water, then the lateral will need to operate for two hours.

An understanding of the precipitation rate and *PR* variance between sprinkler types and nozzle families is a fundamental aspect of sound irrigation system design and management. Too often, irrigation managers have a sense of the amount of water they wish to apply, but no understanding of the rate at which the laterals within the system apply water. Without knowing the *PR* by lateral, the operating time is simply a guess.

The best irrigation designs are accompanied by a table indicating the *PR* for each lateral in the system. The table will then be available when construction is completed to initially schedule irrigations.

Sprinkler Distribution Rate Curves

Ideally, sprinklers would apply water uniformly, like rain. But the basic pattern of a sprinkler is one that applies more water near the sprinkler and less and less water as you move farther from the sprinkler. This is why sprinklers are spaced to complement each other. "Head-to-head" coverage, when one sprinkler throws to the next, is generally good practice, but there may be exceptions.

Knowledge of application patterns can help the designer make sound decisions that improve application efficiency and, thereby, save water. The pattern or curve is called the single-leg **distribution rate curve** (DRC). The term "single-leg" refers to the pattern of a single ray originating at the center of a circle drawn around the sprinkler. All legs or rays exhibit the same DRC in the case of rotor sprinklers operating under no-wind conditions. The single-leg DRC is not so valid for pop-up sprays because of variability between rays. Research suggests that a three-dimensional depiction of a pop-up spray may be preferred to portray and compare pop-up spray performance.

Figure 4.4 depicts a graphic concept of the effect of overlapping and complementing sprinklers. Sprinklers are often spaced at the effective radius recommended by the manufacturer. The DRC for each sprinkler is shown as a smooth curve. The actual depth of application, due to the combined effects of multiple sprinklers, is shown to have high points and low points. The desired minimum application is a flat horizontal line indicating the minimum amount of water that must be applied to keep the turf green and aesthetically appealing.

The low spots of the actual application must be at or above the desired minimum application under a presumption that any turf receiving a lesser application will show stress. This graphic is idealized

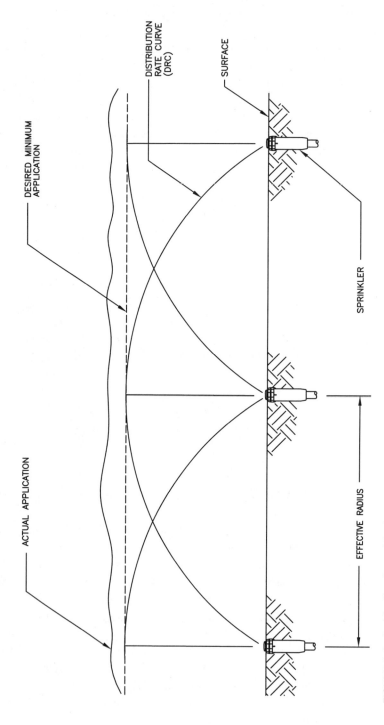

FIGURE 4.4. An idealized graphic showing the effect of overlapping sprinklers. Most sprinkler nozzles apply more water near the sprinkler and less and less water as distance from the sprinkler increases. The shape of the curve, called the distribution rate curve (DRC), is never as smooth or predictable as illustrated here. Sprinklers are spaced not to exceed the manufacturer's recommended effective radius, resulting in so-called head-to-head coverage.

and probably too simplistic in some ways. The shape of the DRC is never so smooth and the actual depth of application varies much more dramatically. But imagine, in general, what happens if the sprinkler spacing is stretched. The DRC will remain the same, but one sprinkler will no longer throw to the other complementing sprinkler and a "dip" in the actual application will form in the middle area between sprinklers. The dip represents less applied water and, consequently, inadequately irrigated turf. Alternatively, the minimum depth of application must be achieved, even between sprinklers where less water is applied; in this case, however, large amounts of water will be wasted near the sprinklers.

Why would anyone stretch sprinkler spacings to exceed the manufacturer's recommended maximum? The answer lies in the process of competitive bidding and irrigation design-build situations, where one sprinkler contractor can underbid another by using fewer sprinklers. Fewer sprinklers also translates to fewer laterals, less piping, less wiring, fewer controller stations, and so forth. An astute buyer would recognize the stretched spacings and contract with a contractor presenting a sound, water-efficient design, but, unfortunately, some buyers take the lowest-cost system, regardless, and are ultimately saddled with poor uniformity and higher annual water bills than they should have.

The DRC for a sprinkler is generally determined in a laboratory, or otherwise indoors, so wind does not distort the sprinkler pattern. For the test, a sprinkler with a given nozzle is operated at a known pressure. **Catch cans** are spaced evenly away from the sprinkler, and the depth of water in each catch can is measured and recorded after the test is completed.

To thoroughly understand what spacing between sprinklers is best, one must use the actual DRC for the sprinkler and nozzle in question, operating at a specified pressure. Figure 4.5 shows several representative distribution rate curves.

DRC "A" is ideal and nonexistent in practice. The shape is that of a wedge. Imagine another sprinkler, with a similar wedge-shaped DRC, located at the tip of the wedge. The two wedges complement each other perfectly, and the resultant application from both sprinklers would be perfectly flat. Unfortunately, this ideal distribution rate curve cannot be achieved in practice.

Now, consider DRC "B." This is a real DRC for a real sprinkler-pressure-nozzle combination. As an irrigation designer, would you use this sprinkler if you were cognizant of the shape of the DRC? The irregularities found in DRC "B" would make it virtually impossible to achieve a high uniformity and high application efficiency.

Consider DRC "C." This is also a real DRC for a real sprinkler-pressure-nozzle combination. You can see that the shape of this DRC is much more uniform and more predictable. A efficient irrigation system can be designed using this sprinkler, pressure, and nozzle.

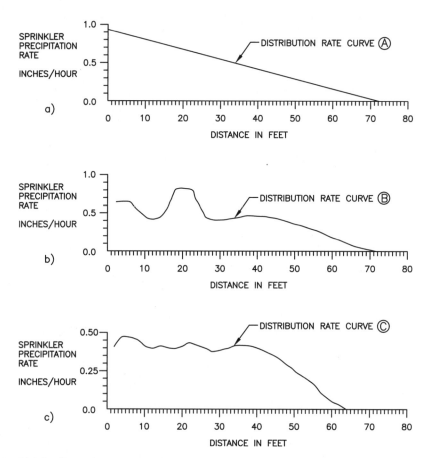

FIGURE 4.5. *Distribution rate curve "A" shows a theoretical, and nonexistent, wedge-shaped DRC. If such a DRC were achievable in practice, the complementing sprinkler, with an identical DRC, would result in a perfectly flat and efficient water application. DRC "B" is an actual DRC obtained from a Center for Irrigation Technology tested sprinkler-pressure-nozzle combination. DRC "C" is an actual DRC obtained from the same tested sprinkler as DRC "B," but at a different operating pressure. Note that DRC "C" is much more uniform and easier to use when attempting to maximize application efficiency. Also, in comparing DRCs "B" and "Cm," note that a change in pressure alone can make a difference in the shape of the curve.*

DRC "C" also exemplifies another aspect of practical DRC use and a special, atypical circumstance with sprinkler irrigation. Many times it is desirable to place sprinklers near the boundary of an irrigated area while avoiding the normal practice of "trimming out" the sprinklers at the boundary. In this way, construction dollars can be saved, and the presumption is that water thrown beyond the irrigated area is not a significant problem. In another case, rotor sprinklers may be placed next to a curb line and throw away without complementing sprinklers beyond. Both scenarios can be used to cause the irrigated landscape conditions to blend into the adjacent unirrigated conditions or native vegetation. What is the "effectively irrigated width" of a single row of uncomplemented sprinklers? In other words, what width of turf will be irrigated in a reasonable fashion and exhibit uniform turf appearance? A common rule-of-thumb answer for this question is "60 percent of the radius of throw." The validity of this rule can be seen in DRC "C"—the DRC is fairly flat out to approximately 36 feet, or 60 percent of 60 feet. Beyond 36 feet, water application begins to decrease and the areas beyond the 36-foot width will be stressed for water.

Conceivably, DRC "B" and DRC "C" may result from the same sprinkler and nozzle operated at different pressures. It is important to not discount a sprinkler or nozzle solely because an unacceptable DRC is found for one operating circumstance. The norm is to pick a sprinkler, then evaluate which nozzle and pressure combinations provide an acceptable DRC.

It is good practice to:

1. Pick a sprinkler model for the attributes of the sprinkler and cost criteria.
2. Pick a nozzle based on the pressure and effective radius found in the manufacturer's catalog.
3. Evaluate the DRC for that sprinkler-pressure-nozzle combination.
4. Iterate with the sprinkler-pressure-nozzle combination and the DRC to achieve an acceptable compromise and a reasonable efficiency.

Because of the high interest in DRCs, and pressure from the irrigation design community and others, there is much more evaluation and scrutiny of DRCs than ever before. DRCs are available from the manufacturer, as well as from independent facilities. It is probably too time-consuming for DRC data to be collected directly by the irrigation designer or end user, so other data sources must be consulted.

For example, the Center for Irrigation Technology (CIT) in Fresno, California, operates an independent testing lab to determine and publish DRC data. CIT can be commissioned to test specific sprinkler-pressure-nozzle combinations for a nominal fee if the data sought are not already in their database. CIT will purchase a sprinkler for you, or you can send it a sprinkler and nozzle to be tested. The data from all of CIT's tests are available through its publications or CIT's database inherent with and integrated with analysis software.

Manufacturers are becoming less reticent to provide DRC data, which are being demanded by irrigation designers and scrutinizing end users involved in equipment selection. The design community has learned to properly evaluate a DRC and use it to the designer's advantage, as well as to the manufacturer's advantage. DRC data may one day be published along with other performance data in catalogs. Inevitably, manufacturers will place increased emphasis on development of nozzles that offer better DRCs, improved performance, and better sprinkler uniformity.

Some manufacturers are using new technologies to improve nozzle development programs while decreasing research and development costs. **Stereo lithography** is a technique for quickly and inexpensively fabricating an irregular shape, like a sprinkler nozzle, from epoxy. A laser is programmed by computer to pass over selected portions of liquid epoxy. The epoxy hardens only in the areas where the laser passes. The result is a plastic-like, three-dimensionally-correct prototype nozzle, which can be used for testing. Stereo lithography dramatically decreases nozzle development and testing time. Almost more importantly, it is easier for design engineers to conceptualize and develop prototypes of very different nozzles having unique shapes and characteristics. Another process, **selective laser centering**, results in a similar, but flexible, end product suitable for tests.

Sprinkler Uniformity

The term **uniformity** refers to how evenly water is applied by overlapping sprinklers. Uniformity can be measured for an irrigation system that has already been built, or it can be evaluated during the design stage using computer programs. With a built and operating irrigation system, catch cans are placed in a grid under the operating sprinklers on a lateral. Water from one or more sprinklers falls into each catch can, the water accumulates, and the depth can be measured. If 0.25 inches falls in a catch can as a result of a 15-minute test, for example, then the sprinkler precipitation rate is 0.25 inches times 4, or 1.00 IPH.

Uniformity can be evaluated on a theoretical basis by using the sprinkler DRC, an assumed sprinkler spacing and pattern, and a suitable computer program. A computer simulation is then run using theoretical "catch cans" gridded out by the computer program. A graphic result from such a computer simulation is called a **densogram.** A dot density pattern is used to depict more or less water in each catch can by gridding in more or less dots. Figure 4.6 shows a densogram created for a sports field using the DRC from a particular sprinkler-pressure-nozzle combination. A disadvantage of densograms is that there is no way to precisely compare one densogram with another. The subtleties between densograms are not easily picked up by the human eye. For this reason, a metric or mathematical comparison can be more enlightening and precise.

Three **uniformity parameters** or **metrics** have been used in landscape irrigation. **Christiansen's Coefficient of Uniformity** (CCU) is the oldest parameter, having been developed for agricultural

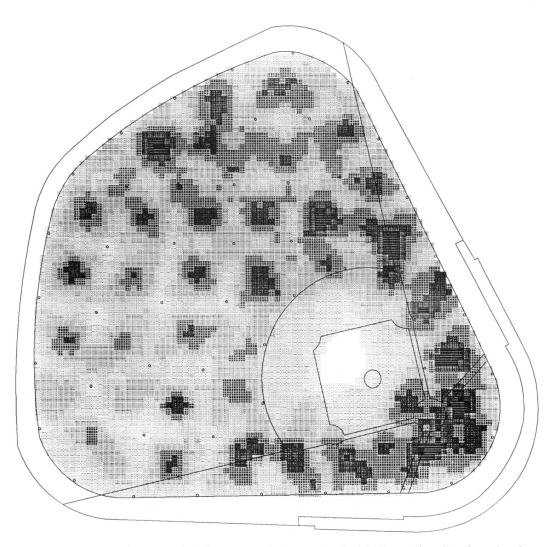

FIGURE 4.6. *A computer-generated densogram. A densogram depicts the uniformity of overlapping sprinklers in a graphic manner using dots. A low dot density indicates less water application, while a higher dot density indicates more water application. Such an analysis can help in comparing different sprinkler layout patterns and differing distribution rate curves. In this case, the densogram is based on actual sprinkler layout and not an equilateral triangle or square pattern.*

sprinkler systems in the 1940s. The **distribution uniformity** (DU) parameter is influenced by the under irrigated areas in the turf and is more widely used than CCU. In recent years, the **scheduling coefficient** (SC) has been recognized as the preferred parameter for turf irrigation because it is sensitive to underwatered areas.

CCU compares the average difference between a measured depth from a catch can and the mean depth. A perfectly uniform (and nonexistent) application will have a CCU of 100 percent. CCU is not sensitive to underwatered areas, so it has little utility in evaluating turf sprinkler performance. Turf appearance, covering the ground fully and uniformly, is a priority in landscapes. Even sprinkler layout patterns with rather high CCU can produce underirrigated areas and stressed turf. Turf can lose aesthetic appeal dramatically with stressed areas; thus, CCU is the poorest indicator of application efficiency for landscape irrigation.

DU corrects for some of the turf-related shortcomings and deficiencies of CCU by evaluating the average precipitation rate of the driest 25 percent of the catch cans divided by the mean precipitation rate. Although DU is a considerable improvement over CCU, it may still cause one to lose perspective of unwatered areas.

SC has come to be the most widely accepted metric for turf sprinkler evaluation because it is very sensitive to underwatered areas. SC was developed at the Center for Irrigation Technology and is simply the average precipitation rate divided by the least precipitation rate extracted from the catch cans. A perfect (and nonexistent) SC is 1.0. Good sprinkler nozzles will have SCs of 1.15 to 1.5.

SC is named from the fact it can be used as a run-time multiplier. For example, assume the SC is 1.2. If a run time of 30 minutes is adequate based strictly on the turf water requirement and the sprinkler precipitation rate, then the actual run time would be 30 minutes times 1.2, or 36 minutes. This is the operating time that is necessary to provide adequate (minimum) water to the relatively dry areas in the layout in order to ensure optimal turf appearance.

The three-dimensional graphic shown in Figure 4.7 exemplifies an approach for presenting the scheduling coefficients associated with different nozzles and operating pressures for a particular sprinkler. A graphic such as this would be one way for a manufacturer to add application efficiency data to its catalog. One can quickly see the operating points that provide the lowest SCs.

Sprinkler Layout

When precipitation rates, distribution rate curves, and uniformity are understood, sprinkler layout should be rather simple, right? Wrong. Now the work begins. The irrigation designer is expected to take the very real, irregular, curvilinear shapes in the landscape and design an efficient irrigation system using available equipment. It is not an impossible task, but skill and experience become very important. A new designer's first sprinkler layouts will be time-consuming, and you should plan to complete several alternatives and pick the best after careful analysis.

There are many philosophical styles and techniques for sprinkler layout. Whatever technique works initially may be dropped, or at least modified, later. The time spent evaluating sprinkler layout patterns will

Scheduling Coefficient Evaluation
(rotor sprinkler, equilateral triangle pattern)

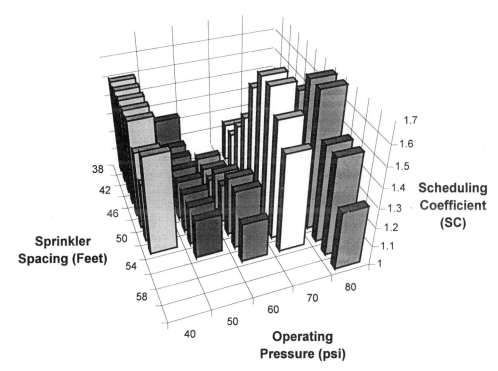

FIGURE 4.7. *A three-dimensional depiction of scheduling coefficient (SC) as a function of spacing and pressure. Such a graphic provides a means to quickly determine which operating points provide for the lowest SC with a given sprinkler and nozzle.*

cause anyone to become more efficient over time. Eventually, poor layout patterns will stand out off the page, almost as obvious as a big blotch of spilled coffee.

The following rules are intended to provide some initial direction and assistance with sprinkler layout:

- Generally, lay in sprinklers around the perimeter of the landscaped area first, then lay sprinklers into the interior of the irregular shape.
- The sprinkler layout patterns should form equilateral triangles, squares, distorted triangles, and distorted squares. All the patterns mentioned are appropriate and can, and probably will, be mixed within the layout.
- Pentagon shapes should be avoided. Pentagons generally indicate a problem—usually stretched sprinkler spacings or a sprinkler left out.

- Place sprinklers in all corners and other obtuse angles of the perimeter. (Today's water costs and public concern about water on hard surfaces dictate utilizing sprinklers in corners.)
- Consider wind. In practice, wind effects in small areas are often ignored. Prevailing wind should be considered on large, open turf areas like parks and golf courses.
- It is preferable for the "flat" layout of the scaled irrigation drawing to show the actual number of sprinklers required, or somewhat more than might be required.
- Sprinkler overspray onto any hard surface should be minimized. Overspray wastes water and can also increase owner and designer liability.
- Spacing is manufacturer- and sprinkler nozzle-specific. (Maximum effective radius is provided in catalog performance data, and distribution rate curve data can be obtained from the manufacturer or from independent testing laboratories.)

Some irrigation designers like to slide a scaled template of either square or equilateral triangles behind the landscape drawing sheet to be a rough guide and to provide a starting point. This can be particularly helpful to new designers looking for the sprinkler layout patterns that are appropriate in a particular irregular shape. Remember, however, there is no panacea in perfect square or equilateral triangle patterns. Distorted squares or triangles are acceptable.

Sometimes sprinkler placement issues or performance characteristics may dictate landscape design changes. For example, a very narrow turf strip might best be mulched instead of even attempting to irrigate it. Ideally, the landscape design and the irrigation design are accomplished in consort and complement each other closely.

A Practical Approach for Perimeter Sprinklers

A simple mathematical approach can help the irrigation designer lay in evenly-spaced sprinklers along a perimeter.

- Measure the dimension of the perimeter or a logical portion of the perimeter.
- Divide the measured dimension by the sprinkler's effective radius (the maximum spacing).
- Round the result *up* to the nearest integer.
- Divide the measured dimension by the number rounded to the nearest integer.
- The result is the exact spacing to use between sprinklers.

For example, assume you wish to lay in sprinklers next to a fence that has a corner-to-corner dimension of 95 feet. You want to use pop-up spray sprinklers with a maximum spacing of 15 feet against the fence line. If you divide 95 feet by 15 feet, the result is 6.33. Thus, there will be 6.33 sprinklers located along the fence. But, there is no such thing as 0.33 or $\frac{1}{3}$ sprinkler. So, round 6.33 up to the nearest integer, which is 7. There will be 7 spaces between sprinklers. Now divide 95 feet by 7 to get the actual spacing between sprinklers, which is 13.6 feet. A spacing of 13.6 feet is less than 15 feet, so the manufacturer's maximum spacing is not exceeded. The sprinkler spacing will be closed up somewhat to accommodate the reality of the 95-foot fence; this is normal and accepted practice.

It is always acceptable to close up the spacing between sprinklers, but it is not acceptable to stretch the spacings. You may ask yourself if it would be acceptable to stretch the spacing slightly to deal with problem dimensions. Consider, again, the roadway median example used previously, but assume the curb-to-curb dimension is 16 feet instead of 15 feet. Is it still acceptable to use half-circle, 15-foot series pop-up sprays at each curb line? The answer is probably yes, because adding a row of fulls would dramatically increase costs, and there would be some inefficiency created by having a spacing of 8 feet between the fulls and the halves. In these situations, irrigation designers must call on their own experience and the manufacturer's experience to make a decision.

A divider—a tool found in most manual drafting sets—is helpful in laying out sprinkler locations on the drawing sheet. Place the divider on the scale edge and set it to the calculated sprinkler spacing. Then, use the divider to "walk out" the sprinkler locations using the point of the divider to make a pinprick on the paper.

A Simple, but Practical, Layout Example

Consider the 100-foot square shape shown in Figure 4.8, and assume you are to determine an sprinkler layout with a high application efficiency. Assume that water cannot be thrown outside the irrigated area.

This shape offers several obvious and very simple solutions, but an understanding of the process involved can help one extrapolate the process to more complex shapes. First, the area must have sprinklers in the corners and evenly spaced along the perimeter. Given this criterion, there are at least three alternatives that one can immediately consider. The area can be irrigated with sprinklers spaced at 25 feet, at 50 feet, and at 33 feet. Each of the resultant patterns is shown in Figure 4.8. Now, the distribution rate curves and the scheduling coefficients of various sprinkler-pressure-nozzle combinations can be considered and analyzed, as was described earlier.

If maintenance personnel were asked to pick the preferred layout given only the three patterns, they would probably pick the layout with the 50-foot spacing. Their decision, strictly from the maintenance person's point of view, would be to pick the layout with the lowest number of sprinklers and the least amount of pipe. This is the obvious

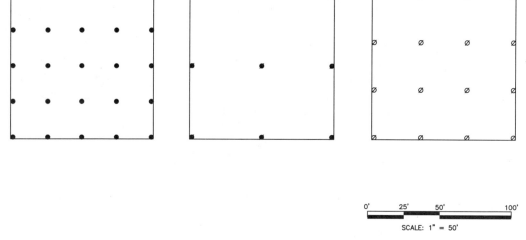

FIGURE 4.8. *Sprinkler layout alternatives in a 100-foot by 100-foot irrigated area. Assuming that sprinklers must "trim out" the irrigated area, three alternatives can be conceptualized using 25-foot-, 33-foot-, and 50-foot-radius rotor sprinklers. After concepts such as these are developed, specific sprinkler-pressure-nozzle combinations can be analyzed to pick the alternative that results in the highest application efficiency. The same process is followed for a more irregular irrigated shape.*

decision for them because fewer sprinklers and less pipe should translate into fewer repairs and less maintenance time.

The 50-foot spacing may very well be the best choice, but, from the irrigation designer's perspective, the decision cannot be made until the DRCs are determined and application efficiency metrics analyzed. The layout with the 25-foot spacing may have superior application efficiency, and it may be possible to pay for the additional sprinklers, pipe, and annual maintenance through annual water savings attributable to the sprinkler layout.

This analytical process can be followed for more complex shapes as well. Sometimes, only one typical shape and spacing within the project needs to be analyzed, as, for example, with a sports complex with lots of open turf to irrigate. Sometimes, two or three shapes and spacings can be spotted as typical of the project. This can lead to the selection of multiple sprinkler, pressure, and nozzle combinations, each selected for the fact that it is appropriate for certain conditions. It is quite possible that sprinklers from different manufacturers may be indicated and warranted through this analysis. The irrigation designer, driven by this process, may find that one manufacturer has the preferred long-range rotor sprinklers, whereas another manufacturer has the preferred short-range rotor sprinklers.

Sprinkler Laterals

A sprinkler lateral constitutes all of the pipe network and sprinklers that are brought together, by virtue of the pipes, and located downstream of the lateral valve. When the valve opens, the pipe gradually becomes pressurized and the sprinklers begin to function.

Small laterals, having very few sprinklers, are desirable from the standpoint of management flexibility. Small laterals let the system manager change the operational program in response to differences in soils, micro-climate, or any other factor that influences when, or for how long, irrigation occurs.

The best example of small laterals is **valve-in-head sprinklers**, which consist of a single valve and sprinkler packaged together—basically a very small lateral. On a golf course, the valve-in-head sprinkler provides the ultimate in operational flexibility; this is why golf superintendents request or demand them.

On the other hand, large laterals tend to be much more economical. A single valve with a control wire and single controller station irrigate a relatively large portion of the site. This reduces the number of valves, the length of wire, and the size or number of irrigation controllers. The effect is to keep costs down.

Lateral Size Limits

The maximum number of sprinklers on a lateral is dictated by available flow, Q_a. If we divide Q_a by the sprinkler flow rate, Q_s, the result is the maximum number of sprinklers on the lateral.

$$\frac{Q_a}{Q_s} = \text{maximum number of sprinklers on the lateral}$$

For example, if Q_a is 18 GPM from a 1-inch POC and Q_s is 2.2 GPM, then the maximum number of sprinklers per lateral is 8.2. However, one cannot have 8.2 sprinklers, so the maximum (integer) number of sprinklers is obtained by truncating the result. In other words, 8 sprinklers is the maximum number for the lateral in this example.

Note then, the flow rate of a lateral is the number of sprinklers on the lateral times the sprinkler flow rate. In the previous example, the lateral flow rate, Q_l, will be 8 times the sprinkler flow rate of 2.2 GPM, or:

$$Q_l = 8 \text{ sprinklers } (2.2 \text{ GPM} / \text{sprinkler}) = 17.6 \text{ GPM}$$

17.6 GPM is less than the Q_a of 18 GPM, so the lateral can be expected to function correctly, assuming lateral hydraulics are correct and support the required flow in each pipe segment within the lateral.

Differing nozzles or arcs within a single lateral require adding up the total flows somewhat differently. In some cases, the flow rate for individual sprinklers on the lateral must be determined based on the nozzle and nozzle arc used, and then the individual sprinkler flow rates are added together to determine the total lateral flow rate.

Lateral Pipe Routing

One technique to use when considering pipe routing is to think of yourself, the designer, as the ditching machine operator completing the excavation for the lateral you have designed. Wanting to complete the trenching work efficiently, you will consider an approach that will minimize the number of "starts and stops," or the number of times you will have to stop, reposition your trenching machine, drop the digging chain boom, and start ditching again. As the ditching machine operator, the more time you spend actually ditching, as opposed to positioning your equipment, the more efficient you can be. As the irrigation designer, it is important to consider the installation techniques and strategy that will be followed during construction. Successful designers get complimentary comments from irrigation contractors who appreciate the thought that went into the design and consideration of the contractor's viewpoint.

Another important consideration with lateral pipe routing is lateral hydraulics. As water flows through pipe and fittings, water pressure is lost due to friction with the pipe and fittings. The goal is to link sprinklers together with a pipe network that is as efficient as possible from both the installation and the hydraulic standpoints. Sometimes the hydraulic and installation considerations are opposed and objectives must be balanced against each other. An "end-fed" lateral, one in which the water flow starts on one end of the lateral and flows to the opposite end, is good from the installation standpoint, as there is only one trenching machine "start" and one "stop." But the lateral can be more hydraulically efficient if the lateral is "center-fed." With center-fed laterals, the amount of pipe may be greater than the end-fed alternative, but the average pipe size can be smaller and the hydraulics better.

Refer to Figure 4.9. Laterals that are center-fed in either a straight or H-shaped pipe layout pattern are preferred over an end-fed pipe layout. Assuming a flat area, an "H" in the figure refers to the sprinkler or sprinklers that will operate at the highest pressure within the lateral, and the "L" refers to the sprinkler or sprinklers that will operate at the lowest pressure. Pipe can be sized for all the layout patterns depicted so as to meet the desired hydraulic criteria. However, the layout patterns of laterals (a) and (b) allow for a smaller average pipe size than laterals (c) and (d).

There is at least one special case to consider: sports fields. Sports fields should not have equipment, other than sprinklers, located on the field because of the injury risk. Turf is a lot more forgiving to an athlete than a hard plastic valve box lid. So, remote control valves, as one example, must be located off the field proper and grouped to the side away from the playing surface in their respective valve boxes. In this case, end-fed laterals may be the lowest-cost approach to balancing the criteria that are imposed on the irrigation designer.

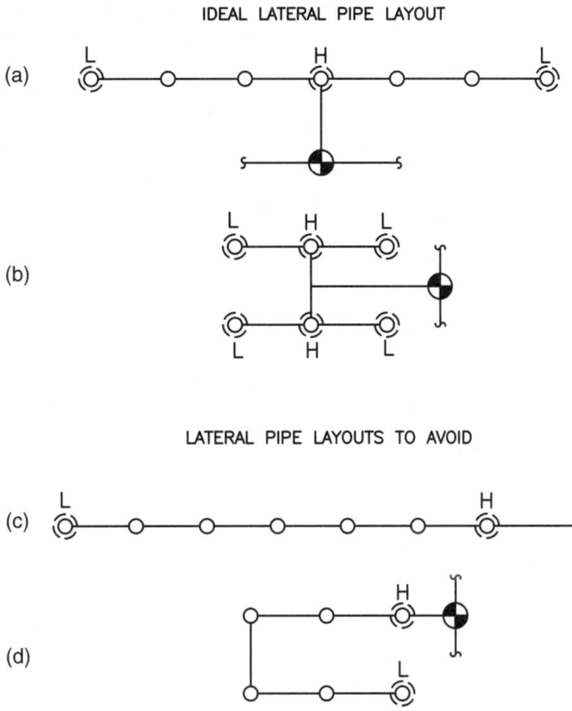

FIGURE 4.9. *Lateral layout alternatives. From the hydraulic perspective, it is always preferred to have "center-fed" laterals that form "T" or "H" patterns. "End-fed" laterals should be avoided, except for special cases.*

IDEAL LATERAL PIPE LAYOUT

(a)

(b)

LATERAL PIPE LAYOUTS TO AVOID

(c)

(d)

The Future for Sprinkler Irrigation

For large areas of turf grass, rotor sprinklers have the lowest **installed unit cost**[4] of any modern irrigation method. Therefore, sprinklers are probably here to stay in turf irrigation applications as long as water costs do not change dramatically. Water costs are rising, however, and a new irrigation method that breaks all the accepted paradigms could be invented. What if a new method was both lower in cost and higher in efficiency? If water costs increased twofold, an additional increment of application efficiency improvement would, in all likelihood, pay for itself and force a basic change in current concepts. For now, though, sprinkler irrigation remains a very appropriate choice for large areas of turf.

Review Questions

Verify both the equilateral triangle and square pattern precipitation rates found for the generic sprinklers found in Appendix A.

---

4. Installed unit cost refers to the total material cost plus the total labor cost divided by the total project area. The result, usually expressed as dollars per square foot or dollars per acre, is the best cost number to use in comparing one irrigation method to another because it considers installation cost (labor and machine) in addition to equipment costs.

Explain the difference between the term "matched precipitation rate" and "balanced precipitation rate."

Procure a DRC for a real sprinkler-pressure nozzle. Consider a grid of 9 catch cans located inside an equilateral triangle pattern with sprinklers spaced at the effective radius for the sprinkler. Use the DRC to determine the amount of water that falls into each of the 9 cans. Calculate the scheduling coefficient for the resulting data.

5

Drip Irrigation

■ **Drip irrigation is advantageous in numerous situations. A drip irrigation system can conserve water, reduce initial construction costs, and enhance plant growth.**

Drip irrigation is also commonly referred to as "trickle" or "low-flow" irrigation. The basic concept of drip irrigation is to provide near-optimal soil moisture on a continuous basis while conserving water.

Agricultural research shows that plants respond favorably to the soil moisture regime afforded with drip irrigation and larger, healthier plants can be expected in a given growth period.

Favorable plant response is well documented in crops such as apples, citrus, grapes, and tomatoes, but these responses must be extrapolated to the landscape environment and an assumption made that most landscape plants also respond favorably. Certainly, the abundance of successfully drip irrigated landscapes supports this extrapolation. Research describes only one variety of oranges in Florida that did not respond favorably to light, frequent irrigations.

The first reported application of drip irrigation in the United States was made in Colorado in 1913. It was noted at that time that the concept was too expensive for practical use. The advent of reliable, inexpensive plastics has changed that, so the conclusion was accurate for that time but misleading concerning the future.

Classically, drip irrigation has been used in agriculture with high-cash-value tree or vegetable crops, or crops grown under extraordinary conditions such as high-cost water, power, or fertilizer situations. Drip irrigation has been in widespread use for roughly three decades and has "come into its own" in application to landscapes. It has been most actively used in landscapes since about 1970.

Drip irrigation is a system that applies water directly to individual plants, as opposed to sprinkler systems, which irrigate all of the surface area. This is accomplished by relatively small–diameter lateral pipes with "emitters" attached to supply each plant with water. Emitters are the key devices within the system, as they afford, through their hydraulic design, the $\frac{1}{2}$- to 2-gallon-per-hour flow rates. Note that these low flow rates, expressed as GPH rather than GPM, are basically different from pop-up spray sprinklers by a factor of 60.

Figure 5.1 shows a section through a tree with emission points on either side and the resulting wetted profile in the soil.

When compared with landscaping, drip irrigation in agricultural applications is relatively simple. The crops are basically homogeneous in nature, usually of the same size, and, for the most part, grown in a single micro–climate. Landscape designers, on the other hand, often must deal with plants of different species and size, all in the same area. This would almost dictate a separate irrigation system for each plant. With drip irrigation and the ability to select emitters of different flow rates and / or vary the number of emitters per plant, a flexibility becomes available to the irrigation designer that no other irrigation method affords.

Landscaping is the arena where drip irrigation is experiencing the greatest growth. Drip irrigation has proved viable in landscapes because

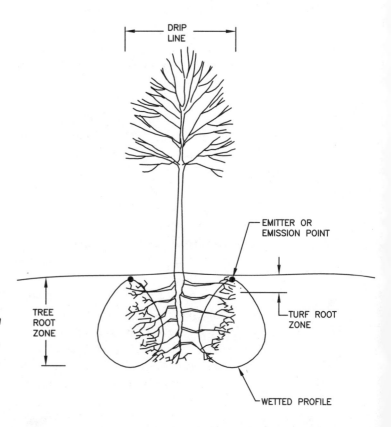

FIGURE 5.1. *A cross section through a drip irrigated tree. Emission points are located in a balanced configuration concurrent with the drip line of the tree. If the tree is planted in turf, drip irrigation can be managed to provide deeper watering to the tree, while sprinklers can be managed for the shallower root zone turf.*

of the ability to save costly water while providing a growth advantage to the plants and reducing initial construction costs.

Drip irrigation is ideally suited to many landscape situations, such as the wide and random spacing of landscape plant materials, the high and rapidly rising costs of water and pumping power, and (in most situations) the lower initial cost of drip irrigation in shrub beds.

In landscapes, drip irrigation is most often used together with sprinkler irrigation, resulting in what is referred to as a combination sprinkler / drip irrigation system. Sprinklers irrigating turf grass offer the lowest cost per irrigated area, but drip irrigation offers numerous advantages over sprinklers on mulched shrub beds, trees, potted plants, and the like. It is particularly cost-effective where plant spacing exceeds 2.5 feet on centers.

The tradeoffs between sprinkler and drip irrigation must be evaluated on a project-by-project basis. Factors include owner preferences, unit installed costs, contractor acceptance, desirability of foliage washing, and relative importance of conserving water.

Emitters

Emitters have come and gone over time, depending on the viability of the manufacturing company, market acceptance, and other subjective factors, such as appropriate applications and popularity. Most emitters available today have been tested and accepted by the market as suitable.

Emitters are the key component of the system. They are availabe in many sizes and shapes. Various emitters incorporate very different hydraulic methods to reduce pressure (or head) and create the one- or two-GPH flow. All emitters should incorporate a UV-inhibiting agent to prevent damage from solar radiation.

Some emitters have multiple outlets, and some multiple-outlet emitters even allow for differing flow rates from individual laterals.

Emitter selection is primarily dependent on factors such as flow characteristics, filtration requirement, cost, and local availability. Local availability is frequently the most critical issue in emitter selection. User familiarity and acceptance of the selected emitter within a locale is very important.

Emitter Types

Emitters can be generally classified into two categories—point source and aerosol. Figure 5.2 shows a cross section through the two types of emitters assuming that the emitter flow rate is equal.

A point source emitter drips water directly to the soil surface. The soil volume directly under the emitter may be saturated during system operation and immediately thereafter.

As implied by the name, the aerosol emitter throws water through the air for some distance before water contacts the soil surface. Some

FIGURE 5.2. *The contrast between point source and aerosol emitters having equal flow rates. Point source emitters drip at one or two gallons per hour (GPH) to a point directly below the emitter. Aerosol emitters, sometimes called mini-sprinklers, throw water through the air for some distance before contracting the soil surface.*

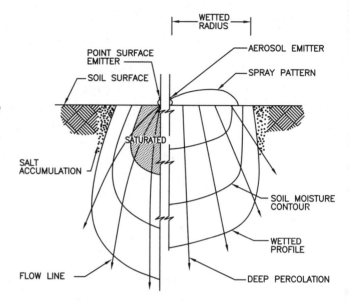

refer to this emitter type as a mini-sprinkler. Unfortunately, aerosol emitters are not as predictable as sprinklers, and distribution rate curves are not readily available to describe their performance.

Within each category, both pressure-compensating and non-pressure-compensating emitters are available. In general, pressure-compensating emitters will be somewhat more expensive than non-pressure-compensating emitters, but pressure-compensating emitters offer the distinct advantage of tolerating significant changes in elevation without materially affecting emitter flow rate.

Figure 5.3 shows the general shape of the performance curves for pressure-compensating and non-pressure-compensating emitters, respectively. With a non-pressure-compensating emitter, the flow rate increases as the pressure increases. As can be seen in the figure, the flow rate as a function of pressure flattens out with the pressure-compensating emitter. Each manufacturer's emitters are different, but 20 PSI to 50 PSI is the most common operating pressure range for pressure compensation.

Some pressure-compensating emitters experience an initial flushing mode, which occurs before the device reaches the normal operating pressure. The POC, the mainline, the remote control valve, and other system components must be sized and suited for the initial flow rate and allow the drip lateral to satisfactorily reach normal operating pressure. The flush mode, depending on the emitter, may show up in the performance curve, as shown in Figure 5.3.

With either type of emitter, salt accumulation can occur if salt is found in either the soil or the water supply. The salt accumulates at the soil surface at the point where surface evaporation occurs.

FIGURE 5.3. *Pressure-compensating versus non-pressure-compensating emitters. Many pressure-compensating emitters provide a consistent nominal flow rate of one or two gallons per hour (GPH) when the emitter operates in the 20 to 50 PSI range.*

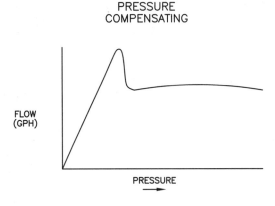

PRESSURE
COMPENSATING

FLOW
(GPH)

PRESSURE

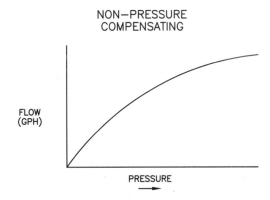

NON–PRESSURE
COMPENSATING

FLOW
(GPH)

PRESSURE

**Emitter Hose
(Line Source)**

Emitter hose products have been available for many years, after having being developed for high–cash–value row crops, such as sugar cane. Sugar cane is burned, along with the emitter hose, after two years of production. Partly for this reason, emitter hose products tend to have a shorter useful life than point source and aerosol emitters. These products can be used in special landscape cases requiring that narrow turf strips be drip irrigated.

Some emitters are factory installed at regular intervals into polyethylene hose. Such a device can be termed an emitter hose as well. Other products are single- or double-walled pipes with laser-drilled orifices. Some products are made from foamed PVC or ground-up, recycled tires re-manufactured into a pipe that sweats water continuously along its length.

**Emitter
Placement**

Guidelines to follow for proper emitter placement include:

- Balanced emitter configuration around the plant
- An even number of emitters

- Emitters placed at or near the drip line of the tree and moved outward as the plant matures and the drip line expands

Placement schemes are noted in Figure 5.4. The very flexible polyethylene or PVC hose used in landscapes lends itself to rather dramatic directional changes and circuitous pipe placement. In fact, the irrigation designer should not attempt to show the irrigation contractor every nuance of pipe placement in the design drawing, but should simply give an indication of routing and pipe quantity.

Construction installation details, presented at a larger scale than the design drawing, can also be used to exemplify emitter placement and pipe routing. Figure 5.5 shows an example of such a detail.

Horticulturalists recommend that the emitter locations move as the drip line expands with maturity. This seldom happens in practice, however, because of the labor and cost involved. Experience suggests that it probably is not absolutely necessary to relocate emitters, and the system can continue to function adequately over time, as long as the emitters are not so close to the plant as to cause excessive moisture and resultant problems with rot or saturated soil.

Advantages and Disadvantages of Drip Irrigation

The advantages of drip irrigation include:

- Precise placement of water in the plant root zone
- Reduced weed growth
- Minimal (even negligible) evaporative losses
- High application efficiency

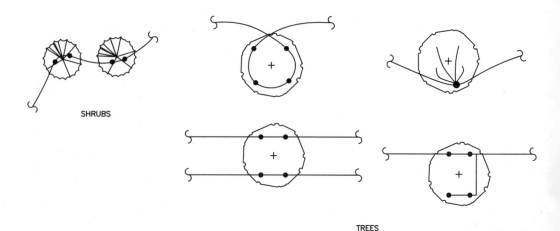

SHRUBS

TREES

FIGURE 5.4. *Various pipe routing alternatives, considering single- as well as multi-outlet emitters.*

FIGURE 5.5. *A pipe routing and emitter placement installation detail to help clarify drip system installation. Not every nuance of pipe routing can be shown on the design drawing.*

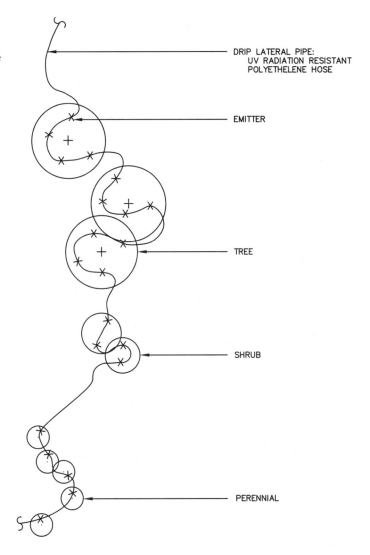

DRIP LATERAL PIPE:
UV RADIATION RESISTANT
POLYETHELENE HOSE

EMITTER

TREE

SHRUB

PERENNIAL

- Low flow rates relative to sprinkler irrigation (this implies smaller POC and lower plant investment fees, fewer valves, smaller controller, and less wire)
- Evaporation and overland flow minimized
- Lower installed unit cost than sprinklers (when stapled on the soil surface in shrub beds and hidden under mulch)
- No evidence of the irrigation system and, therefore, high vandal resistance
- Favorable plant response (larger, healthier plant materials over time)
- Flexible operating hours, considering possible irrigation during daytime hours, high wind conditions, and with pedestrians present (a good way to expand the water window)

- Flexibility to add emitters if plants are added
- Relatively easy to introduce water-soluble fertilizers and chemicals into irrigation system

Disadvantages of drip irrigation:

- Filtration required to prevent emitter clogging
- Proper management more complex
- Adaptation can be more involved than with sprinkler irrigation
- First indication of maintenance problems (emitters clogged) may show up only after plants are stressed

Wetted Profiles in Soil

Wetted profiles will differ quite dramatically in different soils. One of the best ways to determine the wetted profile is to actually set up several emitters of the selected type and flow rate in the field. After the emitters have functioned for an average or normal operating time (approximately one hour), an excavation slice through the soil directly under the emitter will show the size and extent of water movement. It is particularly important to understand the lateral movement.

Figure 5.6 shows the basic shape of the wetted profile in a loam, a clay, and a sand, respectively. This graphic is very generic and assumes a homogeneous soil, equal emitter flow rates, and equal operating times for each soil.

The highly amended soils, the soil stratification, and the excavated pit circumstance in the landscape all cause irregularity in the wetted profile and further support site investigation for assured determination of wetted profile shapes.

Plant Water Requirement Ratios

As compared to sprinkler irrigation, drip irrigation offers a rather unique opportunity. Sprinklers will apply a fairly uniform amount of water to the whole soil surface. Drip irrigation applies water only where it is needed, as dictated by an emitter. The quantity and flow rate of indi-

FIGURE 5.6. *Contrasting wetted profiles in loam, clay, and sand, respectively. The best way to understand the size and shape of the wetted profile in a particular soil is to field-operate an emitter for a typical run time and slice-excavate below the emitter.*

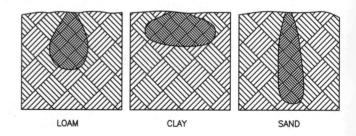

LOAM   CLAY   SAND

vidual emitters irrigating a plant, and as different from another plant in the plant pallet, allow the irrigation designer to develop a scheme to provide different ratios of water to each plant species.

Consider a single-drip lateral scenario using 1 GPH emitters and having two emitters per shrub and four emitters per tree. This scenario implies that the tree water requirement is twice the shrub water requirement, as shown in Table 5.1.

Trees could have 2-GPH emitters as well, or more emitters, to change the ratio. Another approach could be to use multiple-outlet emitters, with half the outlets open initially and all the outlets open at maturity. If this argument were applied to the entire plant list for a project, the number and flow rate of emitters could be specified for every plant in the pallet. In effect, there would be an implied water requirement ratio for each plant relative to all others. Unfortunately, a limitation of this approach is that comparing the relative water requirements of plants is a judgment at best, as the raw research required to accurately compare plant water requirements has not been done.

The combinations offer much flexibility to the drip irrigation designer, but also much complexity to the irrigation manager or maintenance personnel. It is important to achieve a good balance between design and management issues.

Another approach to match differing plant water requirements is to have separate laterals for trees, shrubs, ground cover, and perennials, respectively. Or, taken to the extreme, this argument could be carried through to having separate laterals for each variety of plant in the landscape. Might this approach be necessary or desirable in the future if water cost or availability dictate? The ultimate in flexibility would be achieved, but the unit cost would be high because of more valves, additional wiring, and higher controller station requirements.

System Components

Typical drip irrigation system components, working downstream, are:

- Pump (or pressurized water source)
- Primary filter

TABLE 5.1
An Implied Water Requirement Ratio Considering Differing Numbers of Equal-Flow-Rate Emitters

Shrub (emitter quantity)	Tree (emitter quantity)	Implied Ratio
2	4	$\frac{4}{2}=2$
2	8	$\frac{8}{2}=4$
2	12	$\frac{12}{2}=6$

- Fertilizer injector
- Primary pressure regulator
- Mainline pipe
- Remote control valve
- Secondary filtration
- Secondary pressure regulation
- Lateral manifold pipe
- Zone control valve
- Lateral pipe
- Emitters
- Flush plug

A typical drip irrigation system lateral, indicating many of the components, is shown in Figure 5.7. The lateral manifold is the portion of the pipe between the remote control valve and the zone control valve. This pipe does not have emitters on it, but is used to provide for operational flexibility and system adaptability.

Figure 5.8 indicates how drip lateral pipe is typically routed downstream of a zone control valve. A multi-outlet emitter is used on the tree, while two single-outlet emitters are used on each shrub. Note that the polyethylene lateral culminates at a flush plug. Flush plugs can be very simple and need not be installed in a valve box, but every lateral end should have a flush plug to facilitate periodic flushing to remove any suspended solids that have settled from moving water as the velocity drops.

Figure 5.9 shows a common approach for a remote control valve assembly used in drip irrigation. Working downstream in the detail, note the ball valve for maintenance, the wye filter for secondary filtration, the solenoid valve, and the pressure regulator. The ball valve and the union, utilized together, allow the valve assembly to be removed for maintenance without need to close other valves, which would disrupt operation of the whole system.

The wye filter will need to be flushed periodically. As contamination builds up on the screen, the pressure loss across the screen increases. Because of this, the filter should always be located upstream of the pressure regulator, so that the regulator can deliver the appropriate pressure to the lateral even considering varying pressure loss across the filter. A flush valve on the filter will simplify the flushing operation.

Fixed, in-line pressure regulators are suitable for relatively low flows in the 0.1 to 32 GPM range. A fixed pressure regulator is desirable from the low-cost standpoint, but an adjustable pressure regulator offers much more flexibility. If a number of drip lateral valves are located near one another, a single adjustable pressure regulator can be used upstream of the valve group in lieu of multiple pressure regulators.

Zone control valves are used to isolate selected portions of the lateral for maintenance purposes. A zone control valve installation detail

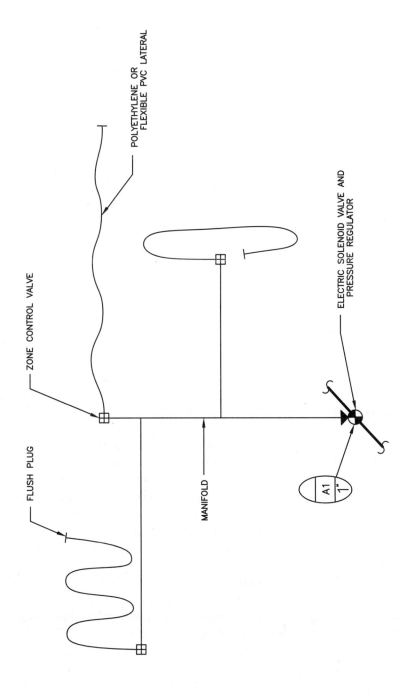

FIGURE 5.7. A typical drip irrigation lateral layout. The lateral manifold can be hydraulically oversized to protect flexibility to add emitters or plant materials in the future. Each polyethylene lateral section should culminate in a flush plug.

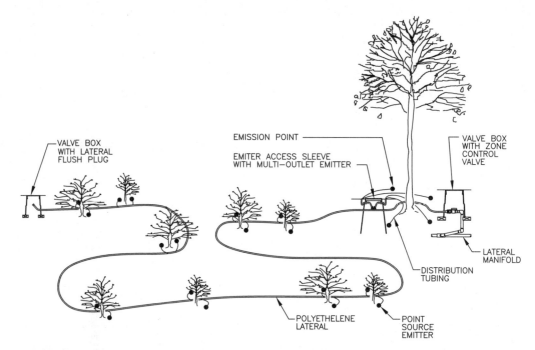

FIGURE 5.8. *A zone control valve and polyethylene or flexible PVC pipe routing concept. Manually operated zone control valves are useful for maintenance purposes when repairs must be made downstream.*

is depicted in Figure 5.10. This concept consists of a manually actuated ball valve at a location where the lateral manifold stops and upstream of the polyethylene or flexible PVC portion of the lateral. The ball valve is shown installed on a conventional swing joint to ensure that the valve and valve box can be easily set to final grade.

A fixed, in-line pressure regulator can be added downstream of the ball valve in Figure 5.10 to further control lateral operating pressure. This approach is desirable on slopes. If primary pressure control for the lateral is accomplished at the top of the slope, secondary pressure regulation can occur downslope to overcome pressure increases due to elevation.

Although ball valves are not generally suitable for flow regulation, they can be used to fine-tune lateral flows at points downstream of pressure regulators. In addition, zone control valves are desirable when maintenance might normally interfere with lateral operation, as the zone control valve can be closed temporarily during repairs on a portion of the lateral.

Small drip irrigation laterals may not warrant zone control valves, but drip laterals can become rather expansive and cover large areas. Consider a large parking lot with drip irrigated shrub bed islands. A single drip lateral may irrigate the entire parking lot, and conveniently

FIGURE 5.9. *A common solenoid valve assembly in a valve box. Note that the filter should always be upstream of the pressure regulator, allowing the regulator to provide a consistent downstream pressure even with varying pressure loss across the filter due to contaminant buildup on the screen.*

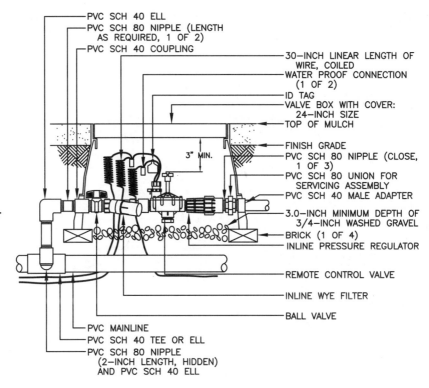

PVC SCH 40 ELL
PVC SCH 80 NIPPLE (LENGTH AS REQUIRED, 1 OF 2)
PVC SCH 40 COUPLING

30–INCH LINEAR LENGTH OF WIRE, COILED
WATER PROOF CONNECTION (1 OF 2)
ID TAG
VALVE BOX WITH COVER: 24–INCH SIZE
TOP OF MULCH
FINISH GRADE
PVC SCH 80 NIPPLE (CLOSE, 1 OF 3)
PVC SCH 80 UNION FOR SERVICING ASSEMBLY
PVC SCH 40 MALE ADAPTER
3.0–INCH MINIMUM DEPTH OF 3/4–INCH WASHED GRAVEL
BRICK (1 OF 4)
INLINE PRESSURE REGULATOR
REMOTE CONTROL VALVE
INLINE WYE FILTER
BALL VALVE

3" MIN.

PVC MAINLINE
PVC SCH 40 TEE OR ELL
PVC SCH 80 NIPPLE (2–INCH LENGTH, HIDDEN) AND PVC SCH 40 ELL

located zone control valves help with maintenance. When maintenance needs to be done, a zone control valve upstream of the problem area can be temporarily closed and maintenance facilitated.

Figure 5.11 depicts a cross section through a drip irrigated tree. An emitter access sleeve is shown to allow ease in locating the emitter in the landscape. Small-diameter (approximately $\frac{1}{8}$-inch) polyethylene or flexible PVC pipe is connected to the emitter to move the emission point to the desired location. Distribution tubing ends can be staked. All piping, emitters, and related equipment should be covered by mulch to discourage vandalism.

Hydraulic Considerations

Most of the hydraulics for drip irrigation is identical with any irrigation system and is covered in the Chapter 6 on hydraulics. However, there are a few important and unique hydraulic characteristics of drip systems.

Always consider the pressure falloff characteristics of the pressure regulator. The manufacturer supplies performance data that indicate the flow that can be expected given the difference between the upstream and downstream pressures.

FIGURE 5.10. *Zone control valve assembly. The PVC ball valve and valve box can be easily set to grade during construction through the use of a swing joint assembly.*

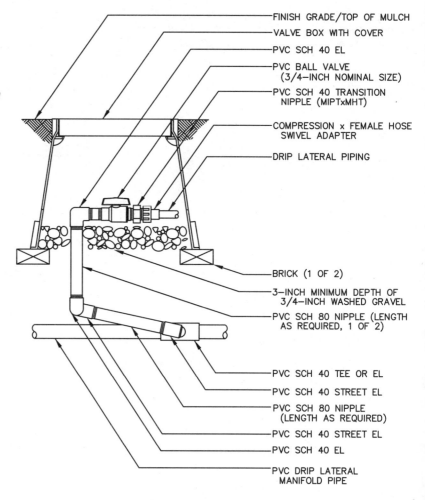

- FINISH GRADE/TOP OF MULCH
- VALVE BOX WITH COVER
- PVC SCH 40 EL
- PVC BALL VALVE (3/4–INCH NOMINAL SIZE)
- PVC SCH 40 TRANSITION NIPPLE (MIPTxMHT)
- COMPRESSION x FEMALE HOSE SWIVEL ADAPTER
- DRIP LATERAL PIPING
- BRICK (1 OF 2)
- 3–INCH MINIMUM DEPTH OF 3/4–INCH WASHED GRAVEL
- PVC SCH 80 NIPPLE (LENGTH AS REQUIRED, 1 OF 2)
- PVC SCH 40 TEE OR EL
- PVC SCH 40 STREET EL
- PVC SCH 80 NIPPLE (LENGTH AS REQUIRED)
- PVC SCH 40 STREET EL
- PVC SCH 40 EL
- PVC DRIP LATERAL MANIFOLD PIPE

Conservative hydraulics is often appropriate in order to allow flexibility for changes and expansion of the system over time. Hydraulically oversized lateral manifolds are desirable for flexibility, and the incremental cost to increase the size of this pipe is small.

The cost of keeping lateral run lengths short is also small relative to the overall cost of the system. Short run lengths improve lateral hydraulics, keep the system simple, and allow for more flexibility to increase flow in portions of the drip lateral if plant material is added.

Polyethylene or flexible PVC lateral pipe may have a smaller inside diameter than is commonly found in hydraulic reference tables. Fittings can also be unique to drip irrigation. The manufacturer's data will be useful, if not absolutely necessary, to deal with differences or nuances between products. Emitter barb size and shape present a unique resistance to water flowing in the lateral pipe and the manufacturer's own tests must be relied on.

FIGURE 5.11.
Emitter access sleeves can be used to protect and identify a multi-outlet emitter used to irrigate a single tree in the landscape. Small-diameter distribution tubing is used to move the emission point to the proper location.

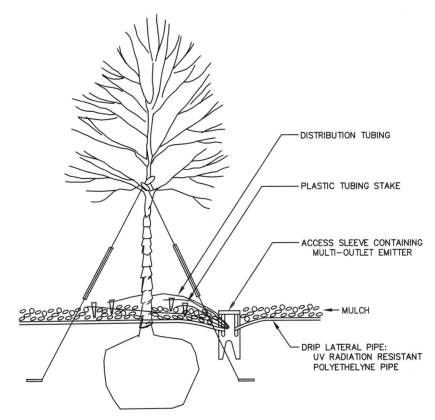

DISTRIBUTION TUBING

PLASTIC TUBING STAKE

ACCESS SLEEVE CONTAINING MULTI—OUTLET EMITTER

MULCH

DRIP LATERAL PIPE: UV RADIATION RESISTANT POLYETHELYNE PIPE

Hydraulic calculations can be accomplished with computer programs designed to handle gradually decreasing flows, slide rules available from manufacturers, or hydraulic reference tables. The simplest method is to use a reference table from the emitter and pipe manufacturer that accounts for pipe pressure losses, emitter barb loses, and gradually decreasing flows (based on plant spacings), all in one table.

Installation

Installation of many drip irrigation system components is identical with sprinklers. There is no difference for backflow devices, mainline, and mainline components. Differences in other parts of the system tend to be concerned with the lateral itself.

The lateral manifold is usually installed at a burial depth of 8 to 14 inches. Polyethylene or flexible PVC lateral pipe is often installed on the soil surface but protected under mulch and staked at 6- to 10-foot intervals with wire stakes.

Management Considerations

With drip irrigation, light but frequent irrigations are usually applied, which presents a favorable soil moisture environment. When the system is properly managed for climatic and soil conditions, the plant root zone is seldom saturated or dry; most plants respond very favorably.

Under proper irrigation system management, drip irrigation saves water because only the plant's root zone is supplied with water, and little water is lost to deep percolation, weed consumption, or soil surface evaporation.

Useful management tools with drip irrigation are tensiometers (see Figure 9.6) and soil probes. Tensiometers can be installed at different depths to monitor relative soil moisture levels. A soil auger is desirable to first ascertain, and then monitor, wetted profiles. With the auger, samples can be taken at regular intervals from the emitter and the shape of the wetted profile can be determined.

Emitter Clogging

A primary disadvantage of drip irrigation is that the small passages required of all emitters make the emitter susceptible to clogging. Therefore, the potential for clogging must be addressed at the design stage and maintenance practices to prevent clogging must be followed after construction.

Clogging is caused by particles in the water, biological growth, precipitation of chemicals, or some combination of these causes.

The prevention of clogging is first addressed through filtration. Pumps should have an intake screen. POCs should have primary filtration, which can take several forms. A device known as a **centrifugal separator** is appropriate for suspended high-density solids, such as sand, in the water. Centrifugal separators should be followed by a screen filter. Algae and other organic contaminants in the water are best removed by a medium such as a sand filter. Any filter must be backflushed, as contaminants cause excessive pressure loss across the filter. Backflushing can be automated or accomplished by manually opening the flush valve if the flushing cycle is not required too frequently.

If clogging occurs, chlorine treatment of the irrigation water is one of the best ways to mitigate the problem. Fortunately, potable water supplies have inherently been injected with chlorine at the recommended rate for clogging mitigation. With any nonpotable water source, chlorine can be injected with a suitable injection system, or the irrigation system could be flushed with chlorinated water from a potable source.

The Future of Drip Irrigation

Consider this: Only 1 percent of the world's water is fresh. Ninety-nine percent of this fresh water is underground. As it becomes more expensive to develop and deliver underground supplies, desalt sea water, or reclaim effluent water, the conservation and efficient use of available water resources becomes increasingly important. Drip irrigation is, and will continue to be, a strong technological tool for mitigating or, in some cases, solving water shortages. The method is undoubtedly here to stay. Therefore, those of us in the landscape irrigation industry need to learn to properly design, install, and manage drip irrigation.

Review Questions

What is a common flow rate for a single drip emitter?

Describe a zone control valve as used with drip irrigation, and the reasons why zone control valves may be useful.

Sketch the wetted profile that would be expected with drip irrigation under a point source emitter for a clay, loam, and sand soil types, respectively.

List the advantages and disadvantages of drip irrigation.

6

Hydraulics

- Understanding the principles of hydraulics is necessary to design a system that will operate correctly and at optimal efficiency.

Important hydraulic calculations in landscape irrigation can be classified as **static hydraulics** or **dynamic hydraulics.** Static hydraulics concerns water at rest and not flowing. Dynamic hydraulics concerns flowing water. An irrigation system with all valves closed is a good example of a static hydraulic situation. The same system is a good example of dynamic hydraulics immediately following the opening of a valve.

Static Hydraulics

In landscape irrigation, we talk about the static pressure at the POC, the operating pressure of the sprinkler, the pressure loss through the valve, the change in pressure due to elevation, and so on. Clearly, pressure and pressure change are key to understanding the hydraulics of irrigation systems.

Pressure, by definition, is a force per unit area, or:

$$\text{Pressure} = P = \frac{\text{Force}}{\text{Area}} = \frac{F}{A}$$

where

P = pressure in pounds per square inch or PSI
F = force in pounds
A = *area in square inches*

Force, in this static case, is equal to the weight of the water. The weight, W, is equal to the volume, V, of the water times the specific weight, S, of water.

$$F = W = VS$$

The specific weight of water is 62.4 pounds per cubic foot (lbs/ft³).
So, referring to Figure 6.1, an imaginary cubic foot of water:

$$P = \frac{F}{A} = \frac{W}{A} = \frac{V \times S}{A} = \frac{(1 \text{ ft}^3)\ (62.4 \text{ lbs/ft}^3)}{(12 \text{ in})\ (12 \text{ in})}$$

$$= \frac{62.4 \text{ lbs}}{144 \text{ in}^2} = 0.433 \text{ lbs/in}^2$$

lbs/in² is commonly abbreviated as PSI. This important derivation (the
only derivation, per se, contained in this book) demonstrates that one
cubic foot of water at rest has a pressure of 0.433 PSI at the base. This
conversion factor is significant to many hydraulic calculations and can
be used to calculate the *static* water pressure for any circumstance where
the vertical distance from a water surface (or datum) is known.
Simply stated as a conversion factor:

$$1 \text{ ft of water} = 0.433 \text{ PSI}$$

The reciprocal of this factor is also good to remember. The reciprocal
of 0.433 is 2.31. One PSI of pressure is created by a vertical column
of water having a height of 2.31 feet.

Or,

$$1 \text{ PSI} = 2.31 \text{ ft of water}$$

Note that the cross-sectional area of the water column is irrelevant
in determining pressure at the base of the column. Refer to Figure 6.2
as an example. The pressure at the bottom of a lake that is 100 feet
deep is 100 times 0.433, or 43.3 PSI. If a 100-foot-long pipe filled with

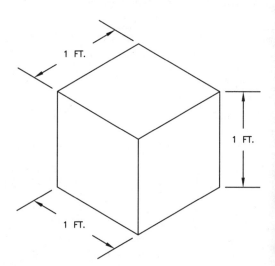

FIGURE 6.1. *A cubic foot of water weighs 62.4
pounds. We can also say the specific weight of
water is 62.4 lbs/ft³.*

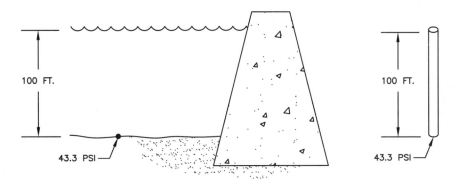

FIGURE 6.2. *The pressure in the lake at a point 100 ft deep is 43.3 PSI. Likewise, the pressure at the bottom of a 100 ft vertical column of water is 43.3 PSI. Whatever the circumstance, the evaluation or the change in elevation in feet can be multiplied by 0.433 PSI/ft to determine the pressure or pressure change due to elevation.*

water is standing on end, the pressure at the bottom is 43.3 PSI. If a town gets its water from a reservoir, and the reservoir's water surface is 200 feet above the town, then the static water pressure in the town is 200 times 0.433, or 86.6 PSI. Any number of additional examples can be conceptualized. Whatever the circumstance, one can multiply the elevation, or the change in elevation, in feet by 0.433 PSI/foot to determine the pressure or pressure change due to elevation.

Static pressure is the pressure of a no-flow, or $Q = 0$, system. The only factor required to determine the various pressures within a static system is the vertical elevation difference between some known pressure, or **datum**, and the point in the system where the static pressure is unknown.

Figure 6.3 shows a water tank and pipe network that ultimately delivers water to a faucet in a house. The vertical dimensions in the figure are provided but are not to scale. The figure should be viewed as simply a graphic representation of a water delivery system.

Note the various points as they relate to the datum, the water surface elevation of the tank. The static pressure at P_0, the datum, is zero because it is located at the water surface elevation. The static pressures at other points in the system can be determined by simply multiplying the vertical elevation difference from the datum by 0.433 PSI/ft.

Thus, the static pressure at P_1 is 60 ft times 0.433 PSI/ft, or 25.98 PSI. The static pressure at P_2 is equal to P_1 because P_1 and P_2 are at the same elevation. The static pressure at P_5 is 145 ft times 0.433 PSI/ft, or 62.79 PSI. The static pressure at P_4 is equal to P_5 and calculated at 86.60 PSI, because P_4 and P_5 are both 200 ft below the datum.

FIGURE 6.3. *A water tank and pipe network typical of many domestic water supplies. The static pressure at P_0, the datum, is zero because it is located at the water surface elevation. The static pressures at other points in this system are determined by simply multiplying the vertical elevation difference from the datum by 0.433 PSI/ft.*

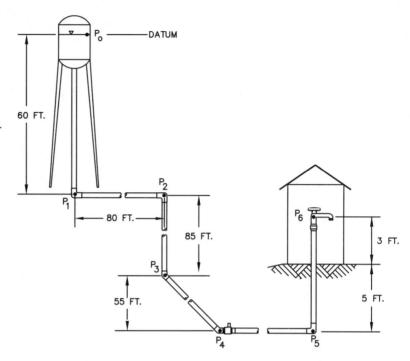

Knowing the static pressure at any one point allows the calculation of the static pressure at another point. For example, the static pressure at P_5 is 86.60 PSI, as noted above. The static pressure at P_6 can be calculated as:

$$P_6 = 86.60 \text{ PSI} - (8 \text{ ft}) (0.433 \text{ PSI/ft})$$

$$= 86.60 - 3.46 = 83.14 \text{ PSI}$$

P_6 also be calculated as:

$$P_6 = 192 \text{ ft } (0.433 \text{ PSI/ft}) = 83.14 \text{ PSI}$$

It does not matter how P_6 is calculated, as either approach gets the same result. It is most important for the designer to understand the calculation, and the most logical thought process and approach for an individual designer will probably be the one to use.

A very important initial piece of data needed to begin any irrigation system design is the pressure.[1] The static pressure at the POC is best determined by querying the water purveyor. The irrigation system must

---

1. Note that any municipal water system has constant demands on the system and, for this reason, the system is never truly static. Even so, the pressure at the POC is referred to as static pressure for landscape irrigation design purposes. Clearly, this term is something of a misnomer, but the irrigation designer can think of the pressure at the POC as a static pressure simply because the POC pressure does not fluctuate rapidly and is predictable at a known point.

be designed to function correctly during the summer months, when evapotranspiration rates are high, others are irrigating, and water pressure is at its lowest. The question for the engineering department in the water purveyor's office is, "What is the worst case (probably July) daytime pressure at my site?" Most water purveyors use mathematical computer models to forecast pressures within their systems, and they can easily advise you as to worst-case pressures.

Conversation notes concerning worst-case pressure, and including the date and name of the person contacted, should be entered into the project file for future reference. The worst-case pressure—the system design pressure—should always be clearly noted on the completed irrigation design drawings. Further, before irrigation construction begins, an affirmation of the pressure and flow from the POC should be made by the irrigation contractor. It is always preferable to learn of a discrepancy between the design pressure and the actual pressure before construction begins. Possible solutions to correct for a pressure discrepancy include:

- Selection of different (lower flow) nozzles for the sprinkler or sprinklers
- Complete redesign of the irrigation system
- Installation of a booster pump at the POC to increase pressure from the POC downstream

A booster pump adds both cost and complexity to an irrigation system. Although booster pumps are frequently used in landscape irrigation, and there is no reason other than cost to avoid them, it should be ascertained that a pump is definitely needed before one is designed into the system.

Many times, if the pressure at the POC drops after the irrigation system is constructed, a pump is the only logical solution. The built irrigation system cannot be easily altered, so a booster pump may offer the lowest-cost corrective action for low pressure.

Note that a pressure booster pump, as the name implies, should not be construed or offered as a means of increasing the available flow from the POC. Available flow is controlled by other factors—maximum flow velocity, for example—as described later in this chapter.

Dynamic Hydraulics and Mainline Pipe

Refer again to Figure 6.3. All of the previous static pressure calculations were based on static, no-flow, conditions. As soon as the faucet (or valve) at P_6 is opened, or some other water demand is created on the system, water begins to flow. When water flows in pipes, the interface between the flowing water and the pipe causes friction, which results in pressure loss. The flowing water loses pressure as fittings are encountered, as well. Further, any mainline component has a pressure loss—sometimes a dramatic pressure loss—associated with it.

A **mainline component** is considered to be any feature in the irrigation system that is not a pipe or a fitting. Remote control valves, curb stop valves, gate valves, and backflow prevention devices are all components by definition.

The key to determining pressures in a dynamic system is simply to use a valid technique and follow a process for determining pressure losses in pipe, fittings, and components. Then elevation, relative to a datum, adds or subtracts pressure in exactly the same way as it does with static pressure calculations.

A good organizational technique is to use the following process, or a similar format, to complete hydraulic calculations to result in a presentation suitable for the project file:

Pressure at P_1
- pipe losses   ← from Hazen-Williams reference tables
- fitting losses   ← from reference materials and tables
- component losses   ← from manufacturer's catalog
± pressure change due to elevation   ← from site plan or survey
= **Pressure at P_2**

Basically, this technique forces the irrigation designer to study each subset of the calculation separately for organizing and presenting the work. The designer should determine a presentation style that suits, and then stick to it over time to ease review of the calculations at a later date.

The pressure at P_1 is determined from measurements, calculated, or otherwise assumed. If P_1 is estimated, the assumptions used should be clearly stated. All the pipe losses can be calculated for each size and type of pipe. Then, all the fittings are counted and total fitting losses are calculated. The components are noted, counted, and the friction loss determined from manufacturer's performance data. Pressure change attributable to elevation gain or loss is then added or subtracted appropriately. Once each of the subportions of the calculation is completed, the dynamic pressure at P_2 can be determined by subtracting the friction loss and adding or subtracting pressure change due to elevation.

Frequently, the irrigated area covered by the lateral, or even the mainline, is flat. In these cases, there is no pressure variation due to elevation. Even though the effect on the calculation is zero, this part of the process should still be accounted for. With this discipline, you will always remember to account for elevation in the calculation, even if the result is zero or negligible.

As a simple example, consider Figure 6.4a. Water is flowing in a pipe, and reference points P_1 and P_2 are shown to be 100 ft apart. Assume the pressure at P_1 is known to be 100 PSI. There are no fittings and no components, so pressure loss is zero for fittings and components, respectively. P_1 and P_2 are at the same elevation, so pressure change due to elevation is zero.

The pressure difference between P_1 and P_2 is attributable to the friction loss in the pipe only. P_2 is clearly going to have a lower pressure than P_1, because it is downstream of P_2. Now assume that the pipe is 4-inch Class 200 PVC and the flow, Q, is 160 GPM. Knowing the type of pipe, the nominal diameter, and the flow rate, the friction factor can be determined. The **friction factor** is pressure loss due to friction per unit length of pipe.

The friction factor for this example can be obtained from the Hazen-Williams loss tables (see Appendix B). From the table, the pressure loss is 0.55 PSI/100 ft. Again, P_1 and P_2 are 100 ft apart, so given that there are no other pressure losses or gains:

a)
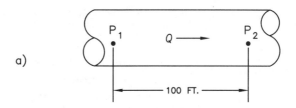

FIGURE 6.4. In 6.4a, water is flowing in a pipe and reference points P_1 and P_2 are shown to be 100 ft apart. There are no findings and no components, so pressure loss is zero for fittings and components, respectively. P_1 and P_2 are at the same elevation, so pressure change due to elevation is zero. The pressure difference between P_1 and P_2 is due only to the pressure loss experienced in the pipe itself. In 6.4b, again there are no fittings or components, so pressure loss is zero for fittings and components. The pressure difference between P_1 and P_2 is due to pipe friction plus the 20 ft of elevation gain.

b)
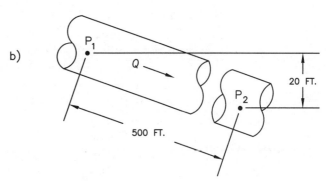

Pressure at P$_1$ = 100 PSI

− pipe losses = 100 ft (0.55 PSI/100 ft)	= −0.55 PSI
− fitting losses	= −0.00 PSI
− component losses	= −0.00 PSI
± pressure change due to elevation = 0 ft (0.433 PSI/ft)	= 0.00 PSI
= Pressure at P$_2$	**= 99.45 PSI**

Or,

$$P_2 = 100 \text{ PSI} - (0.55 \text{ PSI}/100 \text{ ft}) (100 \text{ ft})$$

$$= 100 \text{ PSI} - 0.55 \text{ PSI} = 99.45 \text{ PSI}$$

Consider Figure 6.4*b* and assume that nothing has changed except that P$_1$ and P$_2$ are 500 ft apart and there is an elevation change, specifically an elevation gain, of 20 ft.

Pressure at P$_1$ = 100 PSI

− pipe losses = 500 ft (0.55 PSI/100 ft)	= −2.75 PSI
− fitting losses	= −0.00 PSI
− component losses	= −0.00 PSI
± pressure change due to elevation = 20 ft (0.433 PSI/ft)	= +8.66 PSI
= Pressure at P$_2$	**= 105.91 PSI**

It is good practice, and good discipline, to always use the plus or minus sign in front of the result to emphasize whether the number adds or subtracts pressure.

In this calculation, P$_2$ is greater than P$_1$, even though P$_2$ is downstream and pipe friction loss has been subtracted. In this case, and in many hydraulic calculations, the elevation gain has more than made up for pipe friction loss. Clearly, pressure gain due to elevation can be a benefit and should be used to advantage in the irrigation design.

Mainline Pipe

Almost nothing is more important in an irrigation system than the mainline pipe. Both figuratively and literally, the mainline is the backbone of the irrigation system.

Mainline pipe, by definition, is that portion of the pipe that is pressurized continuously. From the point of connection, the mainline delivers water to the entire irrigated site. The mainline is pressurized continuously, so when a remote control valve is opened, having received 24 volts AC from the controller, water immediately flows into the lateral and sprinklers come up to their normal operating pressure and begin to function.

The mainline must be sized to deliver adequate pressure to all laterals, including, and most importantly, the **hydraulically worst case lateral** or laterals. Further, the mainline must be sized to avoid **water**

hammer or **surge pressures** that could cause damage to mainline pipe or components.

Mainline Routing

The criteria for mainline routing are not stringent, but routing does require some thought and understanding of project requirements. Basically, the mainline is routed so that remote control valves and quick couplers can be strategically located throughout the irrigated site. It is preferable that mainline be located away from structures in case of leakage or a mainline failure. Of necessity, mainline must pass beneath hard surfaces in the landscape, such as sidewalks or parking lots. The number of hard surface crossings should be minimized. Pipe used to accommodate other pipes or wire is called a **sleeve.** Irrigation pipes and wire are "sleeved" inside another pipe for protection and to facilitate repairs.

Quick coupler valves, if used, are located along the mainline and spaced to provide for incidental water needs. Quick couplers may be located at a maximum spacing to avoid long lengths of hose for washing down hard surface or washing plant materials. For this reason, quick couplers frequently dictate where mainline pipe is located.

Portions of the mainline that tee off from the primary mainline are sometimes called **submains.** Submains offer a way of reaching areas of the site that may be somewhat eccentric to most of the irrigated area.

The Point of Connection

Mainline pipe begins at the **point of connection (POC)** for the irrigation system. The size of the POC is dictated by the size of the "tap" into the water supply or the size of the water meter. The size of the mainline pipe is, in turn, dictated by the POC size and pressure loss criteria.

A typical potable-water POC is shown in Figure 6.5. Note that the typical legend symbols and approach to plan-view presentation are shown below the cross section. It is always important, whenever one scrutinizes an irrigation plan view, to be cognizant of the vertical. Fittings, pipe, and other components of the system are often part of a full assembly that is shown on the drawings as a single graphic symbol. Vertically rising pipe and fittings that are coincident to the installation have an important impact on hydraulic calculations.

The term point of connection, or POC, is a contractual as well as technical term. It is the point at which the irrigation contractor begins contract work and is often the point where ownership changes. The water purveyor generally owns the delivery system upstream of the POC, while the owner of the irrigation system owns and maintains everything downstream of the POC.

The **backflow prevention device (BPD)** is used to prevent any backflow of contaminated water into the municipal system. The BPD takes on a number of forms, depending on the degree of hazard. In most cases, it is mounted above grade; hence, it is depicted as such in the figure.

Some piping and valving are located below the **frost line** in cold climates. These valves are closed during the winter months and the system is **winterized** downstream to prevent equipment and pipe breakage. Figure 6.5 indicates a **winterization assembly** between the main irrigation system shutoff valve and the BPD, which would be used as a connection point for an air compressor used to vacate water from the system.

Typically, a transition is made from metallic pipe to plastic pipe just downstream of the BPD, but below grade. Plastic pipe should never be located above grade, because the pipe can easily be shattered by a blow (as from a lawn mower) and because most plastic pipe is not suitable to resist the sun's ultraviolet (UV) radiation.

Most commonly, mainline pipe is polyvinyl chloride (PVC). PVC pipe has a relatively high working pressure rating and is suitable for continuously pressurized service.

If a **master valve** is desired as a part of the POC assembly, it would be located immediately downstream of the BPD. A master valve, as shown in Figure 6.6, offers an advantage in that an additional level of control can be achieved by virtue of a single automated valve, which is opened or closed to cover special situations.

Master valves can be normally open or normally closed. A normally open master valve is opened by the irrigation controller, and held open, for the total operating time required by all laterals. The advantage of a master valve is that the mainline is not capable of flowing until the valve is open. A mainline break downstream of the master valve would flow only during time periods when the valve is open and when irrigation would normally occur.

Some actually perceive master valves as a disadvantage, in that a mainline leak or break may not be observed during normal daytime work hours. The irrigation system is probably programmed to operate at night, so a break would be observed during the night hours but not during daytime hours. Another disadvantage of master valves is that quick couplers cannot be used when a master valve is closed, and one must first activate the master valve from the controller before using quick couplers.

Normally open master valves offer an advantage in that the valve is open continuously, whether the irrigation system is functioning or not. Sensors added to the system and monitored by the control system then allow for master valve closure, if and when programmed parameters are exceeded. A high-flow condition with flows in excess of Q_a (the available flow) might indicate a mainline failure, and a normally open solenoid valve would be closed to prevent flooding or erosion.

There are other disadvantages to using a master valve, whether normally open or normally closed. The valve assembly adds cost to the

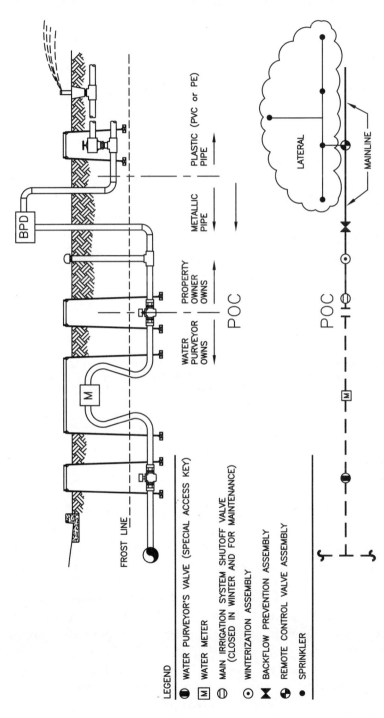

LEGEND

● WATER PURVEYOR'S VALVE (SPECIAL ACCESS KEY)

Ⓜ WATER METER

⊕ MAIN IRRIGATION SYSTEM SHUTOFF VALVE
(CLOSED IN WINTER AND FOR MAINTENANCE)

⊙ WINTERIZATION ASSEMBLY

✕ BACKFLOW PREVENTION ASSEMBLY

⊕ REMOTE CONTROL VALVE ASSEMBLY

● SPRINKLER

FIGURE 6.5. A typical municipal point of connection (POC) for a landscape irrigation system. A "tap" into the potable water supply system is typically made under the asphalt in the street. Valving and a water meter are then brought to a point, usually within or adjacent to the irrigated area, that becomes the irrigation contractor's point of connection. Note that the corresponding legend symbolism that is typical on an irrigation design drawing is shown in plain view.

117

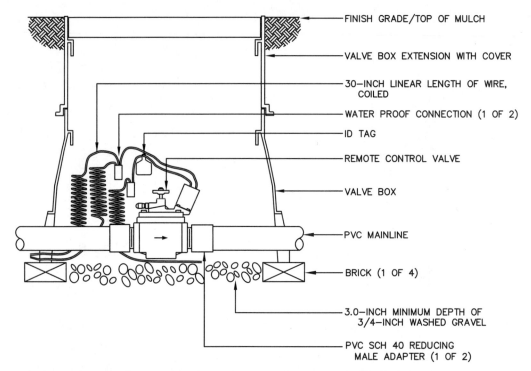

FIGURE 6.6. *A master valve is sometimes used near the POC to mitigate problems due to mainline failure. The master valve is opened by the irrigation controller concurrent with lateral operations. With a master valve in the system, water would flow from a mainline break only when other irrigation is programmed.*

project. Pressure loss through the valve is added on top of other pressure losses and can necessitate upsizing pipe or components or even dictate a booster pump to accommodate the added system pressure loss.

The pressure anticipated at the POC is critical to irrigation design as well as any follow-up hydraulic calculations. This pressure can be measured at a point in time using a suitable pressure gauge, but it is preferable to query the water purveyor. Most water departments or districts use sophisticated computer models to predict the lowest summertime pressures that can be anticipated. Further, engineers with the water department will know if the water pressure will change due to any unforeseen circumstances that the irrigation designer may not be privy to. For example, for a given project the designer may learn that "the water department may soon install a booster pump to increase pressure" or "the pressure can be expected to decrease as future development takes place in the area." This type of information is invaluable and can be learned only through data collection conversations with the water purveyor.

Available Flow The available flow from a POC can generally be calculated knowing the size of the POC.

By definition, **available flow** is the design flow for the irrigation system, which is generally the maximum flow that can be reasonably obtained from the POC. Q_a is the mathematical symbol generally used for available flow.

In the case of a pumped system, Q_a is dictated by the characteristic curve of the pump. The designer would obtain the curve from the pump manufacturer and learn the discharge pressure from the pump at varying flow rates.

The water source for most landscape irrigation systems is a pressurized municipal POC, and in this case, Q_a is dictated by other considerations.

Q_a is a function of:

- The maximum rated flow through the water meter;
- Maximum velocity through the delivery pipe; or
- Maximum flow as dictated and constrained by the upstream delivery system.

A physical measurement of flow is the only way that one can be assured that the delivery system will not constrain Q_a. The POC can be opened and the volume of water per unit time measured by allowing water to flow into a container of known volume, such as a bucket or barrel, for an appropriate length of time. Another approach is to temporarily install a suitably-sized water meter downstream of the POC.

If a physical measurement can be easily made at the time the irrigation design is initiated, it should be done. Many times, however, a physical measurement of flow is not possible, and the designer must make informed assumptions and then clearly state the assumptions on the design.

The delivery system is least likely to affect Q_a because most water systems are designed to deliver flows suitable for firefighting demands. The flows required for landscape irrigation are small compared to firefighting needs.

The water meter is unlikely to affect Q_a because most water meters are designed to accommodate high velocities (well in excess of 10 feet per second (FPS)) and associated high flows.

In any case, the smallest flow due to one of the factors noted becomes the limiting flow and the Q_a that must be used in designing the system. Q_a should always be prominently noted on the design drawing so that it can be checked and confirmed by the irrigation contractor before construction begins.

Available flow is generally a function of the maximum safe flow velocity that convention dictates. Most commonly, the safe flow velocity for a POC is taken to be 7.5 FPS. Q_a, as a function of maximum velocity of the delivery pipe, is calculated using a simple equation called the **continuity equation.**

The continuity equation is:

$$Q_a = VA$$

where

Q_a = available flow in cubic feet per second (CFS)
V = pipe flow velocity in feet per second (FPS)
A = pipe cross-sectional area in square feet (SF)

These units work in the equation as follows:

$$\frac{ft^3}{sec} = \frac{ft}{sec} \times \frac{ft^2}{1}$$

Given the continuity equation, one can easily understand how velocity varies with changes in pipe diameter. See Figure 6.7, where a measurable Q_a is flowing through a water meter and pipes of differing cross section. Immediately downstream of the water meter, the velocity is V_1. V_1 can be calculated knowing the diameter, and therefore the cross-sectional area, of the pipe, and using the continuity equation. The second reach of pipe has a larger diameter and larger cross-sectional area, so V_2 is reduced. The same relative changes in the parameters can be predicted for each of the four pipe segments.

Intuitively, and per the continuity equation, velocity V_2 is less than V_1, which is less than V_3, which is less than V_4.

If units other than CFS are appropriate to express Q_a, then conversion factors are used to change the expression. Cubic feet per second is multiplied by 7.48 gallons per cubic foot and by 60 seconds per minute to get gallons per minute.

As an example, calculate the Q_a for a 1-inch "nominal" pipe size.

Nominal refers to the size of pipe for ordering or discussion. The **nominal size** is different from the **actual inside diameter** of the pipe, which varies according to the type of pipe and pressure rating. Used in this way and in this calculation, it also infers that there is no assumption about the type or material of the pipe when calculating Q_a.

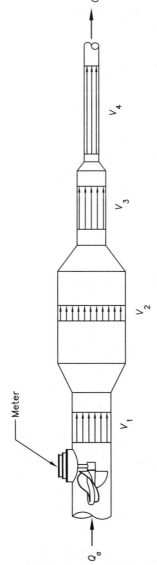

FIGURE 6.7. The continuity equation (Q_a = VA) is best illustrated graphically by four reaches of pipe where the pipe diameter and the cross-sectional area change. The flow through all pipe reaches is constant. When the cross-sectional area increases, velocity decreases, and vice versa. In the figure, velocity V_2 is less than V_1, which is less than V_3, which is less than V_4.

Begin by calculating A. The cross-sectional area of a pipe is:

$$A = \Pi R^2$$

$$= \Pi \left(\frac{0.5}{12}\right)^2 = \Pi \ (0.042)^2 = 3.14159(0.0017) = 0.0053 \ \text{SF}$$

If maximum pipe velocity is 7.5 FPS:

$$Q_a = VA = 7.5 \times 0.0053 = 0.0398 \ \text{CFS}$$

There are 7.48 gallons in a cubic foot and 60 seconds in a minute, so:

$$Q_a = 0.0398 \times 7.48 \times 60 = 17.86 \ \text{GPM}$$

A 1-inch nominal POC is generally considered to have an 18 GPM available flow unless some factor, other than velocity, controls Q_a.

Normally, individual laterals in the irrigation system are designed to operate as close as possible to the available flow. Doing this:

- Minimizes the number of valves in the project and, therefore, the station capacity of the controller needed and the amount of wire.
- Maximizes the use of the investment in the pump or the "plant investment" in the municipal POC.

Municipal POC flow rates for small POC sizes, along with typical plant investment fees, are shown in the Table 6.1. Flow rates in the table are based on approximately 7.5 FPS.

The plant investment fee is the amount charged by the water purveyor for the privilege of tapping into the water system. In addition to the initial plant investment fee, the water district will charge for the actual amount of water used on a volume basis.

Review of Table 6.1 quickly shows why POC sizing is an issue so early in the irrigation design process. The larger the POC, the smaller the irrigation system initial cost because the number of valves is reduced; hence, the quantity of valve wiring is reduced; hence, the station requirement of the controller is reduced. On the other hand, the plant

TABLE 6.1
Comparison of Typical Landscape Irrigation POC Sizes

Nominal POC Size (inches)	Available Flow (GPM)	Typical Plant Investment Fee ($)
0.75	10 to 12	$3,500
1.00	18 to 20	$7,500 to $10,000
1.50	41 to 50	$10,000 to $15,000
2.00	73 to 80	$15,000 to $30,000

investment fee alone can become a substantial portion of the total cost of the irrigation system. Most often, the POC size is chosen to provide for the smallest size that still allows for irrigation to occur within a reasonable period or nighttime **water window.**

Worst-Case Hydraulics

Worst-case mainline hydraulics is a method of sizing mainline pipe and mainline components to ensure adequate pressure and proper operating conditions for the worst-case lateral. Sometimes the worst-case lateral is obvious. Other times, several calculations must be completed to determine which of several laterals presents worst-case conditions.

In general, the worst-case lateral is the one that:

- Has the highest elevation on the project
- Has the highest flow rate
- Is the most remote (longest mainline "run") from the POC
- Requires the highest operating pressure at the sprinkler

Frequently, the worst-case lateral exhibits more than one of these criteria. After the worst-case lateral is determined, mainline pipe and components must be sized to allow pressure in the worst-case lateral to at least meet, and probably exceed, the design pressure for the lateral. The design pressure for the lateral is the pressure (and implied radius) that was assumed for the sprinkler layout.

If the pressure for the worst-case lateral is greater than the minimum requirement, it is presumed that the **flow control feature** on the remote control valve can be used to restrict flow and increase the pressure loss across the valve.

Rotor sprinklers operate at higher pressures than pop-up spray sprinklers, so the worst-case lateral will almost always be a rotor sprinkler lateral.

If the worst-case lateral is not immediately obvious, mainline calculations must be completed for multiple (possible) laterals in order to determine which lateral is the worst-case. The calculations for several laterals frequently complement each other. It is possible to use a diagram or progress plot of the project to complete the calculations in a timely way and record the information for the file.

The worst-case lateral often controls the mainline sizing for the entire project, although, for economic reasons, portions of the mainline can be downsized, assuming hydraulic criteria followed for other portions of the mainline allow downsizing.

Calculation of loss from the POC (P_1) to the worst case lateral (P_2) is accomplished with the procedure outlined previously:

Pressure at P_1

− pipe losses	← from Hazen-Williams reference tables
− fitting losses	← from reference materials and tables
− component losses	← from manufacturer's catalog
± pressure change due to elevation	← from site plan or survey

= Pressure at P_2

Mainline flow velocities are typically held to 5 FPS or less, to avoid surge pressures or water hammer that might damage pipe. It is acceptable, and common, practice for nominal mainline pipe size to be larger than the nominal POC size. Generally, the increased size is only one nominal size, but additional upsizing may be dictated by pressure requirements downstream.

One might logically ask why a 7.5 FPS velocity would be allowed through the POC pipe and components, while mainline velocity is held to 5 FPS maximum. The reasons are that the POC pipe is generally metallic, and components such as the BPD are rated by the manufacturer up to 7.5 FPS.

Note that the P_1 to P_2 calculation process described above is appropriate for mainline calculations when the mainline is not looped. If the mainline is looped, the hydraulic analysis becomes an iterative calculation that is best accomplished using a computer program written to work with pipe networks.

An Example of Mainline Hydraulic Calculations

Refer to Figure 6.8. Assume the pressure at the POC is known and the pressure immediately downstream of a remote control valve is to be calculated. Assume the remote control valve is the valve for which performance data are presented in Appendix A.

P_1, located immediately downstream of the POC, has an assumed pressure of 100 PSI. From the POC, water flows through the BPD, a gate valve, mainline pipe and fittings, and then through the remote control valve and into the lateral. The continuation mark on the downstream side of remote control valve A1 indicates that the pipe continues on. The detail of the lateral is not shown, nor is it needed for this calculation. The valve designator tells us the minimum information necessary, namely, that the valve is a 2-inch valve and the lateral flow is 130 GPM.

The elevation at the POC, called E_1, is 1000 ft. In addition, the contour lines in the figure indicate the elevation. Typically, elevations or contours for hydraulic calculations are available from a grading plan

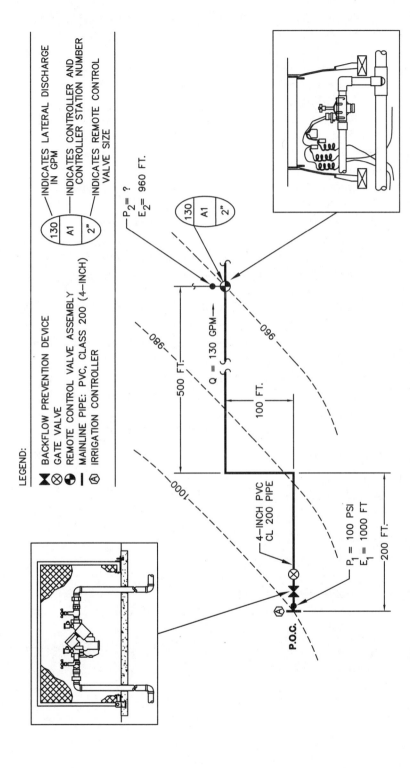

FIGURE 6.8. A mainline system typical of hydraulic circumstances requiring the calculation of the pressure at P_2 when the pressure at P_1 is known. The inset installation details show pipe and fittings that are used in the vertical.

125

or site survey. Elevations will usually not be found on the irrigation drawings.

Other contour lines indicate that E_2 is at an elevation of 960 ft. So, 1000 ft minus 960 ft or 40 ft of elevation head (pressure) are *gained* as water flows from P_1 to P_2.

According to the legend, the mainline pipe is 4-inch Class 200 PVC. There are three mainline segments, which, taken together, total 200 ft plus 100 ft plus 500 ft, for a total of 800 ft. Therefore, water flows through the POC and downstream through 800 ft of pipe before reaching remote control valve A1.

Note the installation assembly details in Figure 6.8, which indicate fittings and pipe used in the vertical. Namely, there are four 90-degree elbows on the BPD, two upstream and two downstream. There is a side-outlet tee at the remote control valve, in addition to a 90-degree elbow between the side outlet tee and the valve. For this calculation, assume that the fitting size is the same as the pipe size on which the fitting is found.

The pressure losses through fittings, for the hydraulic calculations in this book, are computed by relating the fitting to an "equivalent length of standard steel pipe." The reference table used for this purpose is found in Appendix B.

Assume we wish to calculate the pressure at P_2, which is on the downstream side of valve A1. A1 could conceivably be the worst case lateral for this system.

We proceed with the P_1 to P_2 hydraulic calculation as follows:

Pressure at P_1 100.00 PSI

Calculate pipe losses:
4" Class 200 PVC pipe:
$$(800 \text{ ft})(0.38 \text{ PSI}/100 \text{ ft}) = -3.04 \text{ PSI}$$

Calculate fitting losses:
6-4" 90 degree elbows:
$$(6 \text{ els})(11 \text{ ft}_{SSP})(0.85 \text{ PSI}/100 \text{ ft}) = -0.561 \text{ PSI}$$
1-4" side outlet tee:
$$(1 \text{ tee})(23 \text{ ft}_{SSP})(0.85 \text{ PSI}/100 \text{ ft}) = -0.196 \text{ PSI}$$

Calculate component losses:
BPD:
(use specific model & manufacturer's catalog data)
$$= -12.000 \text{ PSI}$$

Gate valve:
$$(1 \text{ valve})(2.3 \text{ ft}_{SSP})(0.85 \text{ PSI}/100 \text{ ft}) = -0.020 \text{ PSI}$$

Remote control valve:
$$(\text{data from Appendix A, RCV-200}) = -7.400 \text{ PSI}$$

Calculate loss or gain due to elevation:
E1 = 1,000 ft
E2 =   960 ft
40 ft of elevation change which *adds* to the pressure at P_2
(40 ft) (0.433 PSI/ft)   = +17.320 PSI
Pressure at P_2   **94.103 PSI**

The technical reference materials used with calculations such as those above are readily available from hydraulic reference books or from the major irrigation equipment manufacturers.

In landscape irrigation, pipe friction or pressure losses are calculated using the Hazen–Williams equation, which is an empirical approach to determining friction loss. A empirical equation is one that is based on laboratory measurements and observations. An empirical equation cannot be derived.

The pipe loss data in the calculation are from a Hazen–Williams pressure loss table that considers 4–inch Class 200 PVC pipe flowing at 130 GPM. Using the Hazen–Williams tables with this information allows one to ascertain a pressure loss of 0.376 PSI per 100 ft of pipe. When this number is multiplied by the total length of 800 ft of 4–inch Class 200 pipe, the result is the total pipe loss due to friction.

Fitting losses in this calculation are determined by equating the fitting to an equivalent length of standard steel pipe; hence the subscript "SSP" attached to the lengths in the calculation.

Component losses are determined, generally, by referring to the manufacturer's catalog data. No attempt is made here to tie these components to specific proprietary equipment, but that is exactly what would be done with a real–world calculation.

Several generalities can be drawn from the calculation. Frequently, component losses will be high relative to other losses. The loss through a reduced pressure principle backflow prevention device will almost always be in the area of 11 to 12 PSI. Fittings will generally yield a small loss as compared to the total pressure loss. It is good to develop an intuitive feel for the total calculation so that any number that appears higher or lower than normal can be given additional scrutiny and a check for errors.

Some techniques, especially those for calculating fitting losses, vary. It is important to receive training in a technique and then to consistently use an accepted approach. Not all hydraulic calculations are as straightforward and relatively simple as this example.

Rules of thumb should be avoided. The previous hydraulic calculation is also good to dispel some invalid rules of thumb. For example, in the past, a common rule of thumb was that "fitting losses are about 10 percent of the pipe loss." This is not valid, as can be noted in the calculation, which shows that fitting losses are about 25 percent of pipe loss. Using a 10 percent rule of thumb would have substantially underestimated fitting loss.

There is another important point concerning this calculation and Figure 6.8. Note that P_2 is downstream of the remote control valve. The pressure at P_2 has been calculated to be approximately 94 PSI. Does this mean that the sprinklers on lateral A1 will operate at high pressure as well? If the remote control valve is left in the full open position, the answer is yes. But most sprinklers, even rotor sprinklers, should not be operated at such high pressure. So, in the field, during construction or during the post-construction walk-through, the flow control on the remote control valve is used to create additional pressure loss across the valve until the sprinklers operate at the desired pressure. Field evaluation of operating pressure at the sprinkler can be done visually. The flow control is adjusted until the radius of flow meets the design performance criteria. Alternatively, the lateral operating pressure can be measured and adjusted while reading a pitot tube.

Lateral Hydraulics

Correct lateral design is an important aspect of an irrigation system design because good hydraulics allows sprinklers to operate at similar pressures and subsequently perform similarly and according to specifications. The greatest opportunity for maximizing application efficiency can be found in understanding the parameters that cause sprinklers to operate in a predictable fashion. Lateral hydraulics is discussed here to include the accepted lateral design standard and a simplifying procedure for using the criteria inherent in the design standard.

Sprinklers, operated at the pressures noted in the manufacturer's catalog, will (almost always) perform as advertised. At a given pressure, the sprinkler and nozzle combination selected will have a given radius of throw and flow at a given rate. The throw radius is expressed in feet and the flow rate as gallons per minute or GPM. The criteria to be used in testing and reporting sprinkler performance are found in standard S398.1 as published by the the American Society of Agricultural Engineers. Use of this standard helps ensure that the data reported by different manufacturers are consistent and comparisons can legitimately be made.

Appendix A shows performance data for typical, but hypothetical, sprinklers. Note that as pressure increases, the radius of throw and the flow rate both increase. Sprinklers are most often laid out in the irregular shapes of the landscape so as to not exceed the radius of throw.[2]

2. The sprinkler manufacturer should note recommended spacing in the catalog along with other performance data. Recommended spacing is usually related to probable prevailing winds, as well as to sprinkler layout pattern.

Sprinklers with similar precipitation rates are then grouped together on a single pipe network called a lateral. Generally, the area irrigated by a lateral is relatively flat, so pressure changes due to elevation are minor or even insignificant.

Now, consider the sprinklers that are all found together on a single lateral. Does the pressure vary within the lateral? Yes. As water flows in a pipe network, pressures vary within the lateral because of pressure losses due to friction and elevation changes. Pressure variation within the lateral means that the sprinklers are not operating at precisely the same pressure. The question of how much pressure variation can be tolerated has been studied, and a design standard was established that has been in use for many years.

The currently accepted lateral design criteria call for understanding the operating pressure difference between the sprinkler operating at the highest pressure and the sprinkler operating at the lowest pressure, and holding the pressure difference at an acceptable level. The design standard for sprinkler laterals is found in the 1983 (fifth edition) of *Irrigation*, published by The Irrigation Association and edited by Claude H. Pair, et al. This design standard is based on the allowable pressure variation in the lateral, and states:

> In order to obtain the high water application efficiencies possible with sprinkler irrigation, it is essential to keep the variation in pressure at a practical minimum. For good design, it is suggested that the variation should be held to ±10 percent of average lateral design pressure. On level ground this would mean holding the pressure drop due to friction to 20 percent between the first and distal sprinkler.

This lateral design standard is written with agricultural water supplies in mind. It can, and should, be "tightened" by using a lower allowable pressure variation when considering high-cost water supplies. Most potable municipal water supplies used with landscape irrigation systems cost three to 10 times more than nonpotable agricultural water.

The question may be asked, "What does water cost have to do with allowable pressure variation in the lateral?" The answer is somewhat complicated. A small variation in pressure means that the sprinklers on that lateral are performing similarly. Similar performance means that the distribution rate curve (DRC) for each sprinkler is similar. Similar DRCs between sprinklers is one means of achieving high application efficiency. High application efficiency means that dollars are saved, assuming the irrigation system is well managed. Briefly restated in a somewhat different way, there is a greater incentive to conserve when you have high-cost water supplies versus low-cost water supplies.

Another question may be asked, "So why not make all the lateral pipe one rather large size to be hydraulically conservative, and achieve a very high application efficiency?" The answer to this question is rather

TABLE 6.2
Allowable Pressure Variation Recommendations

Pressure Variation (%)	Pressure Variation (decimal)	Relative Water Cost
±2-½%	0.05	Very high cost, >$1.00/1,000 gal
±5%	0.10	Medium cost, ±$1.00/1,000 gal
±10%	0.20	Agricultural water, low-cost water, <$1.00/1,000 gal

simple. Lateral pipe is downsized within the lateral to minimize initial construction costs.

Table 6.2 is suggested as a basis for applying the allowable pressure variation inherent in the lateral design standard.

Consider Figure 6.9, which shows a sprinkler lateral with operating pressures noted next to each sprinkler symbol. Assume the design operating pressure for this lateral was 65 PSI. The sprinkler closest to the remote control valve operates at the highest pressure, namely, 68.5 PSI. One sprinkler farthest from the remote control valve operates at 64.5 PSI. The average operating pressure of the lateral is 66.2 PSI.

66.2 PSI ±10 percent provides for a range of 59.6 to 72.8 PSI. 66.2 PSI ± 5 percent provides for a range of 62.9 to 69.5 PSI. Thus, if the criterion is ±10 percent allowable pressure variation, this lateral meets the criterion. If the criterion is ±5 percent, this lateral does not meet the criterion.

Now that the lateral design standard is stated and understood, how is it applied in a practical way? One approach is to design the lateral and then use the Hazen–Williams equation or Hazen–Williams loss tables to calculate the pressure at each sprinkler for conformance with the

FIGURE 6.9. *A lateral indicating the variance in pressures at the sprinkler within the lateral. Pressures could be measured or calculated. Assuming level conditions, the sprinkler closest to the remote control valve will have the highest pressure, and the most distal sprinkler or sprinklers will have the lowest pressure.*

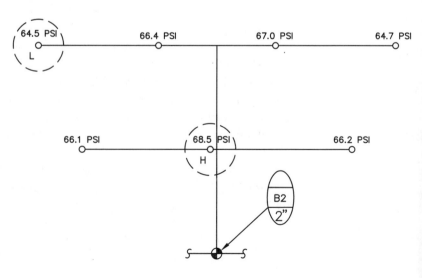

design standard. This approach is time-consuming and potentially iterative in nature, however. Fortunately, a method called the **friction
factor method** for lateral design is available to more quickly size lateral
pipe and hold to the standard.

**The Friction
Factor Method**

The friction factor method of sizing lateral pipe provides a quick, convenient means of determining pipe sizes that meet the criteria. The
friction factor is an indicator of the allowable pressure loss or variation
within the lateral. The **friction factor equation** is:

$$F_f = \frac{(P_O)\,(P_V)}{L_C}$$

where
F_f = *friction factor in PSI / 100 ft*
P_O = design operating pressure for lateral in PSI
P_V = allowable percent pressure variation expressed
    as a decimal ($\pm 10\%$ = 0.20)
L_C = critical length of lateral in 100s of ft
The critical length, L_C, is the pipe run or distance from the valve to
the most distal sprinkler in the lateral.
    After the friction factor is calculated, it is used with Hazen-Williams
friction loss tables to pick the minimum pipe size for each pipe reach
that is less than the calculated friction factor.

**A Practical
Example**

Consider pipe sizing for the sprinkler lateral depicted in Figure 6.10.
Assume that each of the five sprinklers in the lateral has a radius of
throw of 60 feet and a flow rate of 14.8 GPM. The total flow rate for
the lateral is therefore five times 14.8 GPM, or 74 GPM. The sprinklers
are spaced 60 ft apart.
    Assume we want to use PVC Class 160 pipe for the laterals. Assume
level conditions within the lateral. Also assume water costs $1.00 per
1,000 gallons. Referring to Table 6.2, an allowable pressure variation
of ± 5 percent, or 0.10 expressed as a decimal, will be used in the
calculation.
    Calculate the critical length. For this lateral, the distance from the
valve to the most distal sprinkler is shown as shaded. L_C is the sum of
the various pipe segments between sprinklers:

$$L_C = (80 + 30 + 60 + 60)/100 = 230 \text{ ft}/100 = 2.3 \text{ 100s of ft}$$

On a scaled drawing, L_C would simply be measured.
    The friction factor for the lateral is calculated as follows:

$$F_f = \frac{(P_O)(P_V)}{L_C} = \frac{50(0.10)}{2.3} = 2.17 \text{ PSI}/100 \text{ ft}$$

FIGURE 6.10. *A typical sprinkler lateral, for which the friction factor method is used to ensure that pipe is sized to meet or exceed the lateral design criteria. The shaded portion of the pipe indicates the reach within the lateral called the critical length.*

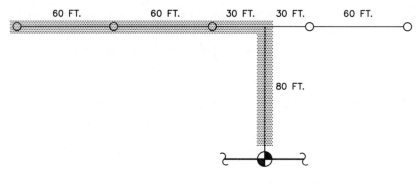

ASSUME: Q_S = 14.8 GPM
PVC CLASS 160 LATERAL PIPE
LEVEL CONDITIONS AND NO ELEVATION CHANGE

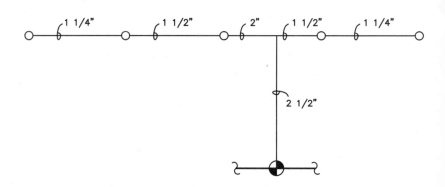

This friction factor, used as a maximum value, can now be used in the Hazen-Williams tables to determine the appropriate pipe size for each reach of pipe. The PVC Class 160 table should be used. Refer to the hydraulic reference tables in Appendix B.

For example, pipe delivering water to a single sprinkler has a flow rate of 14.8 GPM, so all pipe going to a single sprinkler can be sized as 1-$\frac{1}{4}$-inch, because the friction factor for 1-$\frac{1}{4}$-inch pipe at a 14.8 GPM flow rate (round up to 15 GPM for the table) is 0.805 PSI/100 ft. The 0.805 PSI/100 ft is less than 2.17 PSI/100 ft, so 1-$\frac{1}{4}$-inch pipe fits the criteria. (1-inch Class 160 PVC pipe is not generally available.)

Continuing upstream, the pipe reaches that deliver water to two sprinklers have a flow rate of two times 14.8 GPM, or 29.6 GPM. 1-$\frac{1}{4}$-inch pipe cannot be used, because the F_f for 1-$\frac{1}{4}$-inch pipe is 2.905 PSI/100 ft. Considering 1-$\frac{1}{2}$-inch pipe, the next larger nominal size, the F_f is 1.504 PSI/100 ft, which is less than 2.17 PSI/100 ft. So, this reach of pipe can be sized as 1-$\frac{1}{2}$-inch. Continuing with this process, each reach of pipe is sized in turn. All pipe sizes are noted in Figure

6.10 are determined by using the friction factor method and the ±5 percent design criterion.

For any lateral, the friction factor is calculated for the lateral as a whole. Then, each reach of pipe is sized based on the flow rate in the reach.

Similar Laterals   Must the friction factor process be followed for every lateral in a project? No. After pipe sizing is completed on one lateral, a pipe sizing schedule can be used to size pipe on identical or mirror-image laterals. With most landscape irrigation projects, there are few atypical laterals within the system. Many laterals are very similar; an experienced designer can use the size requirements from representative laterals to size pipe for most other laterals in the system.

Review Questions   Calculate the available flow from a 3-inch nominal POC assuming velocity is held to 7.5 FPS.

Determine the plant investment fees in your area for taps sized from $\frac{3}{4}$ inch to 2 inches.

Size lateral pipe for the lateral depicted in Figure 6.10 but using a pressure variation of ±2 ½ percent.

7

Pipe Characteristics

■ **Today's landscape irrigation is defined by plastic pipe. The selection of appropriate piping is a function of budget, working pressures, cyclic system operation, and end user preferences.**

Landscape irrigation, as we know it today, would not be so widely used or have such an impact on our lives if it were not for plastic pipe. **Polyvinyl chloride (PVC) pipe** was introduced in the 1940s; it is now estimated that more than 100,000 miles of PVC pipe are installed each year. **Polyethylene (PE) plastic pipe** is also widely used in landscape irrigation.

PVC and PE plastic pipe is easy to install, lightweight, easy to handle, corrosion resistant, and rated for the typical working pressures found in landscape irrigation. Plastic pipe can be expected to last 40 years, far longer than most irrigation system components.

Commonly used pipe in landscape irrigation systems includes:

- Polyvinyl chloride (PVC) pipe
- Polyethylene (PE) pipe
- Metallic: copper and galvanized steel pipe

In landscape irrigation, pipe is usually installed in a trench that has been excavated using a ditching machine. Several pipes may be installed in a single trench, as shown in Figure 7.1. The pipes should be "snaked" in a shallow S-curve within the trench to allow for expansion and contraction of the pipe as soil temperature changes.

Lateral pipes are generally installed at a somewhat shallower depth than mainline pipes. Mainline pipes are generally installed near the bottom of the trench, but control wiring should be installed beneath the mainline to allow the mainline to protect the wiring. A shovel can easily

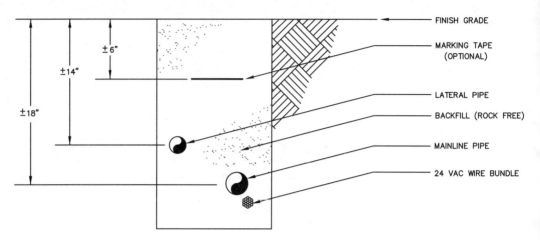

FIGURE 7.1. *Mainline pipe is often placed in the trench in order to protect the low-voltage wire bundle when wiring follows the mainline. Lateral pipes may be buried in the same trench, but at a somewhat shallower depth and favoring the opposite site of the trench. As an option, marking tape at approximately 6 inches can be used to alert maintenance workers that a pipe or pipes are buried below.*

nick the protective coating on a copper wire, or even cut a wire, but pipe is not so easily damaged.

Figure 7.1 also shows optional marking tape that may be installed at a relatively shallow depth above the pipe to provide an early warning to an excavator that pipe or wire is buried beneath. The marking tape may be printed with "IRRIGATION PIPING," "ELECTRICAL WIRING," "BURIED UTILITY," or some other appropriate warning to excavators. Some marking tape also has a wire embedded in the tape. If the integrity of the wire is maintained and continuous, an electronic signal can be induced on the wire and tracked with suitable equipment to assist in pipe and wire location.

Burial depth is defined as the minimum acceptable depth from the soil surface to the top of the pipe or wire. There is no absolute or industry-wide standard for burial depths. Mainline pipe is typically buried at 15 to 24 inches. Lateral pipe is typically buried at 10 to 16 inches. The deeper burial depths allow for additional cover to protect the pipe, but deeper burial depths also add considerably to installation costs, especially when soil conditions are poor. Maintenance over time can also be more time-consuming if burial depths are more than 20 inches because of the overexcavation necessary to conveniently reach and work on pipe and fittings. Clearly, irrigation pipes must be installed deep enough to avoid such routine practices as soil aeration. With this in mind, eight inches is probably the absolute minimum acceptable burial depth.

Installation costs can be quite sensitive to soil conditions. Experienced contractors will always be alert to the extra installation time re-

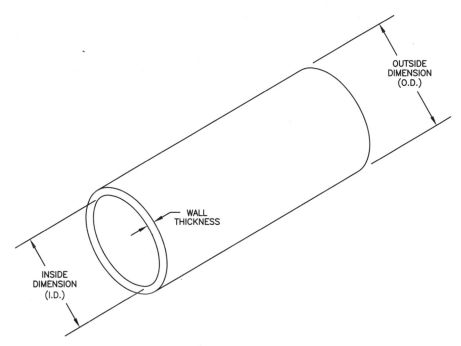

FIGURE 7.2. *Pipe is described by the material from which it is made, the outside diameter (OD), the inside diameter (ID), and the rated working pressure. The wall thickness is the OD minus the ID.*

quired in rocky soils or areas having buried debris, such as old dump sites. Consider, for example, that the irrigation designer learned from the project's soils report that "the presence of a rock layer is noted at the 24-inch depth." By using a burial depth of 18 inches, considerable construction dollars will be saved by avoiding the rock.

Most excavated material from the trench can be used for backfilling the trench as well, but care should be taken to not backfill with rocks or frozen materials. Rough material that contains many small rocks should not be used either. If suitable backfill material cannot be found on-site, it may be necessary to import sand to be used to **bed the pipe.** Sand surrounding the pipe will protect the pipe from damage, and the rough backfill materials can again be used in the upper portion of the trench or hauled off-site for disposal.

Pipe, as shown in Figure 7.2, is described by the material from which it is made, the **outside diameter (OD)**, the **inside diameter (ID)**, and the **rated working pressure.** The **wall thickness** is the OD minus the ID. The **nominal diameter** of the pipe is the closest customary, commonly available, unit size. Most pipe materials are available in $\frac{1}{2}$-, $\frac{3}{4}$-, 1-, $1\frac{1}{4}$-, $1\frac{1}{2}$-, 2-, 3-, 4-, and 6-inch sizes. Note that 5-inch piping is not commonly available.

The measurable ID of most pipes is slightly larger than the nominal size. Referring to Appendix B, for example, note that the actual inside diameter of the nominal 2-inch Class 160 PVC pipe is 2.193 inches. The actual ID is used in the Hazen-Williams equation to compute the friction factor of the pipe.

The standards for pipe materials and the pipe commonly used in landscape irrigation have been developed by the American Society for Testing and Materials in Philadelphia, Pennsylvania. Generally, these standards are referenced in the written construction specifications for the project, an example of which can be found in Appendix C. Section 2.04 of the CSI-format specifications describes pipe and fittings. The ASTM standards describe workmanship, materials, dimensions, tolerances, and testing procedures.

Polyvinyl Chloride (PVC) Pipe

PVC pipe is easily recognized because it is generally white in color, rigid, and delivered in 20-foot sections, which are glued together in the field. Frequently, each pipe segment will have a **belled end**, which is integrally molded with the pipe segment and available to quickly connect pipe segments without using a separate coupler fitting. PVC pipe will have the manufacturer's name, rating, appropriate standard reference, and size printed on the side of the pipe.

PVC pipe is often delivered to the project site and laid out end-to-end adjacent to the trench, preparatory to beginning to glue pipe lengths together. Long runs of pipe may be glued together using the belled ends; then, the installer will go back to cut the pipe in order to glue in non-coupler fittings, such as tees and elbows. The pipe is generally installed in the trench after tees and elbows are installed and after glued fittings have had time to set.

Pipes should be held in place in the trench with periodic placement of soil over the pipe. The soil should firmly hold the pipe in position, but fittings should not be covered, as they will first need to be visually inspected for leaks after the pipe is pressurized. Pipe should not be installed in the trench and left without soil to hold it in place. Rainwater can fill the trench, float the pipe, and require retrenching for proper installation.

PVC pipe is available in sizes ranging from $\frac{1}{2}$-inch to 12 inches. Specifically, PVC pipe is commonly available in nominal sizes of $\frac{1}{2}$, $\frac{3}{4}$ 1, $1\frac{1}{4}$, $1\frac{1}{2}$, 2, $2\frac{1}{2}$, 3, 4, 6, 8, 10, and 12 inches. Some hydraulic reference tables show data for other sizes—5 inches, for example—but 5-inch pipe is not a stocked item for most pipe distributors.

Designers should also be alert to the relationship between rating, and size. For example, $\frac{1}{2}$-inch PVC pipe may be available from the wholesaler at a high pressure rating, but not in a low pressure rating. A small cost difference between two pressure ratings in smaller pipe sizes may motivate the wholesaler to stock only one rated type, usually the pipe with the higher rating. The higher rated pipe, with its smaller ID, will have a higher friction loss per 100 feet of pipe, so the irrigation designer must be alert to the probable situation and assume the higher pressure loss for hydraulic calculations. Experience in given geographic regions or calls to local irrigation distributors will help identify problems of this type.

Fittings

Common PVC pipe fittings are depicted in Figure 7.3. Common tee and ell fittings are shown, as well as reduction and combination fittings, having both glued and threaded connections. The term **slip** refers to a glued fitting, i.e., fitting the "slips" together. **FIPT** refers to "female iron pipe thread" and **MIPT** refers to "male iron pipe thread." Slip is often abbreviated with an "S," so a bullhead tee, for example, may be called out on a material takeoff as a 1″ by 1″ by 2″ (S by S by S) bullhead tee.

Fittings are rated according to their strength. PVC fittings used in irrigation are generally Schedule 40 fittings, although some Schedule 80 fittings might be used in especially difficult or high-pressure situations. Nipples are always Schedule 80 rated, because the wall thickness of Schedule 80 pipe is suitable for threading, while Schedule 40 is not.

The smaller sizes of PVC pipe, although rigid, will in fact bend quite a bit. Trenches can be curved some for changes in direction or 45-degree and 90-degree fittings can be used, singly or in combination, to provide for direction changes. Most PVC connections, if not glued or gasketed, are threaded. A remote control valve, for example, will typically be installed starting from a slip by slip by FIPT (S × S × T) tee, which is also referred to as a **service tee.**

Pipe and Fitting Connections

The gluing process, especially with small diameters, is quite simple; field personnel with little initial experience can be trained over several days to properly glue PVC pipe. Basically, the pipe is cut to length, deburred using a suitable tool, and cleaned. Solvent is applied to both the spigot end and the belled end to further clean and prepare the pipe for glue. Glue is applied liberally to the spigot end of the pipe; some glue is applied, but not liberally, to the bell as well. The pipe is then connected and held until the glue begins to set. No movement between the pipe and the fitting should be observed when the pipe is released. If the glue has not begun to set, the spigot end of the pipe will tend to be forced out of the fitting by the slight bevel in the fitting.

A cement bead should result on the outside of the connection due to the liberal application of cement to the spigot. The cement bead should not be wiped off, but should be left to dry. There should be no significant bead on the inside of the pipe; this would increase friction

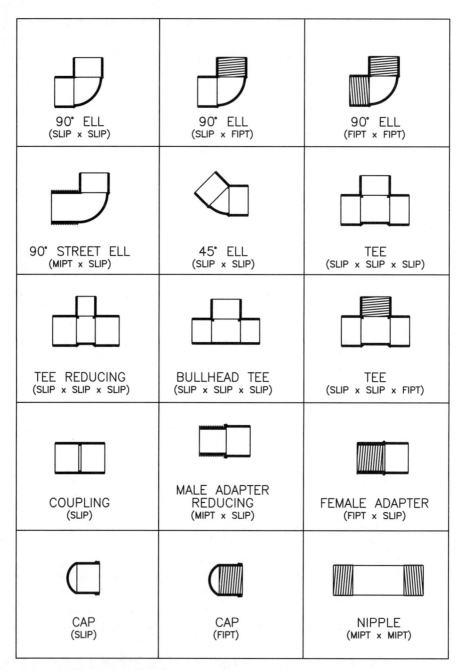

FIGURE 7.3. *Common PVC pipe fittings. The term "slip" refers to a glued fitting. FIPT refers to "female iron pipe thread" and MIPT refers to "male iron pipe thread." Slip is often abbreviated with an "S" and "thread" is often abbreviated with a "T" in material takeoffs or in the descriptive text of purchase orders.*

loss or even run and pool and cause material softening and a weakness in the pipe.

Pigmented (purple) solvent is available to help the installer easily see where solvent has been applied. Clear solvents are available for use when pipe fittings will be exposed. When purple-coated pipe is buried, any aesthetic concerns disappear into the ground. Clear solvent and cement are best used in places where connections will show.

Some pipe cements are intended to dry slowly, for situations requiring long assembly times, or quickly, for situations where a quick-drying joint makes it easier to proceed and assemble the next joint. The pipe manufacturer will recommend specific solvents and cements to be used with pipe of their manufacture under given field or climatic conditions. The project's written specifications should require that the solvent and cement recommended by the pipe manufacturer be used.

PVC pipe may be connected using gaskets. A lubricated gasket, imbedded in the wall of the bell, forms a watertight connection around the pipe spigot. Figure 7.4 shows the basic differences, in profile, between a glued fitting and a gasketed fitting.

Gasketed connections are easier than glued connections to make with large pipe diameters. With this in mind, there is frequently a practical reason to switch from glued to gasketed connection methods with 3-inch pipe. Pipes equal to or less than 3 inches are typically glued, while pipes larger than 3 inches are gasketed. The written project specifications typically call out the specifics of the pipe requirements and the size at which the connection method would change.

Gasketed fittings having a change in direction must be **thrust blocked** to resist thrust forces created by flowing water under pressure. Figure 7.5 depicts typical thrust block configurations. The size of the calculated thrust block is a function of maximum system pressure, pipe

FIGURE 7.4. *PVC pipe can be connected with fittings using suitable glue or by using gaskets. A gasket, imbedded in the wall of the bell, forms a water-tight connection. The basic differences, in profile, between a glued fitting and a gasketed fitting are shown. Gasketed connections are easier to make than glued connections with large pipe diameters. A change from one connection method to the other is often made with 4-inch pipe.*

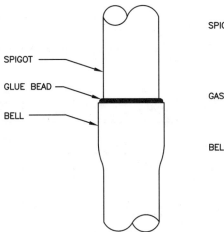
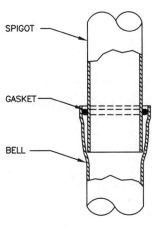

size, appurtenance size, type of fitting, and soil type. The **load bearing strengths** of soils vary widely, with soft clay having a low bearing strength and a mixture of sand, gravel, and clay having a high bearing strength. The table in Figure 7.5 is filled in for a specific project once the variables are known and a calculation of thrust forces is completed. The design of thrust blocking requires calculation of the thrust generated and the bearing strength of the soil against which the thrust block will be placed.

Specialty PVC Pipe

PVC, without any chemical resistance to UV radiation, will deteriorate in sunlight over time. Exposed pipe will become brittle and become less resistant to pressure forces or a blow.

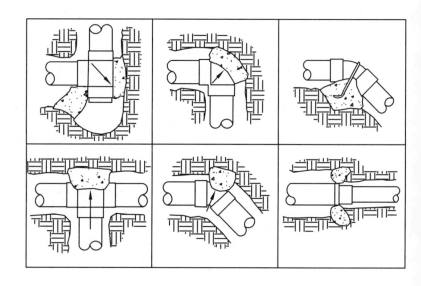

FIGURE 7.5. *Typical thrust block configurations. The size of the thrust block is a function of maximum system pressure, pipe size, appurtenance size, type of fitting, and soil type. The table in the figure is completed for a specific project when the variables are known and calculations completed. The numbers shown are examples only.*

THRUST BLOCK SURFACE AREA
AGAINST UNDISTURBED SOIL (SF)

FITTING SIZE	90° BEND	45° BEND	22 1/2° BEND	11 1/2° BEND	TEE OR DEAD END
3"					
4"					
6"					
8"					
10"					

At least one pipe manufacturer produces PVC that is chemically resistant to UV radiation. This pipe has an off-white, or almost tan, coloration, so it is easily distinguished from other PVC. UV radiation-resistant pipe can be used above ground, assuming the manufacturer's specifications are followed.

Another manufacturer makes small-diameter PVC pipe in flexible, but glueable, lengths, which are delivered in rolls and suitable for drip irrigation. Commonly available Schedule 40 PVC fittings can be used with this flexible pipe.

PVC Pipe Pressure Rating

PVC pipe comes in two somewhat redundant, but parallel, rating systems. When PVC was first manufactured, the pressure rating system was formulated around the criteria established for steel pipe. Steel was, and still is, manufactured as Schedule 40 and Schedule 80. Scheduled steel pipe has a constant wall thickness; Schedule 80 has a thicker wall than Schedule 40, so Schedule 80 steel pipe is therefore stronger and rated for higher pressures.

With PVC pipe, this manufacturing and pressure rating convention was initially applied, and PVC pipe was manufactured with a fairly constant wall thickness. Intuitively, one can surmise that with the same wall thickness, a 4-inch pipe would have more strength than an 8-inch pipe. This is true regardless of material. But, because PVC pipe can easily be manufactured or **extruded** in varying wall thicknesses, manufacturers began to offer PVC with a **constant pressure rating.** This pipe came to be known as **classed pipe.** With classed pipe, a constant pressure rating was achieved by increasing the wall thickness as the pipe size increased. Class 160 and Class 200 PVC pipe are commonly used in landscape irrigation. Class 160 and Class 200 PVC pipe have a working pressure rating of 160 PSI and 200 PSI, respectively.

In summary, scheduled pipe is manufactured with a constant wall thickness; the pressure rating of the pipe goes down as the size goes up. Classed PVC pipe is manufactured with a constant pressure rating, so the wall thickness increases as the pipe size increases.

Note the differences that can be seen in pipe characteristics in Appendix B. Study the Class 160 PVC table and compare it to the Class 200 PVC table. Compare the Class 200 PVC table with the Schedule 40 PVC table.

As an example: two-inch, Class 160 PVC pipe has a wall thickness of 0.091 inches. Two-inch, Class 200 PVC pipe has a wall thickness of 0.113 inches. At 20 GPM, the 2-inch, Class 160 pipe has a friction factor of 0.239 PSI loss per 100 feet of pipe, while 2-inch, Class 200 pipe at the same flow rate has a friction factor of 0.264 PSI loss per 100 feet of pipe. The higher pressure loss with the Class 200 pipe is due to the smaller inside diameter.

Table 7.1 contrasts size and working pressure for classed and scheduled pipe from a single manufacturer. Note that the working pressure for Class 200 PVC pipe remains constant at 200 PSI, while the working pressure of the scheduled pipe falls from 450 PSI to 180 PSI over the sizes compared.

Polyethylene (PE) Pipe

Polyethylene (PE) pipe is black, more flexible than PVC, and connected using a mechanical joint consisting of an insert fitting, which is clamped over barbs to form a watertight seal. PE pipe can be purchased in rolls of 100 feet or 300 feet, depending on the manufacturer. One-thousand-foot rolls are available in the case of the very flexible $\frac{1}{2}$-inch PE tubing used for drip irrigation laterals.

PE pipe is manufactured in sizes ranging from $\frac{1}{2}$-inch to 2-inch. Polyethylene will degrade in UV radiation from sunlight; some manufacturers, though, offer chemically treated pipe suitable for surface applications, such as that which may be required with drip irrigation. It is common for UV radiation–resistant PE pipe to be guaranteed for seven years when installed on the soil surface.

Fittings

Figure 7.6 shows the barbed fittings that are typically available for use with PE pipe. These fittings are commonly referred to as "insert fittings," because the barbed portion is inserted inside the PE pipe. Note that, unlike PVC glued fittings, an insert fitting creates a smaller cross-sectional area for the flow and, therefore, a constriction in the pipe. This constriction naturally increases the friction loss through the fitting, as compared to PVC glued fittings.

Figure 7.7 shows a typical cross section through an insert coupler. Note the clamp that is positioned around the pipe at a point over the fitting barbs. Generally, the installer will slide the clamp over the pipe before the connection is made, and then tighten the clamp afterwards. Alternatively, the gear clamp can be opened and then slid around the pipe. A somewhat less expensive alternative to gear clamps is a "pinch clamp," which is clamped down tight using a special tool. Whether

TABLE 7.1
Comparison of Working Pressures in "Classed" and "Scheduled" PVC Pipe

Nominal Size (inches)	Working Pressure in PSI	
	Class 200	Schedule 40
1	200	450
$1\frac{1}{2}$	200	330
2	200	280
4	200	220
6	200	180

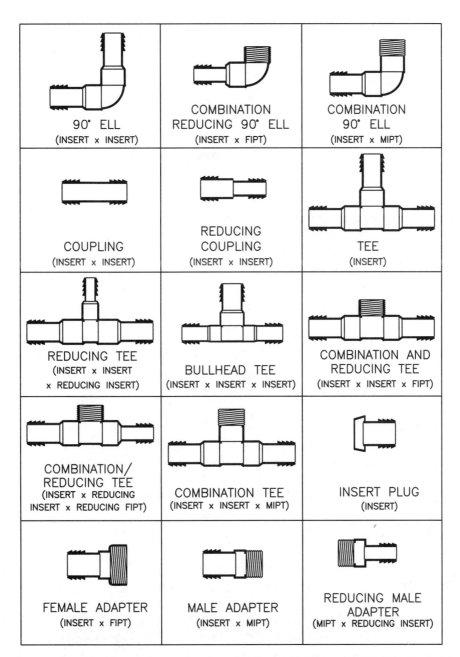

FIGURE 7.6. *Common PE insert fittings. The insert or barbed fittings that are typically available for use with polyethylene pipe are shown. FIPT refers to "female iron pipe thread" and MIPT refers to "male iron pipe thread." Insert is often abbreviated with an "I" and "thread" is often abbreviated with a "T" in material takeoffs or in the descriptive text of purchase orders.*

FIGURE 7.7. *A cutaway cross section of an insert coupler suitable for use with PE pipe and using stainless steel gear clamps.*

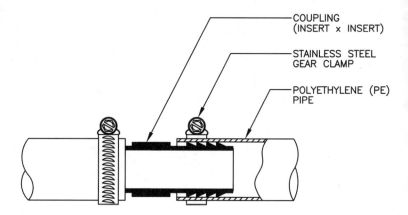

COUPLING
(INSERT x INSERT)

STAINLESS STEEL
GEAR CLAMP

POLYETHYLENE (PE)
PIPE

gear clamps or pinch clamps are used is a matter of personal preference and budget. In either case, the clamp should be manufactured of stainless steel to resist rusting underground.

Fittings that would connect PE pipe to PVC pipe directly are not common, and threaded fittings must be matched up to accomplish the desired effect. For example, if you wish to connect 2-inch PVC pipe to 2-inch PE pipe, it will probably be necessary to purchase two fittings. The first would be a 2-inch PVC Schedule 40 female adapter. The second would be a 2-inch insert male adapter. The two fittings would be joined using the female thread of the Schedule 40 female adapter and the male thread of the insert male adapter.

Pipe and Fitting Connections

PE is quite stiff and hard to connect in cooler temperatures (less than 40°F). It may be necessary to use a rubber mallet to assist in connecting pipe under cooler temperatures. In no case should the pipe be warmed with a torch. Installers are familiar with the fact that black PE pipe warms up nicely in sunlight, and the pipe is much easier to connect after warming a few degrees while the sun rises and the day progresses.

Metallic Pipe

Some metallic pipe is used in landscape irrigation when extra strength or resistance to sunlight or abuse from machinery is required. It is very common to use copper pipe above ground to service the backflow prevention assembly. Copper does not degrade in sunlight and takes on a characteristic tarnished appearance over time, which is aesthetically acceptable in the landscape.

Ductile iron pipe is frequently used for POC assemblies greater than three-inches. Ductile iron fittings with gaskets are in common use on golf courses in the larger pipe sizes. Research has shown that PVC fittings may be subject to a higher rate of failure than ductile iron fittings when frequent changes in pressure are experienced. The new central control systems, which can be programmed for light, frequent irrigations, including syringe cycles, can dramatically increase the frequency of pressure-up and pressure-down conditions. Central control systems offer a great deal of operational flexibility, which can be used to advantage in management, but experience and testing show that piping systems can have shorter lives and can even be damaged by the cyclical pressure variations.

On occasion, it may be desirable to have a bronze fitting or component used with a galvanized fitting. One concern with dissimilar metals in piping is the galvanic action created by dissimilar metals brought into contact in a moist environment. The corrosion of the pipe and fittings can be quite rapid. The solution is a dielectric union, which is a union having a insulator between the two sides of the union. A dielectric union should be used between any dissimilar metal materials.

Pipe Combinations in a Single Irrigation System

It is quite typical, and common, practice for combinations of pipe materials to be used in one irrigation system. For example, PVC Class 200 pipe may be used for the mainline, while PVC Class 160 pipe may be used for the laterals. It is also common, in many areas, for the mainline to be PVC Class 200 pipe and the laterals to be PE pipe. Either of these systems may have copper pipe and fittings used above ground at the backflow prevention assembly.

The selection of appropriate piping system for irrigation is a balance between:

- Construction budget
- Local prevailing practice and end-user preferences
- Maximum working pressures
- Cyclic irrigation system operation

Comparison of PVC and PE Pipe

From the hydraulic perspective, PVC has a lower friction factor, with a Hazen–Williams coefficient of 150 versus 140 for PE pipe. Size is definitely a consideration, as PE is generally not available in sizes larger than two inches. PVC pipe has a much higher-rated working pressure than PE.

From the contractor's perspective, PE can more easily be "pulled in" using a **vibratory plow** because PE is very flexible and comes in long lengths, especially in the smaller sizes. A vibratory plow is a machine that pulls an oscillating shank through the soil. The pipe is attached to the shank and is pulled along behind the shank as the machine moves forward.

On the other hand, PE can be very difficult to work with in cooler weather, when the pipe is stiff and not so easy to connect using insert fittings. PE is considered to be less susceptible to breakage in freezing climates, however, where irrigation systems must be winterized. If a PVC pipe section is full of water and the water freezes, the pipe will be damaged. If a PE pipe section is full of water and the water freezes, the flexible nature of the polyethylene may allow the pipe to expand and potentially not be damaged.

In many areas of the country, especially those in which the irrigation system must be winterized, the most desirable piping system is one using PVC for all continuously pressurized, mainline situations and PE for all lateral piping of two inches or less. There is nothing wrong with mixing PVC and PE pipe on a given project as long as there is good justification.

Threaded Fittings

Threaded fittings, and proper leakproof connections, are important in landscape irrigation. It is impossible to construct a landscape irrigation system without some threaded fittings. Sprinklers are attached to the lateral using threaded fittings. Remote control valves are most often threaded on the inlet and outlet. Most backflow prevention devices are threaded on the inlet and outlet as well.

It is not necessary to use a thread sealant between a sprinkler and the swing joint, swing pipe, or cutoff nipple. All other threaded fittings should be sealed using a thread sealant. A common thread sealant in landscape irrigation is Teflon, which is available as a paste or a tape. The tape is easy to carry, easy to use, and not messy. For these reasons, Teflon tape is generally preferred over Teflon paste by contractors.

All sprinkler manufacturers warn against using a petroleum-based thread sealant with the threaded plastic materials used with plaster sprinklers. If there is ever a question about the type of thread sealant to use, the sprinkler manufacturer should be consulted.

In recent years, the Acme thread has become popular in golf irrigation applications. Acme thread uses a gasket to complete the connection and provide a water-tight seal. Acme thread connections are easy to make, especially under field conditions, and are increasingly requested by contractors.

Winterization

In freezing climates, when pipe is not installed below the frost line, water must be drained or otherwise vacated during the winter. The common approach to irrigation system winterization is a function of personal preferences and acceptance in the region.

If pipes are installed on a grade, drain valves can be installed at low points in the system. Figure 7.8 shows a concept for draining water from low points in the pipe. A sump must be provided and filled with gravel to receive the considerable volume of water held in the pipe.

Some disadvantages of drain valves include:

- Susceptibility to valve clogging (resulting in a slow, imperceptible leak)
- Possibility of valve failure can occur
- Costly assembly, inclusive of piping, fittings, the valve, and a valve box
- Unit installed cost of the irrigation system goes up when the irrigation contractor must grade trenches and pipes to drain

If a particular project has many elevation changes and an undulating terrain, numerous drain valves must be used, and the cost can be quite high. On the other hand, some projects have a uniform grade, and a few correctly located drain valves can provide winterization at rather low cost.

FIGURE 7.8. *A drain valve assembly that might be used to drain water from pipes for the winter. Note that the sump must be suitably sized to accommodate the volume of water held in the pipe. A valve box protects the valve and eases location of the assembly. So-called automated drain valves are available, but they have a tendency to leak and the leak may not be easily detectable. An alternative to drain valves is to winterize irrigation pipes using compressed air.*

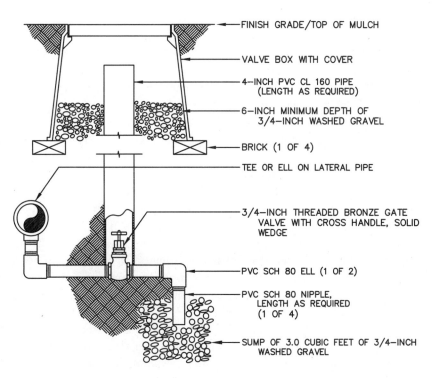

FINISH GRADE/TOP OF MULCH

VALVE BOX WITH COVER

4-INCH PVC CL 160 PIPE (LENGTH AS REQUIRED)

6-INCH MINIMUM DEPTH OF 3/4-INCH WASHED GRAVEL

BRICK (1 OF 4)

TEE OR ELL ON LATERAL PIPE

3/4-INCH THREADED BRONZE GATE VALVE WITH CROSS HANDLE, SOLID WEDGE

PVC SCH 80 ELL (1 OF 2)

PVC SCH 80 NIPPLE, LENGTH AS REQUIRED (1 OF 4)

SUMP OF 3.0 CUBIC FEET OF 3/4-INCH WASHED GRAVEL

An alternative that is quite common in many areas is to winterize the piping system using an air compressor to displace the water with air. Remote control valves will function under air pressure just as well as with water pressure. After the primary shutoff valve is closed, a compressor is connected at or near the water source. When mainline pressure is sufficient, a lateral is opened and water is forced out through the emission devices on the lateral. Generally, a lateral at a low elevation is winterized first and water is pushed out of the mainline, through the remote control valve, and out from the lateral through the sprinklers.

Once the mainline is purged of water, the pipe itself becomes a storage tank for compressed air, and the compressor can be used to fill the mainline before another lateral is opened. For this reason, it is not necessary that the compressor be large. If a wait between valves is not critical, a rather small compressor will work effectively. For example, a $3\frac{1}{2}$- or 5-horsepower compressor is adequate, as a minimum, to winterize most residential and many small commercial projects.

Care should be taken, when winterizing with compressed air, to not cause harmful surges of water or air, to keep air velocity low to avoid heating of system components, and to keep pressures well below the pressure rating of pipe, fittings, and components. In most cases, air pressure should not exceed 50 to 60 PSI, and the output pressure regulator on the air compressor should be adjusted accordingly.

Irrigation Sleeving

Irrigation sleeving was briefly introduced in Chapter 3. A sleeve is a pipe through which another pipe passes. Sleeves allow a mainline, lateral pipe, or control wiring to be installed easily under hard surfaces. The sleeves were probably installed during the construction process long before the landscape and landscape irrigation were constructed. Sleeves are frequently installed on a new project when only curb and gutter are showing.

The correct sizing of sleeving is very important. Imagine trying to install a pipe or pipes through a sleeve that is too small. The hydraulic reference tables, found in Appendix B, can again be used to ensure correct sizing by noting the actual outside diameter of the irrigation pipe, as compared to the actual inside diameter of the sleeve. If the sleeve run length is long, however, then the sleeve must also be sized large enough to accomodate the outside diameter of a Schedule 40 coupling or the pipe's belled end. Accommodation of the coupling necessitates a much larger sleeve size than first meets the eye. It is always good to be conservative and leave more than adequate room in the sleeve for the anticipated pipe and wire. Also, a conservatively sized sleeve will probably allow the polyethylene drip lateral pipe or extra wires that sometimes become mandatory during construction due to changes that must be made during the construction process.

Irrigation wiring is generally installed in sleeves under hard surface as well. The outside diameter of the bundled wire must be anticipated and, again, a comfortable margin left for installation of the wire bundle inside the sleeve. It is best to isolate 24 VAC wiring in a separate sleeve from irrigation pipes; some jurisdictions require this. Further, 110 VAC electrical wiring must be in a separate sleeve, and local electrical codes may dictate specifics concerning the electrical conduit that must be used.

It is not absolutely necessary that pipe used as a sleeve be glued, but gluing does ensure that the pipe will not easily separate. It may be desirable to use PVC sewer and drain pipe or PVC pipe with a lower pressure rating than the mainline or lateral irrigation pipe. Such a decision would be made to save money, but one should also consider the compressive strength of the pipe. PVC sewer and drain pipe may not hold up to the impact of heavy machinery and compacted pressures of the overburden soil. The pipe manufacturer should be consulted concerning the structural strengths of the pipe to be used.

The locations of sleeves, whether for irrigation or for wiring, should be shown on the design drawing, logged on an as-built drawing, and marked during construction in some obvious way. One approach to use in the field during construction is to make a subtle mark, just a simple line, on concrete curb or sidewalk above the sleeve. Another approach is to pass a "pull rope"—used to pull the pipe or wire through the sleeve—into the sleeve and attach wooden stakes to each end of the rope. The stakes can remain above grade for easy future location. Sleeve ends should be taped or capped with a PVC cap to prevent soil from filling the sleeve.

Figure 7.9 shows a sleeving concept and a burial depth hierarchy that might be used to accomodate lateral pipe, mainline pipe, and electrical wiring, all in one trench that would have been excavated prior to the installation of concrete or asphalt. Sleeves should be graded to positively drain to one end or other of the pipe segment and to avoid water being held in a low area inside the sleeve.

If sleeving was not installed or inadvertently left out before hard surfaces were installed, the recourses are to reroute the pipe or wire to avoid the crossing, to cut the hard surface and install the sleeving, or to horizontal bore. Generally, the cutting of finished asphalt or concrete is the least desirable fix for a missing sleeve. Horizontal boring, also call "pipe jacking," is often the least costly approach. With horizontal boring, a special boring tool and connecting stems are driven from a ditching machine's power take-off and used to bore a hole in the soil, which is somewhat larger than the sleeve or pipe that must pass through. The process is similar to drilling a well, only conducted in the horizontal.

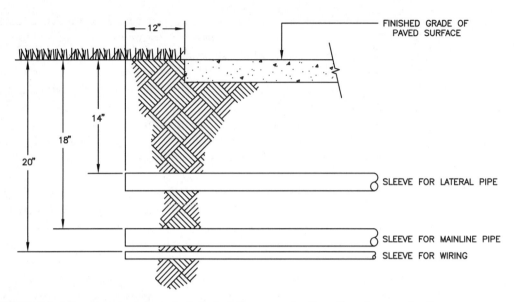

FIGURE 7.9. *Irrigation sleeves are installed at the same depth as the pipe or wire they are intended to accommodate. Sleeve locations should be noted on irrigation as-built drawings; it may be desirable to mark the concrete or curb discretely as well.*

Short horizontal bores are easily accomplished, but longer bores under streets or parking lots are best done by experienced personnel.

**Review
Questions**

Sixty feet of 2-inch Class 200 belled-end PVC machine piping is to be installed under an asphalt parking lot. Recommend an appropriate sleeve size to accommodate the 2-inch mainline.

Call the local irrigation distributor in your area and get current pricing for Class 160 PVC pipe and PE pipe rated at 100 PSI in various sizes. Contrast the size, price, pressure rating, installation labor, and installation process between PVC and PE to be used as lateral pipe.

What is a dielectric union and when would one be used?

8

Control Systems

■ **Irrigation control systems are becoming increasingly more sophisticated, while prices are falling. Computers can make flow control and maintenance efforts function more smoothly.**

Most landscape irrigation systems are automated by using electrically or hydraulically actuated valves. Almost all new systems utilize electric valves because the latest solid-state controllers provide so many desirable features and value for the cost—features that simply cannot be provided in an electromechanical hydraulic controller.

The best commercial controllers have gone down in cost over the past decade, while the features list has increased rather dramatically. In other words, we get a lot of "bang for the buck" in today's irrigation controllers.

This chapter presents current features and electrical aspects of the independent irrigation controllers. The concepts of centralized irrigation control are described as well.

Independent Controllers

The term **independent irrigation controller** is applied to controllers that are completely separate (and independent) from other controllers. In other words, there is no "feedback" or communication link between these controllers, as there can be with **centralized irrigation control.**

Figure 8.1 illustrates an overview of the manner in which irrigation control systems function. The controller is an electronic device, which, in its most basic form, is an electronic calendar and clock housed in a suitable enclosure for protection from the elements. A low-voltage output (24 volts AC) is provided, as programmed, to certain "posts" or "stations" within the controller; valves open, and stay open, when voltage is applied.

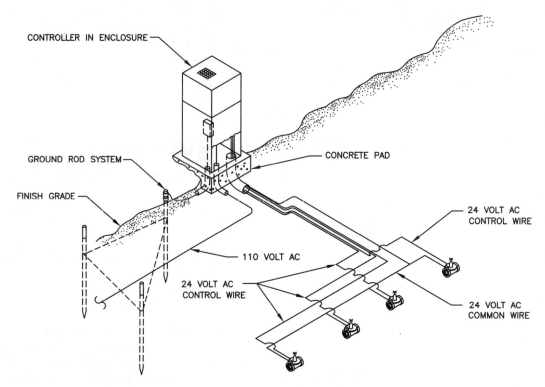

CONTROLLER IN ENCLOSURE

GROUND ROD SYSTEM

FINISH GRADE

CONCRETE PAD

24 VOLT AC
CONTROL WIRE

110 VOLT AC

24 VOLT AC
CONTROL WIRE

24 VOLT AC
COMMON WIRE

FIGURE 8.1. *An "independent controller" is independent from all other controllers and has no "feedback" or communication capabilities to the user or other controllers. Low-voltage wiring (24 VAC) connects the controller with lateral valves.*

Controllers are powered by 110 volts AC. Valves are opened by 24 VAC. Most remote control valves are "normally closed," meaning that the valve is closed until the solenoid is actuated by 24 VAC. A "normally open" remote control valve remains open until the solenoid is actuated.

The pedestal-type controller enclosure is generally bolted to a concrete pad. Sweep elbows in the pad protect the incoming power wire, as well as the low–voltage wires to the valves. Controllers can be wall–mounted in a garage, pump house, or maintenance building. Most maintenance personnel prefer that the controller be pedestal-mounted outdoors, however, to ease access.

When evaluating controllers to pick an appropriate system for a particular project, the following factors should be considered:

- Cost, quality, and warranty
- Programming features
- Station capacity (maximum as well as station increments)
- Enclosure (suitability to outdoor or indoor installation)
- Repair alternatives

Controllers should be grounded according to the manufacturer's instructions. Figure 8.1 indicates a grid of three grounding rods that are grounded together and, thus, to the controller's ground.

As shown, this controller is clearly not a "satellite controller," because there is no communication link (hard wire, telephone, or radio) depicted that would tie this controller to other controllers under a centralized system.

Features

The basic features of any independent irrigation controller are to provide the time of day, a day-of-the-week calendar, the ability to change the time setting on each station, and a means of physically connecting stations to valve wiring.

Some new features are important to irrigation managers because of the positive implication to an irrigation scheduling strategy. For example, a desirable feature is **percent scaling.** This feature allows a multiplier to be applied to the time setting on every station. Older-model controllers without such a feature require that every station's time be set individually, which is time-consuming and frustrating to the user.

With percent scaling, the system operator can go to the controller, key in a new percent scaling factor, and know that the time settings on all 12 or 16 or 32 stations on the controller have been automatically reset for the time setting on that station multiplied by the percentage.

For example, assume a certain station has a time setting of 25 minutes. If the percent scaling factor is 100 percent, the valve will stay open for 25 minutes when that station is powered. Alternatively, if the percent scaling factor is programmed to be 40 percent, then the valve will open for 25 minutes times 0.4, or 10 minutes. There is a strong incentive for maintenance personnel to implement more frequent program changes when a percent scaling feature is available on the controller. For this reason, this simple feature is very important.

It is possible, and often desirable from the "keep it simple" philosophy, to set each station for the time setting that would allow the lateral to apply one full inch of water when the percent scaling is set to 100 percent. Then, 0.25 inches equates to a 25 percent scaling factor, 0.50 inches equates to a 50 percent scaling factor, and so on. This approach can provide a further incentive for maintenance personnel to implement program changes and adhere closely to prevailing evapotranspiration rates.

Other new features that are important in the latest controllers include:

- Multiple programs so that sprinklers, drip emitters, bubblers, and outdoor lighting can be on completely separate operating programs
- Extended, flexible calendars that adapt to every-third-day schedules or other imposed restrictions that are local-area-specific

- Non-volatile memory, which holds the time settings and program in the event of 110 VAC power loss
- Easy adaptability to rain, freeze, or moisture sensors

Some controllers allow every station to be programmed independent of other stations; some irrigation managers consider this feature to be quite important. Programming such a controller can be more complex and time-consuming, but the flexibility may be worth it.

Another new feature provides for a single irrigation event to be broken up for brief periods of operation followed by brief periods of "rest." Irrigating in this way makes use of the characteristic curve (intake rate) of the soil and allows the sprinkler precipitation rate to match the soil's intake rate more closely. Specifically, if certain rotor sprinklers need to operate for 35 minutes in total, the 35-minute duration might be broken into three 10-minute cycles followed by one 5-minute cycle, for the total of 35 minutes. The required amount of water is applied and more water infiltrated under this scenario, as opposed to a continuous 35-minute operating cycle.

Some controllers allow the addition of a handheld remote to facilitate repairs. For example, if a maintenance person completes a repair and wants to check the valve or the sprinkler performance, a handheld remote device can be used to start the valve without going back to the controller. The time-saving aspects of such a device can often show a direct payback.

Electrical considerations

Figure 8.2 graphically depicts a typical independent controller with two of six stations wired to valves.

Schedules are maintained within the controller's logic by programming the controller. When a given station or valve is to be opened, a 24 VAC source is provided between the controller's "common" position on the terminal strip and the valve station. A volt-ohm meter can be used to verify in practice that the 24 VAC is available and that the controller is functioning as intended.

A "terminal strip" with a screw for each station provides the easiest approach to wire connections inside the controller. Some controllers have a labeled wire bundle, and valve wires are attached to the appropriate controller wire using a wire nut.

Controllers are powered by 110 VAC. The amperage requirement is small, on the order of 1.5 amps, and can often come directly from a 110 VAC outlet or from power grids for street lighting. 110 VAC wiring, unless available from a standard 3-prong electrical outlet, should be installed by an electrician, but 24 VAC wiring may be installed by the irrigation contractor in most areas.

FIGURE 8.2. *In this figure, station 1 is depicted as opening one valve only. Station 2 opens two valves wired in parallel, with the assumption that the two laterals have identical or similar precipitation rates and irrigate the same plant material.*

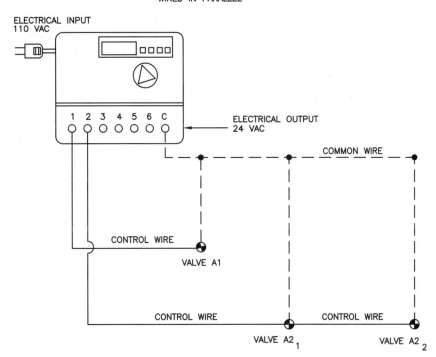

The 24 VAC output is a standard in the irrigation industry. This is important for several reasons. One is that the same personnel who install irrigation systems can also install the low-voltage wiring. It is not necessary that the work be done by electricians. Second, because all controllers output 24 VAC and all electric solenoid valves open with 24 VAC, controllers and valves in a system need not be of the same manufacturer. Valves, as well as controllers, can be selected for their prices and features and packaged. (Note that some manufacturers do have an extended warranty when their valves and controllers are used together.)

Remote Control Valve Wiring

Figure 8.2 depicts a single valve wired to station 1 on the controller. When 24 VAC is applied to the station, the solenoid on the valve is actuated and allows a small water passage to open. The water pressure upstream of the valve is used to hydraulically open the valve. The 24 VAC continues to be applied from the controller and the solenoid stays active, or "holds," for the full time increment set on the controller.

Station 2 has two valves wired to it in parallel. The implication is that the sprinkler laterals downstream of the valve have identical, or very similar, precipitation rates and, further, they irrigate plant material having similar or identical water requirements. Generally, this also means the two laterals have identical sprinklers and the sprinklers have identical nozzles.

It should be noted that, although the wiring scheme shown for station 2 is electrically acceptable, many would argue that each valve should have a separate wire between the controller and the valve. Each wire would then be attached to the terminal strip and to each other at station 2. This allows for increased flexibility, in that the two valves could be easily separated in the future by simply moving one wire off of the station 2 post on the terminal strip. When two wires are used, the two valves are completely independent from one another except for the station on the controller required to activate them.

Grounding and Surge Protection

In general, a controller should be grounded and should be protected from electrical surge. The manufacturer should be consulted as to its specific recommendations. Solid-state electronics are more susceptible to lightning and power fluctuations than the older electromechanical designs, but consideration of these factors should not deter one from considering solid-state. Again, a lot of "bang for the buck" is found in solid-state controllers.

Controller manufacturers will generally recommend:

- 6- or 8-foot copper-clad ground rods installed next to the controller with the controller wired to ground using heavy-gauge wire and suitable connectors
- A metal oxide varistor (MOV) on each station to protect against electrical surge
- MOV on the primary input side to protect the controller's electronics

24 VAC Wire Characteristics

Wiring used between the controller and the electric valve must be suitable for direct burial and rated as such. UF or "underground feeder" describes wire that is suitable for direct burial.

Wire comes in AWG, or "American Wire Gauge," sizes. Typical sizes are 18 to 8 AWG, with 18 being the smallest (approximately 0.04 inch diameter) and 8 the largest (about 0.13 inch diameter).

For smaller projects having short wire runs, it may be practical to consider multistrand cable, which is 18 AWG wire bundled together into a single cable. Multistrand cable is commonly available with 4-, 6-, 8-, 10-, and 12-wire cables. Each wire in a single cable is color-coded differently from all other wires. (So-called multistrand thermostat cable should never be used in lieu of multistrand cable suitable for direct burial. Thermostat cable is the wire that might be used inside building walls to wire thermostats to heating or cooling systems, and it is clearly not manufactured for burial.)

The common wire is often white, while control wire is typically red or some other unique color. Although it takes longer to install, each control wire can be a different color/stripe to uniquely identify it within the wire bundle. From the maintenance perspective, imagine exposing a wire bundle hundreds of feet from the controller and easily finding a uniquely colored wire, as opposed to a bundle of wires having the same color. In the latter situation, wires must be checked one at a time to find the desired wire. An applied voltage from a transformer, a battery, or the irrigation controller, along with a volt-ohm meter, can be used to identify wiring.

Wires coming into the controller should be labeled to indicate the valve to which they are attached. Sequentially numbered wire labels are available for this purpose.

Wire Sizing   24 VAC wiring is sized based on the following electrical properties:

- Allowable voltage drop
- Inrush current
- Wire resistance

The **allowable voltage drop** is the controller output voltage (approximately 24 VAC) minus the minimum solenoid operating voltage (manufacturer-specific). The **inrush current** is the current necessary to initially open the solenoid valve; this current increases as the water pressure increases because the solenoid works against the pressure. Wire resistance increases as the cross-sectional area of the wire decreases and the length of run increases.

The major valve manufacturers have developed wire sizing procedures for their valves to assist irrigation system designers. It is best to use their resources when available because some of the procedure is based on empirical (observation) testing of their valves and using their performance criteria. Toro Irrigation Division, for instance, provides a document entitled *24 Volt & 115 Volt Electrical Product Application Guide.* Rain Bird provides a document from the Golf Division entitled *New Wire Sizing Procedures from Rain Bird.*

Interestingly, 24 VAC wire is often sized through a criterion that has nothing to do with electrical properties. Many maintenance personnel consider 14 AWG wire to be the minimum acceptable size for a purely subjective reason—they believe a heavier (14 AWG or 0.06-inch diameter) wire is less likely to be damaged or cut when mainline or wire repairs are made. They are probably right, and it is hard to argue against this consideration from the maintenance perspective.

Wire Installation   Low-voltage, 24 VAC wiring should be installed below the mainline pipe in the irrigation system. The mainline pipe can protect the more damage-susceptible wiring from cutting or nicking, as shown in Figure 7.9.

Wire not protected by the mainline should be installed in conduit. A warning tape installed about six inches deep in the trench can provide further protection and an alert to excavators.

Any 110 VAC or 24 VAC wiring installed above grade should be in electrical conduit. Examples are the 110 VAC wire into the controller, whether wall-mounted or post-mounted, and the control wires into the controller. High-voltage and low-voltage wire should always be installed in separate electrical conduits.

Control and common wire should be looped at 45- and 90-degree turns in the trench to provide for expansion and contraction of the wire as the ground temperature changes. The wire bundle should be taped at 6- to 10-foot intervals to keep the wire together as a bundle.

An advisable installation technique at the valve is to produce an expansion coil in the valve box by wrapping two to four feet of wire around a shovel handle or 1-inch pipe to produce a coil, which has the appearance of a spring. A further benefit of this technique is to allow the valve top to be removed from the valve box without disconnecting the wires. An installation of this type is shown in Figure 2.10.

All underground wire connections are made with waterproof connectors. There are many styles available; all allow for a firm connection of the two (or three) wire ends and a sealing of the connection in silicon rubber or a similar durable, waterproof material.

In larger systems with long wire runs, wire splices may be necessary at places along the mainline where there are no valves. In this case, wire splices should always be grouped together and installed in a valve box, which can be shown on the irrigation record drawings at completion.

Troubleshooting

Understanding the electrical characteristics of control systems allows and facilitates troubleshooting of problems. Necessary tools and supplies include a volt-ohm meter, wire cutters and strippers, waterproof wire connectors, and wire in various gauges and colors.

Equipment distributors offer classes, and manufacturers offer telephone support and advise in electrical wiring repairs and troubleshooting. Some irrigation controllers provide hints, or even station lights, which indicate shorts to ground in the control wire for a particular valve.

Broken wires can often be tracked with equipment designed to find faults and shorts to ground. This equipment can also assist in finding valve boxes that have disappeared into the landscape or valves that were buried with no valve box.

Centralized Irrigation Control

Rising water and power costs demand increased attention to sound management of landscape water. Large projects, such as school or park districts, functioning under one management group should be particularly alert to their water management strategy. Centralized irrigation control is not only an appropriate tool for improving water management, but other objectives can be accomplished at the same time.

There are many central control systems to choose from; the user base is very large and geographically diverse, with hundreds of systems throughout the country. Basic technical capabilities, reliability, and cost-effectiveness have been demonstrated repeatedly to the satisfaction of even the most skeptical.

Most central control systems run on IBM or IBM-compatible computers. In general, a faster computer with more RAM is required than in the past. Most new users purchase a high-speed computer that has plenty of hard disk capacity, additional RAM, floppy disk drives, and a streaming tape backup system.

Certain minimum capabilities can be assumed from most of the central control systems available now. Most systems provide reliable radio and telephone communication with remote sites, percent scaling to quickly accomplish day-to-day changes in scheduling, and greatly expanded instrumentation possibilities that are limited only by imagination and budget. Percent scaling is usually possible at multiple levels. For example, a percent scaling factor may be applied globally to the entire system, and another percent scaling factor may be applied to individual sites.

Figure 8.3 is a diagrammatic representation of a central control system coupled with an on-site weather station or an accessible local weather station network. Together, the control system and the management system offer the potential of scheduling irrigations more closely and reactively than with any other approach. In the representation, climatic data are gathered from a weather station, and the daily reference evapotranspiration rate (ET_0) is calculated and used in making irrigation decisions. Irrigations can be rescheduled daily, or even during the course of a single day, to accommodate rainfall, changes in ET, or even subjective judgments on the part of the system operator or water manager.

In the figure, the **water manager** is depicted between the management system and the control system. In fact, many central control systems can be configured to automatically pass ET_0 data to cause run time adjustments. Whether or not a given project should be configured to perform in this way is a function of people and management philosophies. There is good reason to keep the people in the loop and not allow a circumstance where the control system is left alone, without overview and overseeing of knowledgeable operators.

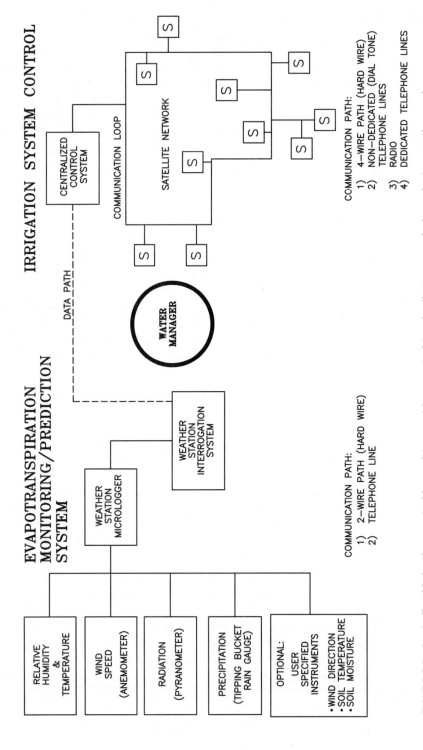

FIGURE 8.3. Centralized irrigation control is used to provide a control "umbrella" over one management group. All parks in a city, for example, can be controlled from one place and reactive decisions made to alter irrigation scheduling.

New Capabilities and Spinoff Support Services

Users do have numerous new capabilities to consider in central control. The "look and feel" of systems have been constantly improved—some dramatically improved. Pull-down menus, point-and-click (mouse) applications, and icon-driven menus are now common. New capabilities come quickly in response to wish lists from current or potential users.

Specialized consultants are available to help with initial data input and long-term modifications and advice. Their services include determination or measurement of lateral precipitation rate, soil infiltration rates, lateral flow rates, and system hydraulic limitations. The initial program for the control system can be developed and entered based on design drawings, fieldwork, or a combination of both. Most consultants are available to provide follow-up support, training, and troubleshooting.

Some manufacturers provide an accreditation program to train and expand the knowledge base of consultants actively working with central control systems. Certification by the manufacturer is a means of promoting the service and an indication of the competence and proficiency of the consultant.

Differing Philosophies

A look at the overall philosophy of system operation can be enlightening and helpful in evaluating different systems. The control or management hierarchy built into the system and components is indicative of the system's basic philosophy. It is important as a potential user, for the designer, to understand this philosophy to assure that it can be used and applied or adapted to current irrigation practices. A change in management style to match the imposed style of the system is probably not desirable.

The philosophy of some systems is exemplary of a system with "middle management." The central system communicates with a site having a field unit (FU) at the site. The FU, in turn, is linked by hard wire or radio to a satellite controller. The satellite controller contains the terminal strip, where the 24 VAC control and common wires are connected to valves. The FU contains a computer (making it programmable and "smart") and provides the middle management role in placement and hierarchy within the communication link. The FU may be programmed to adjust for certain actions, such as closing a valve or valves in response to a high-flow condition, without the necessity of communication with the central.

In contrast, other systems are exemplary of a direct central to satellite management and communication philosophy. The central communicates by radio or telephone directly to satellite controllers. The satellite controller may see an alarm condition (say, a high-flow condition at a flow meter) and the satellite initiates a call back to the central.

The central itself is programmed to react to the alarm. This communication process is full two-way communication between the central and the satellite controller. The central can communicate with the satellite in the field and the satellite can initiate communication back to the central.

Distinguishing Capabilities

Exciting new features have become available, including:

- Communication approach configured by site (telephone to a park, radio to a streetscape, etc.)
- Alarms or alphanumeric messages sent directly to pagers worn by maintenance personnel
- Automated interrogation of weather station(s) and automatic ET_0 data utilization
- Prediction of soil moisture storage based on the checkbook or water balance method of irrigation scheduling
- User-developed condition statements (if-then-else commands) used to create specific alarms
- Multitasking environments, which set the stage for dramatically expanded features in the future

Additional comment is appropriate concerning multitasking. Multitasking allows several computer applications or processes to run simultaneously on the same computer. Multitasking, as the name implies, gives the program and the user the ability to do several things at once. Multitasking, in essence, breaks the computer CPU up into multiple computers. Multitasking is a natural for central control applications. The control system, the weather station interrogation system, the communications process, the off-site support program, and even user-specific applications can all function simultaneously and in concert. The potential for expanding control systems under a multitasking environment is enormous.

Sensor Possibilities

The measurement of flows at the irrigation point of connection is the most popular sensor requested by users. Flows that are out of range, either high or low, can be reported and acted on.

Figure 8.4 shows a **flow sensor** that can be easily retrofitted into existing irrigation systems. This sensor can be installed on a tapping saddle on the existing mainline pipe. A valve box is provided to protect the sensor and facilitate maintenance. The flow sensor can be read remotely by the control system hardware directly or by adding interface hardware.

The flow sensor depicted in Figure 8.4 uses a paddle, the revolutions per minute being a function of the flow velocity. One full rev-

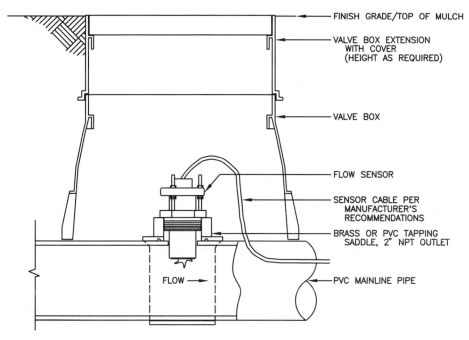

FINISH GRADE/TOP OF MULCH

VALVE BOX EXTENSION
WITH COVER
(HEIGHT AS REQUIRED)

VALVE BOX

FLOW SENSOR

SENSOR CABLE PER
MANUFACTURER'S
RECOMMENDATIONS

BRASS OR PVC TAPPING
SADDLE, 2" NPT OUTLET

FLOW →

PVC MAINLINE PIPE

FIGURE 8.4. *A paddle-type flow meter can easily be retrofitted into an existing irrigation system using a saddle. When the flow meter is integrated with the control system, instantaneous flow can be monitored and high or low flow alarms generated.*

olution of the paddle is counted as a pulse by the control system, and one pulse equates directly to flow velocity. Remotely read flow meters of this type are often added even if existing manually-read flow meters are already installed. High-flow or low-flow alarms are possible when the flow meter is integrated with the control system.

A logical response to a high-flow condition is for the control system to discontinue operation of the valve or valves showing high flow. But what if the mainline pipe has failed and high flow rates are causing erosion in addition to wasting water? A further response would be to close the system's master valve. A master valve, such as that depicted in Figure 8.5, is a valve located at or near the POC or, alternatively, on significant portions of the mainline. A high-flow condition, recognized by the central controller, can activate the master valve circuit, close the valve, and prevent further flow. Such action, when coupled with an alarm report issued to the central computer operator, can be quite effective in responding to a high flow and subsequently leading to a timely repair.

Wind sensors can prevent or terminate irrigation if the specified and sustained winds develop. Rain sensors can prevent irrigation during or after significant rain. Soil moisture sensors can prevent irrigation

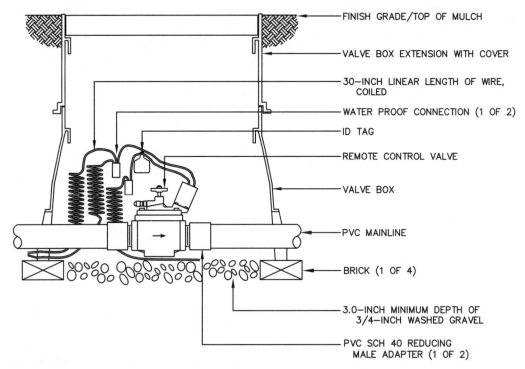

FINISH GRADE/TOP OF MULCH

VALVE BOX EXTENSION WITH COVER

30-INCH LINEAR LENGTH OF WIRE, COILED

WATER PROOF CONNECTION (1 OF 2)

ID TAG

REMOTE CONTROL VALVE

VALVE BOX

PVC MAINLINE

BRICK (1 OF 4)

3.0-INCH MINIMUM DEPTH OF 3/4-INCH WASHED GRAVEL

PVC SCH 40 REDUCING MALE ADAPTER (1 OF 2)

FIGURE 8.5. *A master valve is a valve located at or near the POC or, alternatively, on significant portions of the irrigation system's mainline. A high flow condition, recognized by the central controller, can activate the master valve circuit, close the valve, and prevent further flow.*

when adequate soil moisture is already present. Pressure sensors can prevent irrigation if the minimum pressure at the POC or pump is not found.

Figure 8.6 shows a simple, low-cost rain sensor. Rain causes the porous disks in the device to swell and open a microswitch. The switch remains open as long as the disks are swollen. When the rain has passed and the ET rate is back up, the disks dry out and the switch again closes.

This device can be implemented in two ways. With central control, the switch closure can be read by the central system, which, in turn, can be programmed to effect a rain shutdown at one or more sites. Or, with any control system, even an independent controller, the device can be installed at or near the controller and as a switch on the common wire. In this way, irrigation is prevented because the circuit is not completed when the switch is open.

How to Determine What Central System Is Right

In determining the best central control system for a specific project and management group, the first thing to recognize is that an informed decision will be time-consuming. If the end users already have preconceived notions about the control system, the manufacturer, or the dis-

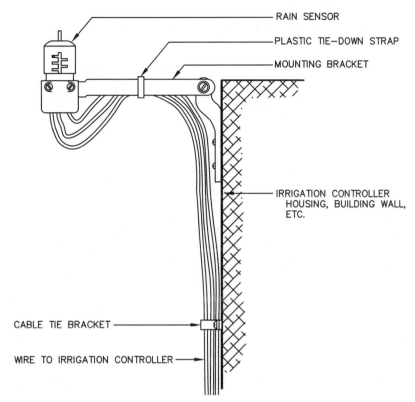

FIGURE 8.6. *A simple, low-cost rain sensor can be used with independent controllers or integrated with central control. In this device, rain causes porous disks to swell and open a microswitch. When the device is installed on the controller's common wire, irrigation is prevented if the switch is open. Subsequent drying of the disks allows the switch to close; irrigation can again occur as programmed from the controller.*

tributor, then they should probably act on their preconceptions. If the end users are open and unbiased and wish to make a sound decision based on an objective evaluation of capabilities, costs, and overall effectiveness, then they should be prepared to put appropriate time into the effort.

Some have chosen to accept on-site, fully installed demonstrations. Nothing compares to a relaxed, on-site evaluation, especially if you can communicate with an existing site. However, the cost of on-site demonstrations is high to the manufacturer and distributor of the equipment. The prospective user should complete an evaluation on paper first and have a sense of the requirements and potential economies. Any on-site demonstrations should then be limited to the one or two systems that have the highest potential for implementation. Be ready to tell manufacturers that are not in the running—most will appreciate and respect candor.

Implementation Economics

A computer model allows for analysis and comparison of the management models and control alternatives. The model is depicted graphically in Figure 8.7.

Any project issues can be broken down into six categories, each of which has components that are noted in Figure 8.7:

IRRIGATION CENTRAL CONTROL FEASIBILITY MODEL

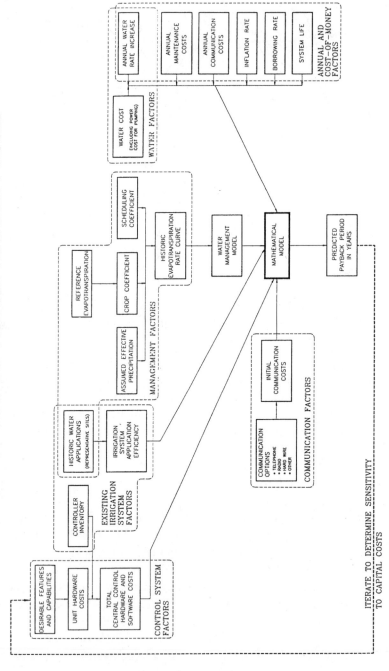

FIGURE 8.7. A flow chart of an economic model showing the interaction of the irrigation, control, communication, water, management, and cost-of-money factors influencing central control implementation.

- Control system factors
- Communication factors
- Existing irrigation system factors
- Management factors
- Water factors
- Economic, or annual cost-of-money, factors

The primary control system factor, from the economic perspective, is cost. What is the initial, installed cost of the control system?

The cost issue also must be considered in terms of communication, in that the initial cost and annual cost of communication must be determined to fully understand the respective cost implications. Telephone tends to have a lower initial cost than radio, but radio tends to have a lower annual cost. Only a thorough analysis indicates which is most cost-effective over the economic life of the system. Further, if a particular control system is suitable only with radio or with telephone, then the system must be analyzed with this limitation in mind.

An inventory of the existing irrigation system is necessary. The number, location, and relative size of existing independent controllers must be known before a replacement concept can be developed. Historic applications and practices must be known in order to compare past practice with future practice.

Water factors include the current unit cost of water and projected future rate increases. It is not uncommon for water rates to increase annually at one to two times the annual rate of inflation.

The historic ET rate for the area must be known to ascertain management alternatives and develop a water management strategy. The annual costs that may be affected by central control implementation must be determined and economic factors, such as rate of inflation, cost of money, and economic life, must be estimated.

All of these factors can best be analyzed in a mathematical model that can be built, at its simplest, in a spreadsheet program. The primary reason to have the analysis computer-based is to facilitate iterative work. A sensitivity analysis on the data can often provide much insight into the decision process. If water rates were to triple instead of double over the 10-year life of the project, does the decision change? If System "A" is half the cost of System "B," how does the payback period compare?

Interestingly, the initial cost of the system is sometimes a minor factor. What if System "A" gives a projected 2-year payback and System "B" is indicated to have a 3.5-year payback? System "B" may have superior alarm condition reporting, which does not reduce the payback period but which makes life easier for maintenance personnel. If either system can be paid off this quickly through water savings, most decision makers can justify increased cost for additional, and sometimes subjective, benefits.

**Review
Question**

You are the (young, dynamic, aggressive) director of the Parks and Recreation Department for the city of Murietta in southern California. You have held your present position for one year, just long enough to identify a significant problem that is developing for you and your department. Your department's already high annual water bills are expected to increase by 40 percent over the next three to four years, and that rate of increase can be expected to continue in the years beyond.

Water use restrictions have occurred in the past and may occur in the future. Restrictions have included irrigation constraints, such as irrigating only every third day, and fines for applying more water than can be justified by the irrigated area. Maintenance people have experienced great difficulty in dealing with these restrictions, and turf quality suffers. You do have confidence in the basic capabilities of your maintenance personnel.

Your park and streetscape irrigation systems vary in age, quality, number of failures, and types of equipment. Some of the oldest irrigation systems were designed inadequately.

Older streetscape irrigation systems have some overspray, which is particularly troublesome from the water conservation standpoint, as well as the risk of irrigation occurring when the temperature drops below 32 degrees. High wind exacerbates the overspray problem, and drivers call on their cellular phones and complain.

The unit rate for water is presently $1.55 per 1,000 gallons. Each site and irrigation point of connection is metered, and monthly reports of volumes are received on water bills.

Currently, all irrigation scheduling is performed by maintenance people, who also mow, trim, pick up trash, and fertilize. There is no formal means of scheduling irrigations. Irrigation controller time settings are often set and left for several months at a time. Your own investigations indicate that your department is overirrigating by 35 percent to 45 percent, depending on the site. You have as-built drawings of only approximately 10 percent of the irrigation systems.

The historic evapotranspiration rate curve, or ET_0 curve, is available from the local extension service. You have heard that the extension service has some good material available on crop coefficients, determination of lateral precipitation rates, soil moisture management, measuring soil infiltration rates, and other irrigation subjects.

The Parks Department irrigates streetscapes, parks, and golf courses as described in Table 8.1.

Fortunately, you have just attended a landscape and irrigation conference, which reminded you of new and readily available technology your department can apply. Further, you were exposed to the latest equipment in centralized control and the latest techniques in water management. You have a number of ideas that could help control present and future water costs.

TABLE 8.1
Irrigated Areas for Various Projects in the City of Murietta

Project	Description	Irrigated Area (acres)	Comments
Parks	82 sites varying in size from 2 to 80 acres, irrigation systems are 2 to 17 years old, and many are in need of replacement.	790	This rather large irrigated area is a significant part of the annual water bill.
Streetscapes	75 city blocks are irrigated with numerous small POCs and an equal number of independent irrigation controllers, some of which only have two to six valves on the controller.	55	Public calls concerning irrigation during rainfall, broken sprinklers, and water on hard surface is an ongoing problem.
Golf Courses	Two 18-hole golf courses	320	Maintenance of overall turf quality is of utmost importance to keep or increase the rounds of play.
Total		1,165	

You know that the way in which you present your ideas to the city council will be critical to your success in getting programs funded and implemented. You determine to write a proposal memorandum to the council that will be succinct and hard-hitting. Irrigation technical subjects must be presented so "non-irrigators" can understand what is proposed. You determine that if the memorandum is more than 10 pages in length, you will lose some council members in the detail. You know that graphics may help get the point across.

Develop a document that will have an important bearing on your success as director and your career.

9

Management

■ **Proper irrigation management requires knowledge of the parameters involved, such as evapotranspiration and infiltration rates. Water audits can help ensure that a system is being managed appropriately.**

With water rates and public awareness of wasted water increasing, irrigation managers are becoming more concerned with annual water use, system operating constraints, and total annual irrigation costs. Good irrigation managers recognize that the greatest potential for reducing water costs is implementation of a strategy to match irrigation applications to landscape water requirements. This process is known as **irrigation scheduling.** To implement an irrigation scheduling program, irrigation managers must have local and current evapotranspiration rate and rainfall data, and they must employ a number of tools, some remedial, to assist in their efforts.

The evapotranspiration (ET) rate, the combined loss of water from soils by evaporation and plant transpiration, has become something of a household word in some areas because of the frequent exposure to the term on television or in the newspaper. Homeowners, and, more importantly, turf managers understand that knowing the seasonal and day-to-day variation in ET is key to proper irrigation. ET is generally expressed as inches per day (IPD).

Potential ET and Reference ET

Potential evapotranspiration, by definition, is the ET rate of the unstressed plant material. Potential evapotranspiration is measured by growing plant material in a closed box called a **lysimeter.** This box has a maintained water level from which the plant roots can draw. Because water is so readily available, the plant is never subjected to moisture stress.

173

Figure 9.1 shows the concept of a weighing lysimeter. The day-to-day changes in the weight of the lysimeter are a function of one factor—soil moisture. Soil moisture increases due to irrigation and rainfall, and decreases due to ET. If there have been no rainfall and no irrigation, then the weight change is attributable solely to ET.

Reference evapotranspiration (ET_0), by definition, is the potential ET rate for a specific crop, most commonly grass or alfalfa, and a specific set of surrounding, or advective, conditions. Reference evapotranspiration can be calculated using empirical equations developed for this purpose.

A typical evapotranspiration rate curve is shown in Figure 9.2. The average (smooth curve) is shown. The actual scatter associated with the curve is highly variable and can change 50 percent, or even 100 percent, from one day to the next.

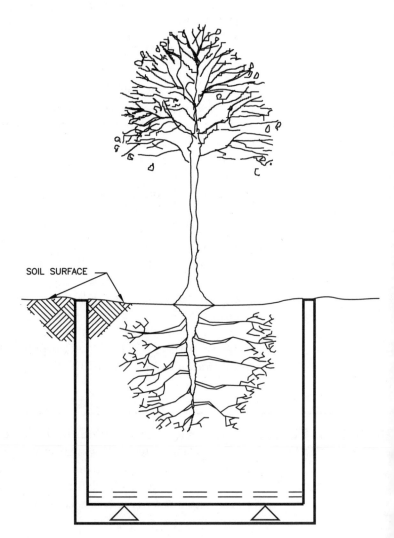

SOIL SURFACE

FIGURE 9.1. *A lysimeter is a closed box that can be weighed. Weight varies because of changing soil moisture related to irrigation, rainfall, and ET. When irrigation and rainfall are known, ET can be calculated.*

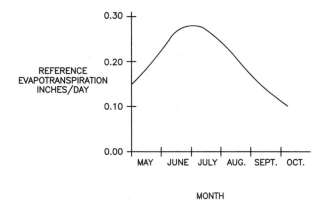

FIGURE 9.2. *A historical ET rate curve is smooth because many years of ET data are averaged. Day-to-day variation in ET can, in fact, be quite marked due to changing temperatures, wind, humidity, and solar radiation.*

The ideal management or irrigation scheduling program should come as close as possible to providing the precise amount of water required over a given time period. Important factors in an irrigation scheduling program include ET_0, rainfall, and soil moisture storage.

One way of monitoring the evapotranspiration rate on any given day is to interrogate an on-site or nearby weather station as an integrated part of the scheduling program. The climatic parameters required are obtained from the weather station, and the ET rate for the day can be calculated.

The commonly used ET rate equations in landscape irrigation are:

- Jensen–Haise
- Blaney–Criddle
- Penman
- Penman–Monteith

The Penman or Penman–Monteith equations are preferable, and are most widely accepted in landscape irrigation, because they are calibrated for "clipped grasses" and, more importantly, they are valid for relatively short time periods—namely, one day. One day is the critical time element for landscape irrigation scheduling because the turf root zone is relatively shallow and holdover soil moisture storage is not significant. For this reason, irrigation must be done on a relatively frequent basis.

The equation that one must use is driven by the following factors:

- Historical climatic data available for the area
- Time period for which ET is needed
- Locality (some equations perform better in certain localities)
- Plant type and condition

Specifically, the Penman equation requires climactic input of:

- Maximum and minimum temperature
- Relative humidity
- Wind movement
- Net radiation

Precipitation data are also needed in order to understand the amount of rain that may have contributed to meeting the ET rate.

Weather Stations

A typical weather station used in landscape irrigation scheduling is shown in Figure 9.3. Instruments are housed on the horizontal cross arm, and the "data logger" is housed inside the vertically rising portion of the housing.

The data logger is essentially a programmable computer suitable for the adverse outdoor conditions in which one might place a weather station. The data logger is programmed to interrogate each instrument every five seconds and store the data.

Weather stations can be powered by 110-volt AC power, solar power, or even 12-volt DC wet-cell batteries. The data logger requires very little power, so even a 12-volt DC car battery can effectively power the weather station for up to a year.

The minimum instruments for an ET-based irrigation scheduling program are:

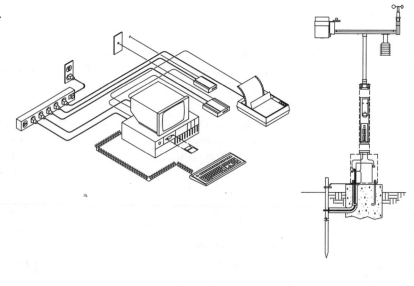

FIGURE 9.3. *The hardware required for an on-site weather station consists of a microcomputer and a pedestal-mounted weather station. Hard wire or a dial-tone telephone can be used for communication between the two. The microcomputer can run a centralized irrigation control system as well, and data can be automatically and seamlessly passed from the weather station interrogation system to the control system.*

- A pyranometer for solar radiation
- A temperature sensor for maximum and minimum temperature
- An anemometer for wind speed
- A relative humidity sensor for relative humidity
- A tipping bucket rain gauge for rainfall

Other desirable instruments, depending on needs, are one or more soil temperature probes, a wind direction sensor, a soil moisture sensor, and water quality sensors.

If the weather station is near a pump station, it may be desirable to measure pressure, flow, and power availability at the pump but using the expandable capabilities of the weather station data logger.

If there is a demand for rainfall intensity measurements, then a somewhat more expensive, but appropriate, rain gauge is needed. Tipping bucket rain gauges tend to underreport rainfall when the rain intensity exceeds two inches per hour. So, if the water department or others would like rainfall intensity for predicting storm water runoff, an additional rain gauge can be added or substituted for the tipping bucket rain gauge.

The flexibility to interrogate additional instrumentation using the weather station data logger is basically limited only by imagination and budget.

Instruments require periodic maintenance and recalibration. Specifically, the anemometer bearings wear out and some probes deteriorate in time, depending on the level of air pollutants. Tipping bucket rain gauges require cleaning and service. The pyranometer should be checked and the surface cleaned. All instruments should be checked at intervals, conceptually every two to three years, and recalibrated as necessary. (Generally, it is appropriate to budget $300 to $500 per year for weather station maintenance and calibration.)

Weather Station Location

Ideally, the weather station is located in a position that is indicative and representative of the landscape, not shaded from sun or shielded from wind, and having little or no potential for vandalism. The weather station should be surrounded by irrigated turf grass. Figure 9.4 shows weather station position relative to an obstruction, such as a building or tree canopy, that could affect readings from the various instruments. In the figure, the height of the obstruction is X. Air disturbance occurs $2X$ distance upstream, X distance above the obstruction, and $6X$ distance downwind.

What if no location is found to be suitable? What if vandalism is an overriding issue? The most important factor for landscape irrigation management purposes is to find a location and leave the weather station there. An irrigation scheduling program requires many assumptions and adjustments for subjective factors. It is best to use the data in a sched-

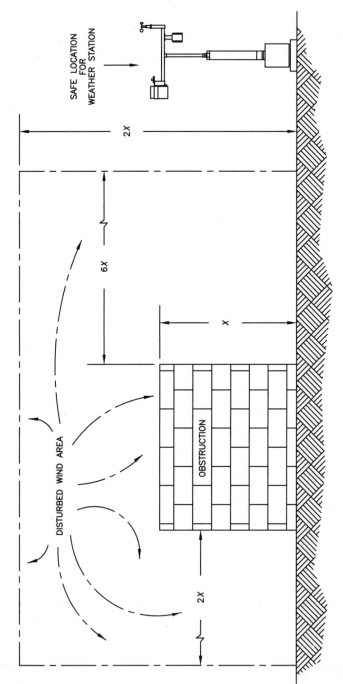

FIGURE 9.4. *Weather station position relative to an obstruction having a height of X. The weather station should be positioned to avoid influences from a building or tree canopy that would adversely affect instrument readings.*

uling scheme and allow smaller anomalies to be filtered in with all the other subjective factors of the irrigation scheduling program. In brief, precision is not as important as developing a historical database that one can relate to.

An existing irrigation system may need to be modified to accommodate the weather station. Sprinklers should not throw onto the instruments, nor should water deflected off the weather station housing strike them. It is still possible to place the weather station approximately six to seven feet from a rotor sprinkler and allow the water stream to pass under the cross arm holding the instruments. Usually, it is not possible to locate the weather station between rotor sprinklers because the highest point of trajectory from the sprinkler is about the midpoint of its radius. The best circumstance is probably several part-circle pop-up spray sprinklers located at the base of the weather station and throwing away from it.

Interrogation Software

At the absolute minimum, the interrogation software should provide a report of ET_0 and rainfall. These data are essentially all that is needed for irrigation scheduling, and irrigation scheduling is what will likely pay for the weather station, the control system, and other irrigation efficiency improvements.

If the investment has been made in the weather station hardware and instruments are interrogated frequently, one might like to know if some parameter or group of parameters is met or exceeded. This level of sophistication may be called "alarm conditions," and it is desirable that they be reported in a timely manner.

The alarm conditions, or "events," that might be of interest are:

- Rainfall in excess of a predetermined and appropriate amount
- Rainfall in excess of a predetermined rate
- Temperature has dropped below 32° F
- Wind speed has increased to 25 MPH and held that level or higher for 20 minutes

Conditions of this type are generally based on a data threshold, or a rate of change, and the weather station interrogation system can respond to these requirements.

Assume a project has centralized irrigation control. ET and rainfall can be evaluated and manually entered into the control system. The percent scaling feature of any control system can be used to apply an amount of water intended to make up for recent ET. However, most operators now prefer that the ET and rainfall data automatically pass to the control system for automatic scaling of run times. Most, but not all, control systems allow this interaction.

The alarm conditions mentioned above are fairly intuitive. What if local researchers have completed research that indicates that the climatic or soil conditions encourage a certain disease or pest? These disease or pest models, also called **phenology models**, can be programmed and an alarm created. The weather station and weather station interrogation system are justified from the irrigation perspective, but other beneficial uses are important if they make turf management easier.

Area-Wide Weather Station Networks

There are low-cost options to having an on-site weather station and the expense associated therewith. Many areas have existing weather station networks, which can be accessed at low or no cost.

In California, for instance, the California Irrigation Management Information Service (CIMIS) can be accessed and data downloaded for one or more of the many weather stations located throughout the state.

Other networks are not so large. In Denver, for example, local irrigators or others can call the Denver Water Department's ET Bulletin Board System. Anyone can call in at no cost, log on as a user, and download data for any of eight weather stations positioned throughout Denver.

When ET rates are known, irrigation managers have a key part of the information available for a successful irrigation scheduling program. An understanding of soil moisture storage is also important in developing a scheduling program.

The Checkbook Method of Irrigation Scheduling

One of the simplest, and oldest, irrigation scheduling techniques is the **checkbook method**, also called the **water-balance method** in irrigation technical literature. Basically, the irrigator monitors and uses knowledge of the soil, irrigation application depth, effective rainfall, evapotranspiration rates, and deep percolation below the root zone. These parameters allow the irrigator to predict the amount of water available in the root zone on a given day and, further, to judge when the next irrigation should occur.

The term "checkbook method" describes this scheduling process because the inflows (irrigation and rainfall) and outflows (evapotranspiration and deep percolation) of water in the soil profile are monitored and logged just as one would monitor the inflows and outflows from a checking account. On any given day, the amount of water, or the balance in the checking account, can be computed.

The irrigator can then predict when water will be needed, just as you might predict when more money will be needed in your checking account.

In conceptualizing how the checkbook method of irrigation scheduling works, the soil profile can also be likened to a sponge. At some point in time, there is a given amount of water in the sponge. Water evaporates from the surface of the sponge, drains out, or is stored in the sponge. Water is added as the sponge is allowed to soak up water, assuming it can hold more water.

In the soil profile, the root zone of the plant is synonymous with the sponge. At a certain time, the soil moisture content can be determined by field measurement. Soil moisture changes because water is added or subtracted. Water is added by rainfall and irrigation and is subtracted by ET.

The Method   Figure 9.5 shows the checkbook method of irrigation scheduling graphically. The soil water content is shown on the vertical axis, and the time, in days, is shown on the horizontal axis.

The allowable depletion is the percentage of the available soil moisture in the root zone that corresponds to a management-acceptable crop stress. One would not want the soil moisture content to drop below the allowable depletion level, because of excessive stress to the plant, but water conservation benefits are gained by letting the soil moisture drop toward allowable depletion.

The heavy dots in the graph are points in time when the soil moisture content is measured. Measurements can be made by weighing the soil before and after drying, or by using a soil moisture measurement device such as a tensiometer, neutron probe, or other method.

A line or curve drawn through the points graphically indicates a trend that can be extrapolated into the future. If ET rates of the recent

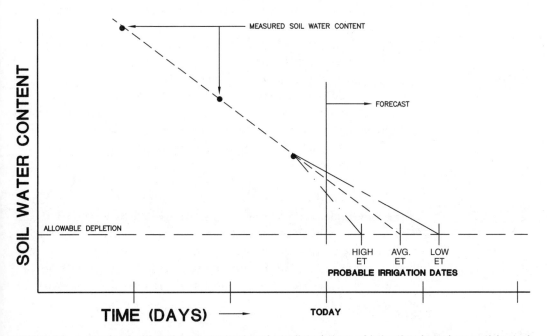

FIGURE 9.5. *A graph of soil moisture content and predicted time of irrigation based on anticipated (high, average, or low) ET rates.*

past are similar in the future (average ET), the probable irrigation date is predicted by the continued line that passes through the measured data.

A higher-than-average ET in the near future will cause the soil moisture content to drop more rapidly, and the next irrigation will need to occur sooner. Conversely, a lower-than-average ET rate will cause the soil moisture content to stay higher, and the time of the next irrigation can be extended.

Why is the checkbook method of irrigation scheduling and determining the probable date of the next irrigation good management information? Some of the more important reasons are:

- If the project has a surface or raw water source, it may be necessary to schedule or "call on" the water delivery with the water supplier's "ditch rider." By knowing the probable irrigation date, the irrigator can more easily schedule the water delivery in advance.
- Prolonging the time between irrigations encourages plants to develop a deeper root system. The checkbook method allows for a methodical analysis, which is much better than a guess or uninformed judgment.
- Rainfall may occur to help meet ET requirements without irrigation. The irrigation manager can make judgments based on the probability of rain. The manager may feel, "Why not hold off on irrigating today because there is acceptable soil moisture and the local meteorologist is suggesting a 40 percent chance of rain?"
- Data monitored with the checkbook method helps managers better understand the overall soil and water system they are dealing with, or the "big picture." It is often found that the intuitive judgments of the past are not accurate enough and definitely not insightful enough, considering today's water costs.
- Controlled **deficit irrigation** schemes can be implemented to put the plant under some stress for moisture, while avoiding excess stress that would increase disease or pests. Knowledge of soil moisture content helps to determine the appropriate allowable stress and then manage based on it.

If all the parks within a city, or all the schools within a school district, are under one manager, it is not necessary to develop a checkbook method worksheet for each site. Rather, it would be appropriate to develop a worksheet or worksheets that represent all the sites. If there are two basic types of soil and two basic microclimates, for instance, four worksheets may adequately represent all the sites having one variety of turf grass.

A Practical Example

The process for the checkbook method of irrigation scheduling is easily facilitated with any of the commonly available spreadsheet programs for microcomputers. Or, if preferable, a calculator and a columnar pad can be used as well.

Table 9.1 illustrates the computations for the checkbook method on a day-to-day basis. Although the table indicates daily computations, it is not necessary to compute on a daily basis but, rather, on an interval basis that makes practical sense.

A good time to start the procedure is in the spring, when the soil moisture is at field capacity after spring rains or initial spring irrigation. In Table 9.1, note that the water content at the start of Day 1 is 3.00 inches. For this example, assume that the field capacity of the soil is 3 inches and that our allowable depletion is 2 inches. We want to manage soil moisture content in order to stay between 2 and 3 inches.

Field capacity can be approximated given the soil texture, or it can be measured for a specific soil by a soils laboratory. The charge for a test to determine field capacity for one soil sample is nominal. A local university extension agent will generally be able to provide data for valid assumptions or information on local soils laboratories to perform tests.

Note the various columns in the worksheet. A plus or minus in the column indicates whether the data in the column add or subtract from soil moisture content.

Irrigation applications add to soil moisture content, as does effective rainfall. Effective rainfall, by definition, is rain that enters the soil profile. Some rain will be lost to runoff if the intensity of the rain exceeds the intake rate of the soil. The local extension agent can help with initial estimates of effective rainfall. With experience in observing rainfall intensity and runoff, and using the checkbook method, irrigators can easily make their own empirical observations and estimates.

Evapotranspiration pulls water from the soil profile, so ET subtracts from soil moisture.

Refer again to Table 9.1. On Day 1, the water content is 3 inches, which is field capacity as determined based on the soil type and the root depth. The evapotranspiration was 0.25 inches on Day 1, so the water content at the end of the day is 3.00 minus 0.25, or 2.75 inches, as there was no rainfall and no irrigation. This scenario continues on Day 2, and the day ends with 2.47 inches stored in the soil and available to the plant.

On Day 3, 0.10 inches of rain falls, which is assumed to be 100 percent effective. The rain falls at a low rate, and the soil absorbs the rain without runoff occurring. Day 3 ends with 2.37 inches stored in the soil. On Day 4, the ET rate is 0.32 inches, so the day ends with 2.05 inches stored.

On Day 5, 0.75 inches is applied by irrigation, the ET rate is 0.32 inches, and the day ends with 2.48 inches stored.

On Day 6, rain falls. It is estimated that 3.55 inches of rain are effective, but 2.5 inches go to deep percolation. Adding 3.55 inches of

TABLE 9.1
Example Worksheet for the Checkbook (or Water Balance) Method of Scheduling Irrigations

Day or Date	Irrigation Depth (inches) (+)	Effective Rainfall (inches) (+)	ET (inches) (−)	Deep Percolation (inches) (−)	Water Content at the beginning of the Time Period (inches)	Water Content at the End of the Time Period (inches)	
1.	—	—	0.25	—	3.00	2.75	← Day starts with soil moisture at field capacity but ends at less than field capacity because of ET
2.	—	—	0.28	—	2.75	2.47	
3.	—	0.10	0.20	—	2.47	2.37	← Effective rainfall adds to soil moisture and helps make up for some of the loss due to ET
4.	—	—	0.32	—	2.37	2.05	
5.	0.75	—	0.32	—	2.05	2.48	
6.	—	3.55	0.08	2.50	2.48	3.00 (3.45)	← Predicted soil moisture above field capacity is not possible so effective rainfall was estimated too high or deep percolation was estimated too low and soil moisture is adjusted back to field capacity
7.	—	—	0.31	—	3.00	2.69	
8.	—	—	0.40	—	2.69	2.29	
9.	—	—	0.35	—	2.29	1.94	
10.	0.50	—	0.35	—	1.94	2.09	

rain, subtracting 0.08 inches of ET, subtracting 2.5 inches of deep percolation, suggests that 3.45 inches is stored in the root zone. However, the field capacity, as noted earlier, is 3.00 inches, so the water content at the end of the day is adjusted back down to 3.00 inches. Any water content in the soil that exceeds field capacity is assumed to go to drainage, or deep percolation below the root zone, and the water is lost from the standpoint of being stored in the soil and meeting the plant's ET requirements.

At this point the process begins again with the soil profile at field capacity.

Periodic field checks help to ensure that the procedure has a practical meaning. Despite some limitations, the checkbook method of irrigation scheduling gives a good approximation of soil water content, as well as other useful information. By measuring the actual soil moisture content at intervals, the table can be reconciled (just as one reconciles a checkbook) with actual conditions.

In landscapes, one concern—and a practical limitation of the checkbook method—is the depth of the plant's root zone. As a worst case, if the root zone is only 6 inches deep, all the soil moisture may be needed to meet peak season ET, and frequent, even daily, irrigations may be necessary. This problem is further complicated if the maximum available flow is lower than it should be and if a limited water window combines to limit management alternatives.

However, any efforts to manage soil moisture and extend the time between irrigations can prove useful, because the plant is encouraged to develop deeper roots. A deeper root zone means that total soil moisture storage is increased, along with root zone depth. When this happens, management will become easier in the future.

Soil Moisture Measurement

One of the least expensive and most accurate, methods of measuring soil moisture is to simply extract a sample, weigh the sample, oven-dry the sample, weigh the sample a second time, and determine the moisture content on the basis of weight change. Samples can be obtained from deeper levels by using a soil auger, a stainless steel device with rod extensions, to allow sample extraction from depths of up to four feet.

Another device that has been used in agriculture, and later in landscapes for many years, is a **tensiometer.** The basic device is shown in Figure 9.6. Tensiometers are often installed in pairs, with one tensiometer at a shallow depth and the other at a deeper (bottom of the root zone) depth. The primary disadvantages of tensiometers are that they require fairly frequent servicing and they do not work well with coarse-textured (sand or sandy loam) soils.

FIGURE 9.6. *A tensiometer is a useful device for measuring relative soil moisture levels in finer-textured soils. Soil is in close contact with the porous cup on the end of the liquid-filled tube. Relative soil moisture levels are measured on the attached vacuum gauge.*

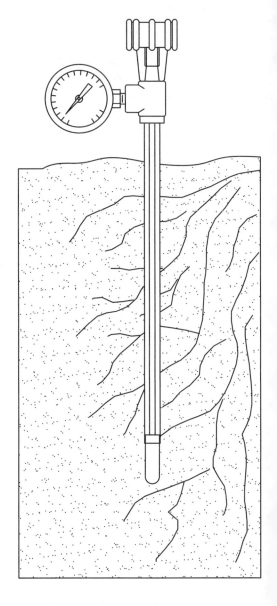

Many irrigation scheduling techniques and decisions are related to **soil texture.** The textural name of a soil is based on the relative percentages of sand, silt, and clay. Figure 9.7 shows the textural triangle, which can be used to determine the textural name by simply entering the percentages of sand, silt, and clay.

Figure 9.8 shows how field capacity and wilting point tend to change as a function of soil texture. **Field capacity** is the soil moisture content immediately after wetting. The **wilting point**, or **wilting coefficient**, is defined as the soil moisture content below which plants will wilt permanently. Wilting point is generally taken to be the lower

FIGURE 9.7. *A soil triangle showing the naming scheme for soils having varying percentages of sand, silt, and clay.*

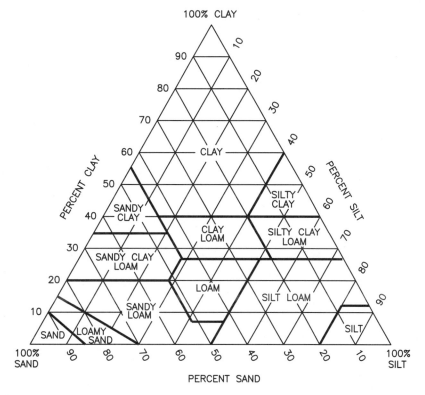

FIGURE 9.8. *A graphic showing the relationship between key soil moisture parameters and soil texture.*

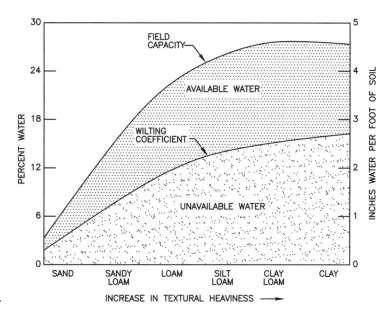

limit of available water, although it is dependent on the plant involved as well.

Intuitively, one can conceptualize an irrigation scheduling program that is entirely based on monitoring and then responding to soil moisture. There are two practical reasons why this approach alone is not widely used. First, the variability in the soil is high, both spatially and in profile. This implies that the location of the soil moisture measurement is critical. Landscape soils, especially, are highly variable because of soil amendments that may or may not be added throughout the site during construction. Secondly, the devices or probes for monitoring soil moisture have disadvantages, which include cost, the need for service, inaccuracy, and reliability. Most soil moisture measurement devices cannot be installed and left through the winter months. Many devices have been manufactured over the years and they later disappear because they did not receive wide acceptance or the manufacturing company failed.

Soil moisture measurement definitely has a valid place in an irrigation scheduling program, but it is most effectively used in conjunction with the checkbook method, as described previously.

Water Management Models

It is helpful to consider irrigation applications in direct relationship and comparison to the turf ET rate curve, as shown in Figure 9.9.

Not so many years ago, it was common practice to simply set the irrigation controller at the beginning of the season for an application rate that far exceeded the ET rate, even the peak season ET rate. This rather gross approach to irrigation scheduling is shown graphically in Figure 9.9a. All of the application above the historic ET rate curve is lost, as it cannot be beneficially used by the plant. Water wastage with this model is extremely high.

Figure 9.9b suggests a model that includes changing applications by resetting the irrigation controller on three occasions during the season. This model indicates a substantial improvement over the previous model, but much of the annual application is still over and above the historic ET rate.

A concept of rescheduling irrigations every two to four weeks during the season is shown in Figure 9.9c. The time lapse between rescheduling events changes because the slope of the historic ET rate curve changes. For example, the peak season application is shown to be approximately four or five weeks long, because the slope is fairly flat and actually starting to turn downward at peak season. On the other hand, scheduling intervals are shorter early and late in the season, because the slope of the curve is steeper and the ET rate is changing faster.

Figure 9.9d shows a deficit irrigation concept, where irrigation applications are held below the ET rate. The premise here is that a busi-

FIGURE 9.9. *Water management models. When irrigation applications are superimposed over the historic ET rate curve, it is visually easier to project when schedule changes should occur. It is not necessary that scheduled time periods be equal and, in fact, they should have a relationship with the slope of the ET rate curve.*

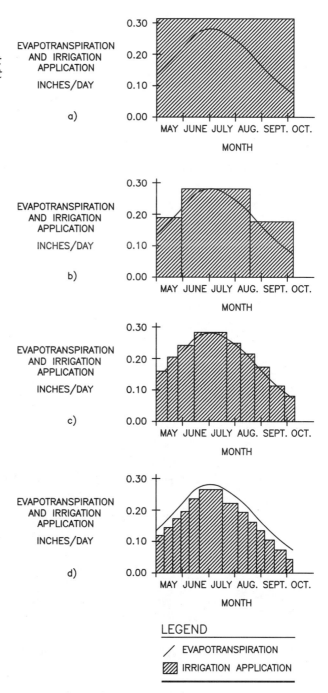

ness decision can be made to save water and not apply the amount of water the plant would ideally like to see. The plant is subjected to some moisture stress, but not so much stress as to increase the chance for diseases or pest infestations.

Because the irrigation applications are portrayed in each model as being flat, there is an implication that each of these models is accomplished using an independent irrigation controller. It is probably too time-consuming and expensive to go to every independent controller in the system every day, so time intervals are chosen that balance the rescheduling cost against the savings.

It is important to consider what might be accomplished with the models if centralized irrigation control is available and if irrigation scheduling is done on a reactive basis, with schedule changes occurring frequently, even on a daily basis. Consider Figure 9.9*b* again. If daily schedule changes using a centralized control system are possible, then the series of plateaus below the historic ET rate curve become a curve themselves. The assumption is that lateral run times are changed daily to account for the ET rate and the deficit irrigation scheme.

Deficit irrigation, especially when it is accomplished with centralized control, offers one of the greatest opportunities for landscape irrigators to save significant amounts of water as compared to past practices.

Soil Infiltration Rate

Few irrigators actually know the **infiltration rate** for their soil or soils. It is very important to match the sprinkler application rate to the soil infiltration rate, and, yet, the infiltration rate is seldom known. Further, the infiltration rate for a given soil can be substantially higher initially, but decreases until it reaches a steady state. This is known as the **characteristic curve** for the soil. Irrigation durations can be timed, through programming suitable controllers, to irrigate for a time period that matches the higher infiltration rate of the soil, wait for a time, then irrigation again. The idea is that the full water requirement can be applied, but in short durations with a waiting period in between.

Infiltration rates are expressed as inches per hour (IPH), just as with sprinkler application rates.

Even with an existing landscape and irrigation system, it is desirable to measure the infiltration rate to help determine maximum run times and the need for programmed repeats.

A very inexpensive and simple device called a **ring infiltrometer** can be used to measure infiltration rates. This test can be done in the off-season as well, when maintenance personnel can more easily find the time.

A steel pipe segment is driven into the soil to the maximum depth possible using a sledgehammer (see Figure 9.10). It helps if the end of

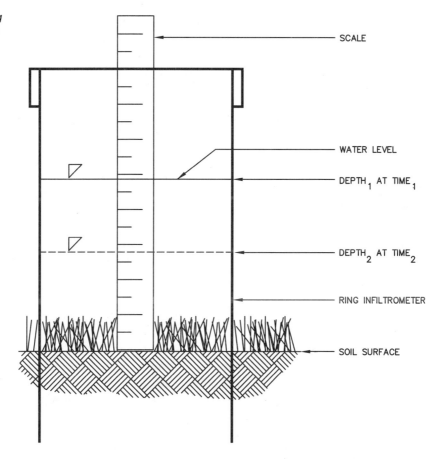

FIGURE 9.10. *A ring infiltrometer used to determine soil infiltration rates.*

SCALE

WATER LEVEL

$DEPTH_1$ AT $TIME_1$

$DEPTH_2$ AT $TIME_2$

RING INFILTROMETER

SOIL SURFACE

the pipe to be driven into the soil is tapered at a 45-degree angle. Once installed, a polyethylene sheet is placed in the cylinder so that water can be poured in and a scale or staff gauge set. At time zero, the polyethylene sheet is pulled, a stop watch started, and an initial depth is recorded. Subsequent lapsed times and depths are recorded until the infiltration rate is observed to become constant. With some soils, a constant infiltration rate takes several hours to achieve, or it may not stabilize.

Once the test is complete, the data are plotted. The value in the plotted data is that one can learn, specific to the tested soil, just what application rate the soil can take and for what time period. This allows the irrigation manager to see what maximum time interval should be used with sprinkler irrigation, and a cycle followed by a soak period can be conceptualized.

Irrigation Evaluation or Water Audits

In recent years, the process of gathering data and making recommendations for irrigation improvements and irrigation scheduling has come to be known as **water audits.** The need has come about, and the support service born, because the project owner or the maintenace personnel may not understand their irrigation system. Whether the data collection is done in-house or a consultant is hired, the goal is to learn more about the existing irrigation system and the existing landscape, and to either make improvements or otherwise better understand the constraints under which one is operating.

One can argue that the data collection is best done by maintenance personnel because they will learn much more about their system. On the other hand, routine maintenance duties may totally consume personnel time, or maintenance personnel may not understand the data collection requirements. The best of all worlds is often a consultant who can educate maintenance personnel in data collection and evaluation techniques so that the actual data collection can be done during work lulls. Conceivably, the consultant could also be asked to return to evaluate data or develop recommendations.

However it is accomplished, an irrigation evaluation or water audit typically includes work efforts such as those noted in Table 9.2.

The appropriate work efforts should culminate in a better understanding of the irrigation system, how it is best operated, how much it costs annually to operate and maintain, and so on. One piece of the puzzle that is often missing in an older system is a replacement plan. Most systems should be evaluated, and a replacement plan formulated, by the time the system is 10 years old or so. A replacement plan projects when replacement would become necessary or cost-effective, benefits that would be achieved, phasing, and probable costs.

Operational and Management General Notes

Because we live in a litigious society, and landscape irrigation is by no means exempt, every irrigation designer must be cognizant of the design intent and a strategy for effective long-term management. Maintenance, after the project is built, is often the responsibility of people who were not involved in the design process and who may not appreciate what was supposed to happen. Notes, called operation and management general notes, are one of the best ways to communicate with unknown persons taking responsibility for repair, maintenance, and adjustments in the future.

The following notes are presented as a general guideline:

OPERATIONAL/MANAGEMENT GENERAL NOTES

1. It is the owner's responsibility to supply these construction documents in their entirety, including the plans, specifications, de-

TABLE 9.2
Typical Water Management, Water Conservation Program, or Water Audit Scopes of Work

Scope of Work	Description
Control system data collection	■ Precipitation rates by lateral ■ Planting by lateral ■ Appropriate lateral sequencing ■ Flow rates by lateral (estimated or measured)
Control system programming	■ Detailed operational programming ■ Follow up field observations and program fine tuning ■ Sensor parameters
Site and irrigation system data collection	■ Evaluate historical practices ■ Ring infiltrometer tests ■ Catch can tests ■ Efficiency evaluation (CCU, scheduling coefficient, etc.)
Whole project or site reference maps	■ Whole project site locations ■ Control designator (station requirement, site number, etc.) ■ CAD-produced site maps with POC location, control system location, and other pertinent features
As-built drawings	■ Triangulation measurements to valves, sprinklers, etc. ■ "Bubble diagram" of laterals and implied pipe routing ■ CAD produced drawings
Development of historic ET rate curve	■ Collect climatic data ■ ET rate calculations (2- to 4-year basis) ■ Prepare historic ET rate curve and equation for the curve ■ Estimate crop coefficients ■ Deficient irrigation recommendations
Central control feasibility study	■ Control system evaluation and costs ■ Development of model assumptions ■ Forecast future operations scenarios ■ Computer economic model ■ Report ■ Presentation to city council, governing board, etc.
On-site weather stations or weather station networks	■ Weather station siting ■ Interrogation software license, training, support
Scheduling program for independent controllers	■ Computerized programs by controller for full season ■ Software license, training, support, etc. ■ Data collection by lateral
Irrigation replacement plan	■ Estimate remaining life ■ Establish replacement priorities ■ Costs and recommendations ■ Report

tails, these notes, and the contractor-drawn "as-built" plans, to any future owner, maintenance company, or homeowners' association.

2. The purpose of this irrigation system is to provide water to supplement natural precipitation, such that the plant life is sufficiently maintained. The amount of water applied shall be the minimum amount necessary to result in plant life of acceptable

health and vigor. The irrigation application shall be in accordance with the local historical evapotranspiration (ET) rate curve and modified in response to recent ET rates. Although during periods of extreme ET the amount of water applied will need to be greater than the historical ET value, at no time shall it exceed the historical ET by more than 30%. ET rate curves and data are available from the local extension service.

3. Soil moisture conditions shall be routinely monitored by a qualified individual with a suitable soil sampling tube and auger. This shall be performed in order to determine if acceptable moisture conditions, as defined above, are being maintained. The irrigation schedule shall be adjusted accordingly, depending on the results of this monitoring.

4. Short, multiple irrigation cycles shall be utilized as necessary to minimize ponding and runoff.

5. At no time shall water be applied to cause soil saturation. Overwatering can result in death of plants and soil expansion, causing possible damage to pavement and foundations. A qualified structural engineer shall be retained on at least an annual basis to inspect pavement and structures for damage due to excessive soil moisture.

6. Inspections of the irrigation system shall be made on a daily basis to observe and provide repairs or remedies to the following unacceptable problems:

   A. Overspray on sidewalks, streets, paved areas, fences, walls, buildings, or other structures.

   B. Drainage or runoff across sidewalks, streets, or paved areas.

   C. Irrigation ponding on any landscape surface, sidewalk, street, or paved area.

   D. Damaged, leaking, or improperly operating sprinklers, pipe, valves, controllers, or other irrigation equipment.

7. Only qualified landscape contractors and landscape maintenance personnel shall provide or make repairs to the irrigation system.

8. At all times, the landscape contractor or maintenance contractor shall assign a qualified individual or individuals to inspect and monitor the irrigation system. Owner's representatives shall be supplied with 24-hour emergency phone numbers for use in reporting broken or damaged irrigation equipment.

9. All irrigation equipment requires continuous maintenance, cleaning, adjustment, parts inspection, and replacement. It is the responsibility of the owner or owner's contractor to provide these services on a continual and regular basis.

10. The responsibility of ensuring that the above precautions, repairs, and continuing maintenance are properly performed is that of the owner. The irrigation engineer has been retained to pre-

pare these construction documents only and does not provide post-construction reviews nor reviews of on-site maintenance. The irrigation engineer does not assume responsibility or liability for ongoing maintenance of the irrigation system.

Review Questions

Determine the reference evapotranspiration rate and the recommended crop coefficients for turf growth in your area.

Develop a blank worksheet suitable for monitoring soil moisture using the checkbook method of irrigation scheduling.

Appendix A

Generic Performance Data

The component performance data presented here are generic and fabricated to look and feel like real performance data. These data are utilized in the calculations herein and are the minimal data necessary to follow through the hydraulic examples in this textbook.

Catalogs and more complete information are readily available from major irrigation equipment manufacturers and should be used to complement course work and in practice.

Pop-up Spray Sprinklers: 10-Foot Series   *15° trajectory*

NOZZLE	PRESSURE (PSI)	RADIUS (Feet)	FLOW (GPM)	PRECIP■ (IPH)	PRECIP▲ (IPH)
10F-LA	15	7	1.16	2.27	2.63
	20	8	1.30	1.96	2.26
	25	9	1.44	1.72	1.98
	30	10	1.57	1.52	1.75
10H-LA	15	7	0.58	2.27	2.63
	20	8	0.65	1.96	2.26
	25	9	0.72	1.72	1.98
	30	10	0.79	1.52	1.75
10T-LA	15	7	0.58	2.27	2.63
	20	8	0.43	1.96	2.26
	25	9	0.48	1.72	1.98
	30	10	0.52	1.52	1.75
10Q-LA	15	7	0.29	2.27	2.63
	20	8	0.33	1.96	2.26
	25	9	0.36	1.72	1.98
	30	10	0.39	1.52	1.75

■ Square spacing based on 50% diameter of throw.
▲ Triangular spacing based on 60% diameter of throw.

Pop-up Spray Sprinklers: 12-Foot Series   *30° trajectory*

NOZZLE	PRESSURE (PSI)	RADIUS (Feet)	FLOW (GPM)	PRECIP■ (IPH)	PRECIP▲ (IPH)
12F	15	9	1.80	2.14	2.47
	20	10	2.10	2.02	2.34
	25	11	2.40	1.91	2.21
	30	12	2.60	1.74	2.01
12TQ	15	9	1.35	2.14	2.47
	20	10	1.58	2.02	2.34
	25	11	1.80	1.91	2.21
	30	12	1.95	1.74	2.01
12TT	15	9	1.21	2.14	2.47
	20	10	1.41	2.02	2.34
	25	11	1.61	1.91	2.21
	30	12	1.74	1.74	2.01
12H	15	9	0.90	2.14	2.47
	20	10	1.05	2.02	2.34
	25	11	1.20	1.91	2.21
	30	12	1.30	1.74	2.01
12T	15	9	0.60	2.14	2.47
	20	10	0.70	2.02	2.34
	25	11	0.80	1.91	2.21
	30	12	0.87	1.74	2.01
12Q	15	9	0.45	2.14	2.47
	20	10	0.53	2.02	2.34
	25	11	0.60	1.91	2.21
	30	12	0.65	1.74	2.01

■ Square spacing based on 50% diameter of throw.
▲ Triangular spacing based on 60% diameter of throw.

Pop-up Spray Sprinklers: 15-Foot Series   *30° trajectory*

NOZZLE	PRESSURE (PSI)	RADIUS (Feet)	FLOW (GPM)	PRECIP■ (IPH)	PRECIP▲ (IPH)
15F	15	11	2.60	2.07	2.39
	20	12	3.00	2.01	2.32
	25	14	3.30	1.62	1.87
	30	15	3.70	1.58	1.83
15TQ	15	11	1.95	2.07	2.39
	20	12	2.25	2.01	2.32
	25	14	2.48	1.52	1.87
	30	15	2.78	1.58	1.83
15TT	15	11	1.74	2.07	2.39
	20	12	2.01	2.01	2.32
	25	14	2.21	1.62	1.87
	30	15	2.48	1.58	1.83
15H	15	11	1.30	2.07	2.39
	20	12	1.50	2.01	2.32
	25	14	1.65	1.62	1.87
	30	15	1.23	1.58	1.83
15T	15	11	0.87	2.07	2.39
	20	12	1.00	2.01	2.32
	25	14	1.10	1.62	1.87
	30	15	1.23	1.58	1.83
15Q	15	11	0.65	2.07	2.39
	20	12	0.75	2.01	2.32
	25	14	0.83	1.62	1.87
	30	15	0.93	1.58	1.83

■Square spacing based on 50% diameter of throw.
▲Triangular spacing based on 60% diameter of throw.

Rotor Sprinkler: Performance

PRESSURE (PSI)	NOZZLE	RADIUS (Feet)	FLOW (GPM)	*PRECIP■ (IPH)	*PRECIP▲ (IPH)
40	1	40	3.5	0.42	0.34
	2	44	6.4	0.64	0.51
	3	50	10.2	0.79	0.63
	4	56	13.1	0.80	0.65
50	1	40	3.9	0.47	0.38
	2	44	7.4	0.74	0.59
	3	52	11.6	0.83	0.66
	4	58	14.8	0.85	0.68
60	1	40	4.4	0.53	0.42
	2	46	8.2	0.75	0.60
	3	54	12.8	0.85	0.68
	4	60	16.3	0.87	0.70
70	1	40	4.7	0.57	0.45
	2	46	8.9	0.81	0.65
	3	56	13.9	0.85	0.68
	4	62	17.8	0.89	0.72
80	1	42	5.1	0.56	0.45
	2	46	9.6	0.87	0.70
	3	56	14.9	0.92	0.73
	4	62	19.0	0.95	0.76

*Precipitation rates are based on half-circle operation.
■Square spacing based on 50% diameter of throw.
▲Triangular spacing based on 60% diameter of throw.

Remote Control Valve: Valve Pressure Loss (PSI)

FLOW (GPM)	RCV-100 1-Inch (PSI)	RCV-150 1 1/2-Inch (PSI)	RCV-200 2-Inch (PSI)
1	—	—	—
5	2.0	—	—
10	2.2	—	—
20	2.5	1.5	—
30	5.0	1.5	—
40	9.3	3.3	—
50	15.5	3.5	1.2
75	—	3.9	2.4
100	—	7.0	4.2
125	—	11.3	6.8
150	—	16.2	9.8
175	—	—	13.3
200	—	—	17.7

1. Pressure loss data are for valves with the flow control fully open.
2. Flows with no loss data shown are not recommended.
3. Data presented here are fictional and are not to be used for any purpose other than the example calculation herein.

Appendix B

Reference Data

The hydraulic reference data presented here are the minimal data needed to follow through the hydraulic examples in this textbook. More complete hydraulic reference materials are readily available from major irrigation equipment manufacturers or other sources and should be used in practice.

The data presented *should not be used* for purposes other than following the examples in this book.

Friction Loss Characteristics
PSI Loss per 100 Feet of Pipe (PSI / 100 FT)
PVC Class 160 IPS Plastic Pipe
(1120, 1220) SDR 21 C = 150

SIZE	1-1/4"		1-1/2"		2"		2-1/2"		3"		4"		6"		
OD	1.660		1.900		2.375		2.875		3.500		4.500		6.625		OD
ID	1.532		1.754		2.193		2.655		3.230		4.154		6.115		ID
WALL THK.	0.064		0.073		0.091		0.110		0.135		0.173		0.225		WALL THK.
FLOW (GPM)	V (FPS)	LOSS (PSI per 100 ft.)	V (FPS)	LOSS (PSI per 100 ft.)	V (FPS)	LOSS (PSI per 100 ft.)	V (FPS)	LOSS (PSI per 100 ft.)	V (FPS)	LOSS (PSI per 100 ft.)	V (FPS)	LOSS (PSI per 100 ft.)	V (FPS)	LOSS (PSI per 100 ft.)	FLOW (GPM)
1	0.2	0.005													1
2	0.3	0.019	0.3	0.010											2
3	0.5	0.041	0.4	0.021	0.3	0.007									3
4	0.7	0.070	0.5	0.036	0.3	0.012	0.2	0.005							4
5	0.9	0.105	0.7	0.054	0.4	0.018	0.3	0.007							5
6	1.0	0.147	0.8	0.076	0.5	0.026	0.3	0.010							6
7	1.2	0.196	0.9	0.102	0.6	0.034	0.4	0.014	0.3	0.005					7
8	1.4	0.251	1.1	0.130	0.7	0.044	0.5	0.017	0.3	0.007					8
9	1.6	0.313	1.2	0.162	0.8	0.055	0.5	0.022	0.4	0.008					9
10	1.7	0.380	1.3	0.197	0.8	0.066	0.6	0.026	0.4	0.010					10
11	1.9	0.453	1.5	0.235	0.9	0.079	0.6	0.031	0.4	0.012					11
12	2.1	0.532	1.6	0.276	1.0	0.093	0.7	0.037	0.5	0.014					12
13	2.3	0.617	1.7	0.320	1.1	0.108	0.8	0.043	0.5	0.016	0.3	0.005			13
14	2.4	0.708	1.9	0.367	1.2	0.124	0.8	0.049	0.5	0.019	0.3	0.006			14
15	2.6	0.805	2.0	0.417	1.3	0.141	0.9	0.055	0.6	0.021	0.4	0.006			15
16	2.8	0.907	2.1	0.470	1.4	0.158	0.9	0.062	0.6	0.024	0.4	0.007			16
17	3.0	1.015	2.3	0.525	1.4	0.177	1.0	0.070	0.7	0.027	0.4	0.008			17
18	3.1	1.128	2.4	0.584	1.5	0.197	1.0	0.078	0.7	0.030	0.4	0.009			18
19	3.3	1.247	2.5	0.645	1.6	0.218	1.1	0.086	0.7	0.033	0.4	0.010			19
20	3.5	1.371	2.7	0.710	1.7	0.239	1.2	0.094	0.8	0.036	0.5	0.011			20
22	3.8	1.636	2.9	0.847	1.9	0.286	1.3	0.113	0.9	0.043	0.5	0.013			22
24	4.2	1.922	3.2	0.995	2.0	0.336	1.4	0.132	0.9	0.051	0.6	0.015			24
26	4.5	2.229	3.4	1.154	2.2	0.389	1.5	0.153	1.0	0.059	0.6	0.017			26
28	4.9	2.557	3.7	1.324	2.4	0.446	1.6	0.176	1.1	0.068	0.7	0.020			28
30	5.2	2.905	4.0	1.504	2.5	0.507	1.7	0.200	1.2	0.077	0.7	0.023			30
35	6.1	3.865	4.6	2.001	3.0	0.675	2.0	0.266	1.4	0.103	0.8	0.030	0.4	0.005	35
40	7.0	4.950	5.3	2.562	3.4	0.864	2.3	0.341	1.6	0.131	0.9	0.039	0.4	0.006	40
45	7.8	6.157	6.0	3.187	3.8	1.075	2.6	0.424	1.8	0.163	1.1	0.048	0.5	0.007	45
50	8.7	7.483	6.6	3.873	4.2	1.306	2.9	0.515	2.0	0.199	1.2	0.058	0.5	0.009	50
55	9.6	8.928	7.3	4.621	4.7	1.559	3.2	0.615	2.2	0.237	1.3	0.070	0.6	0.011	55
60	10.4	10.489	8.0	5.429	5.1	1.831	3.5	0.722	2.3	0.278	1.4	0.082	0.7	0.012	60
65	11.3	12.165	8.6	6.297	5.5	2.124	3.8	0.838	2.5	0.323	1.5	0.095	0.7	0.014	65
70	12.2	13.954	9.3	7.223	5.9	2.436	4.1	0.961	2.7	0.370	1.7	0.109	0.8	0.017	70
75	13.0	15.856	9.9	8.208	6.4	2.768	4.3	1.092	2.9	0.421	1.8	0.124	0.8	0.019	75
80	13.9	17.869	10.6	9.250	6.8	3.120	4.6	1.231	3.1	0.474	1.9	0.139	0.9	0.021	80
85	14.8	19.993	11.3	10.349	7.2	3.490	4.9	1.377	3.3	0.530	2.0	0.156	0.9	0.024	85
90	15.6	22.225	11.9	11.504	7.6	3.880	5.2	1.530	3.5	0.590	2.1	0.173	1.0	0.026	90
95	16.5	24.566	12.6	12.716	8.1	4.289	5.5	1.692	3.7	0.652	2.2	0.192	1.0	0.029	95
100	17.4	27.014	13.3	13.983	8.5	4.716	5.8	1.860	3.9	0.717	2.4	0.211	1.1	0.032	100
110	19.1	32.229	14.6	16.683	9.3	5.626	6.4	2.219	4.3	0.855	2.6	0.251	1.2	0.038	110
120			15.9	19.600	10.2	6.610	6.9	2.607	4.7	1.004	2.8	0.295	1.3	0.045	120
130			17.2	22.732	11.0	7.666	7.5	3.024	5.1	1.165	3.1	0.342	1.4	0.052	130
140			18.6	26.076	11.9	8.794	8.1	3.469	5.5	1.336	3.3	0.393	1.5	0.060	140
150					12.7	9.993	8.7	3.942	5.9	1.518	3.5	0.446	1.6	0.068	150
160					13.6	11.261	9.3	4.442	6.3	1.711	3.8	0.503	1.7	0.077	160
170					14.4	12.600	9.8	4.970	6.6	1.915	4.0	0.563	1.9	0.086	170
180					15.3	14.006	10.4	5.525	7.0	2.128	4.3	0.626	2.0	0.095	180
190					16.1	15.482	11.0	6.107	7.4	2.352	4.5	0.692	2.1	0.105	190
200					17.0	17.024	11.6	6.715	7.8	2.587	4.7	0.761	2.2	0.116	200
225					19.1	21.174	13.0	8.352	8.8	3.218	5.3	0.946	2.5	0.144	225
250							14.5	10.152	9.8	3.911	5.9	1.150	2.7	0.175	250
275							15.9	12.112	10.8	4.666	6.5	1.372	3.0	0.209	275
300							17.4	14.229	11.7	5.482	7.1	1.611	3.3	0.246	300
325							18.4	16.503	12.7	6.357	7.7	1.869	3.5	0.285	325
350									13.7	7.293	8.3	2.144	3.8	0.327	350
375									14.7	8.287	8.9	2.436	4.1	0.371	375
400									15.6	9.339	9.5	2.745	4.4	0.418	400
425									16.6	10.448	10.0	3.072	4.6	0.468	425
450									17.6	11.615	10.6	3.415	4.9	0.520	450
475									18.6	12.838	11.2	3.774	5.2	0.575	475
500											11.8	4.150	5.5	0.632	500
550											13.0	4.952	6.0	0.754	550
600											14.2	5.817	6.5	0.886	600

1. Shaded areas indicate velocities greater than 5 FPS
2. Pressure losses based on Hazen-Williams equation
3. Pipe Sizes 3/4 and 1-inch are CL 160 PVC pipe

Friction Loss Characteristics
PSI Loss per 100 Feet of Pipe (PSI / 100 FT)
PVC Class 200 IPS Plastic Pipe
(1120, 1220) SDR 21 C = 150

	3/4"		1"		1-1/4"		1-1/2"		2"		2-1/2"		3"		4"		6"		SIZE
	1.050		1.315		1.660		1.900		2.375		2.875		3.500		4.500		6.625		OD
	0.930		1.189		1.502		1.720		2.149		2.601		3.166		4.072		5.993		ID
	0.060		0.063		0.079		0.090		0.113		0.137		0.167		0.214		0.316		WALL THK.
FLOW	V	LOSS	V	LOSS	V	LOSS	V	LOSS	V	LOSS	V	LOSS	V	LOSS	V	LOSS	V	LOSS	FLOW
(GPM)	(FPS)	(PSI per 100 ft.)	(FPS)	(PSI per 100 ft.)	(FPS)	(PSI per 100 ft.)	(FPS)	(PSI per 100 ft.)	(FPS)	(PSI per 100 ft.)	(FPS)	(PSI per 100 ft.)	(FPS)	(PSI per 100 ft.)	(FPS)	(PSI per 100 ft.)	(FPS)	(PSI per 100 ft.)	(GPM)
1	0.5	0.061	0.3	0.018	0.2	0.006													1
2	0.9	0.219	0.6	0.066	0.4	0.021	0.3	0.011											2
3	1.4	0.464	0.9	0.140	0.5	0.045	0.4	0.023	0.3	0.008									3
4	1.9	0.790	1.2	0.239	0.7	0.077	0.6	0.040	0.4	0.013	0.2	0.005							4
5	2.4	1.194	1.4	0.361	0.9	0.116	0.7	0.060	0.4	0.020	0.3	0.008							5
6	2.8	1.673	1.7	0.506	1.1	0.162	0.8	0.084	0.5	0.028	0.4	0.011							6
7	3.3	2.226	2.0	0.674	1.3	0.216	1.0	0.112	0.6	0.038	0.4	0.015	0.3	0.006					7
8	3.8	2.851	2.3	0.862	1.4	0.277	1.1	0.143	0.7	0.048	0.5	0.019	0.3	0.007					8
9	4.2	3.545	2.6	1.073	1.6	0.344	1.2	0.178	0.8	0.060	0.5	0.024	0.4	0.009					9
10	4.7	4.309	2.9	1.304	1.8	0.418	1.4	0.216	0.9	0.073	0.6	0.029	0.4	0.011					10
11	5.2	5.141	3.2	1.556	2.0	0.499	1.5	0.258	1.0	0.087	0.7	0.034	0.4	0.013					11
12	5.7	6.040	3.5	1.828	2.2	0.586	1.7	0.303	1.1	0.103	0.7	0.041	0.5	0.016					12
13	6.1	7.006	3.8	2.120	2.4	0.680	1.8	0.352	1.1	0.119	0.8	0.047	0.5	0.018	0.3	0.005			13
14	6.6	8.036	4.0	2.431	2.5	0.780	1.9	0.403	1.2	0.136	0.8	0.054	0.6	0.021	0.3	0.006			14
15	7.1	9.131	4.3	2.763	2.7	0.886	2.1	0.458	1.3	0.155	0.9	0.061	0.6	0.024	0.4	0.007			15
16	7.5	10.291	4.6	3.114	2.9	0.999	2.2	0.516	1.4	0.175	1.0	0.069	0.7	0.027	0.4	0.008			16
17	8.0	11.514	4.9	3.483	3.1	1.117	2.3	0.578	1.5	0.196	1.0	0.077	0.7	0.030	0.4	0.009			17
18	8.5	12.799	5.2	3.872	3.3	1.242	2.5	0.642	1.6	0.217	1.1	0.086	0.7	0.033	0.4	0.010			18
19	9.0	14.147	5.5	4.280	3.4	1.373	2.6	0.710	1.7	0.240	1.1	0.095	0.8	0.036	0.5	0.011			19
20	9.4	15.557	5.8	4.707	3.6	1.510	2.8	0.781	1.8	0.264	1.2	0.104	0.8	0.040	0.5	0.012			20
22	10.4	18.560	6.3	5.616	4.0	1.801	3.0	0.931	1.9	0.315	1.3	0.124	0.9	0.048	0.5	0.014			22
24	11.3	21.806	6.9	6.597	4.3	2.116	3.3	1.094	2.1	0.370	1.4	0.146	1.0	0.056	0.6	0.017			24
26	12.3	25.290	7.5	7.652	4.7	2.454	3.6	1.269	2.3	0.429	1.6	0.170	1.1	0.065	0.6	0.019			26
28	13.2	29.010	8.1	8.777	5.1	2.815	3.9	1.456	2.5	0.493	1.7	0.195	1.1	0.075	0.7	0.022			28
30	14.2	32.965	8.7	9.974	5.4	3.199	4.1	1.654	2.7	0.560	1.8	0.221	1.2	0.085	0.7	0.025			30
35	16.5	43.856	10.1	13.269	6.3	4.256	4.8	2.201	3.1	0.745	2.1	0.294	1.4	0.113	0.9	0.033	0.4	0.005	35
40	18.9	56.161	11.5	16.992	7.2	5.450	5.5	2.818	3.5	0.954	2.4	0.377	1.6	0.145	1.0	0.043	0.5	0.006	40
45			13.0	21.133	8.1	6.778	6.2	3.505	4.0	1.186	2.7	0.469	1.8	0.180	1.1	0.053	0.5	0.008	45
50			14.4	25.687	9.0	8.239	6.9	4.261	4.4	1.442	3.0	0.569	2.0	0.219	1.2	0.064	0.6	0.010	50
55			15.9	30.646	9.9	9.830	7.6	5.083	4.9	1.720	3.3	0.679	2.2	0.261	1.4	0.077	0.6	0.012	55
60			17.3	36.005	10.9	11.548	8.3	5.972	5.3	2.021	3.6	0.798	2.4	0.307	1.5	0.090	0.7	0.014	60
65			18.8	41.758	11.8	13.394	9.0	6.926	5.7	2.344	3.9	0.926	2.6	0.356	1.6	0.105	0.7	0.016	65
70					12.7	15.364	9.7	7.945	6.2	2.689	4.2	1.062	2.8	0.408	1.7	0.120	0.8	0.018	70
75					13.6	17.458	10.3	9.028	6.6	3.055	4.5	1.207	3.1	0.464	1.8	0.136	0.9	0.021	75
80					14.5	19.674	11.0	10.174	7.1	3.443	4.8	1.360	3.3	0.523	2.0	0.154	0.9	0.023	80
85					15.4	22.012	11.7	11.383	7.5	3.852	5.1	1.521	3.5	0.585	2.1	0.172	1.0	0.026	85
90					16.3	24.470	12.4	12.654	8.0	4.282	5.4	1.691	3.7	0.650	2.2	0.191	1.0	0.029	90
95					17.2	27.047	13.1	13.987	8.4	4.733	5.7	1.870	3.9	0.718	2.3	0.211	1.1	0.032	95
100					18.1	29.743	13.8	15.381	8.8	5.205	6.0	2.056	4.1	0.790	2.5	0.232	1.1	0.035	100
110					19.9	35.485	15.2	18.350	9.7	6.209	6.6	2.453	4.5	0.942	2.7	0.277	1.3	0.042	110
120							16.5	21.558	10.6	7.295	7.2	2.882	4.9	1.107	3.0	0.325	1.4	0.050	120
130							17.9	25.003	11.5	8.461	7.8	3.342	5.3	1.284	3.2	0.377	1.5	0.058	130
140							19.3	28.682	12.4	9.706	8.4	3.834	5.7	1.473	3.4	0.433	1.6	0.066	140
150									13.3	11.028	9.0	4.356	6.1	1.674	3.7	0.492	1.7	0.075	150
160									14.1	12.429	9.6	4.909	6.5	1.886	3.9	0.554	1.8	0.085	160
170									15.0	13.905	10.3	5.493	6.9	2.110	4.2	0.620	1.9	0.095	170
180									15.9	15.458	10.9	6.106	7.3	2.346	4.4	0.689	2.0	0.105	180
190									16.8	17.086	11.5	6.749	7.7	2.593	4.7	0.762	2.2	0.116	190
200									17.7	18.789	12.1	7.421	8.1	2.852	4.9	0.838	2.3	0.128	200
225									19.9	23.369	13.6	9.231	9.2	3.547	5.5	1.042	2.6	0.159	225
250											15.1	11.219	10.2	4.311	6.2	1.267	2.8	0.193	250
275											16.6	13.385	11.2	5.143	6.8	1.511	3.1	0.231	275
300											18.1	15.726	12.2	6.042	7.4	1.776	3.4	0.271	300
325											19.6	18.239	13.2	7.008	8.0	2.059	3.7	0.314	325
350													14.2	8.039	8.6	2.362	4.0	0.360	350
375													15.3	9.134	9.2	2.684	4.3	0.409	375
400													16.3	10.294	9.8	3.025	4.5	0.461	400
425													17.3	11.517	10.5	3.385	4.8	0.516	425
450													18.3	12.803	11.1	3.763	5.1	0.574	450
475													19.3	14.152	11.7	4.159	5.4	0.634	475
500															12.3	4.573	5.7	0.697	500
550															13.5	5.456	6.2	0.832	550
600															14.8	6.410	6.8	0.978	600

1. Shaded areas indicate velocities greater than 5 FPS
2. Pressure losses based on Hazen-Williams equation

Friction Loss Characteristics
PSI Loss per 100 Feet of Pipe (PSI/100 FT)
Schedule 40 IPS Plastic Pipe C = 150
(1120, 1220) C = 150

	1/2"		3/4"		1"		1-1/4"		1-1/2"		2"		2-1/2"		3"		4"		
SIZE OD	0.840		1.050		1.315		1.660		1.900		2.375		2.875		3.500		4.500		SIZE OD
ID	0.622		0.824		1.049		1.380		1.610		2.067		2.469		3.068		4.026		ID
WALL THK.	0.109		0.113		0.133		0.140		0.145		0.154		0.203		0.216		0.237		WALL THK.
FLOW (GPM)	V (FPS)	LOSS (PSI per 100 ft.)	V (FPS)	LOSS (PSI per 100 ft.)	V (FPS)	LOSS (PSI per 100 ft.)	V (FPS)	LOSS (PSI per 100 ft.)	V (FPS)	LOSS (PSI per 100 ft.)	V (FPS)	LOSS (PSI per 100 ft.)	V (FPS)	LOSS (PSI per 100 ft.)	V (FPS)	LOSS (PSI per 100 ft.)	V (FPS)	LOSS (PSI per 100 ft.)	FLOW (GPM)
1	1.1	0.429	0.6	0.109	0.4	0.034	0.2	0.009											1
2	2.1	1.549	1.2	0.394	0.7	0.122	0.4	0.032	0.3	0.015									2
3	3.2	3.282	1.8	0.835	1.1	0.258	0.6	0.068	0.5	0.032	0.3	0.010							3
4	4.2	5.591	2.4	1.423	1.5	0.440	0.9	0.116	0.6	0.055	0.4	0.016	0.3	0.007					4
5	5.3	8.452	3.0	2.151	1.9	0.664	1.1	0.175	0.8	0.083	0.5	0.025	0.3	0.010					5
6	6.3	11.847	3.6	3.015	2.2	0.931	1.3	0.245	0.9	0.116	0.6	0.034	0.4	0.014	0.3	0.005			6
7	7.4	15.761	4.2	4.011	2.6	1.239	1.5	0.326	1.1	0.154	0.7	0.046	0.5	0.019	0.3	0.007			7
8	8.4	20.183	4.8	5.137	3.0	1.587	1.7	0.418	1.3	0.197	0.8	0.059	0.5	0.025	0.3	0.009			8
9	9.5	25.103	5.4	6.389	3.3	1.973	1.9	0.520	1.4	0.245	0.9	0.073	0.6	0.031	0.4	0.011			9
10	10.5	30.512	6.0	7.765	3.7	2.399	2.1	0.632	1.6	0.298	1.0	0.088	0.7	0.037	0.4	0.013			10
11	11.6	36.403	6.6	9.264	4.1	2.862	2.4	0.753	1.7	0.356	1.1	0.106	0.7	0.044	0.5	0.015			11
12	12.7	42.768	7.2	10.884	4.4	3.362	2.6	0.885	1.9	0.418	1.1	0.124	0.8	0.052	0.5	0.018	0.3	0.005	12
13	13.7	49.602	7.8	12.623	4.8	3.899	2.8	1.027	2.0	0.485	1.2	0.144	0.9	0.061	0.6	0.021	0.3	0.006	13
14	14.8	56.899	8.4	14.481	5.2	4.473	3.0	1.178	2.2	0.556	1.3	0.165	0.9	0.069	0.6	0.024	0.4	0.006	14
15	15.8	64.654	9.0	16.454	5.6	5.083	3.2	1.338	2.4	0.632	1.4	0.187	1.0	0.079	0.7	0.027	0.4	0.007	15
16	16.9	72.862	9.6	18.543	5.9	5.728	3.4	1.508	2.5	0.712	1.5	0.211	1.1	0.089	0.7	0.031	0.4	0.008	16
17	17.9	81.520	10.2	20.747	6.3	6.408	3.6	1.687	2.7	0.797	1.6	0.236	1.1	0.100	0.7	0.035	0.4	0.009	17
18	19.0	90.623	10.8	23.063	6.7	7.124	3.9	1.876	2.8	0.886	1.7	0.263	1.2	0.111	0.8	0.038	0.5	0.010	18
19	20.0	100.17	11.4	25.492	7.0	7.874	4.1	2.073	3.0	0.979	1.8	0.290	1.3	0.122	0.8	0.042	0.5	0.011	19
20			12.0	28.033	7.4	8.659	4.3	2.280	3.1	1.077	1.9	0.319	1.3	0.134	0.9	0.047	0.5	0.012	20
22			13.2	33.444	8.2	10.331	4.7	2.720	3.5	1.285	2.1	0.381	1.5	0.160	1.0	0.056	0.6	0.015	22
24			14.4	39.292	8.9	12.137	5.1	3.196	3.8	1.509	2.3	0.447	1.6	0.188	1.0	0.065	0.6	0.017	24
26			15.6	45.571	9.6	14.076	5.6	3.706	4.1	1.751	2.5	0.519	1.7	0.219	1.1	0.076	0.7	0.020	26
28			16.8	52.275	10.4	16.147	6.0	4.251	4.4	2.008	2.7	0.595	1.9	0.251	1.2	0.087	0.7	0.023	28
30			18.0	59.400	11.1	18.348	6.4	4.831	4.7	2.282	2.9	0.676	2.0	0.285	1.3	0.099	0.8	0.026	30
35					13.0	24.411	7.5	6.427	5.5	3.036	3.3	0.900	2.3	0.379	1.5	0.132	0.9	0.035	35
40					14.8	31.259	8.6	8.230	6.3	3.887	3.8	1.152	2.7	0.485	1.7	0.169	1.0	0.045	40
45					16.7	38.879	9.6	10.237	7.1	4.835	4.3	1.433	3.0	0.604	2.0	0.210	1.1	0.056	45
50					18.5	47.256	10.7	12.442	7.9	5.877	4.8	1.742	3.3	0.734	2.2	0.255	1.3	0.068	50
55							11.8	14.844	8.7	7.011	5.3	2.079	3.7	0.875	2.4	0.304	1.4	0.081	55
60							12.9	17.440	9.4	8.237	5.7	2.442	4.0	1.028	2.6	0.357	1.5	0.095	60
65							13.9	20.226	10.2	9.553	6.2	2.832	4.4	1.193	2.8	0.415	1.6	0.110	65
70							15.0	23.202	11.0	10.959	6.7	3.249	4.7	1.368	3.0	0.475	1.8	0.127	70
75							16.1	26.364	11.8	12.452	7.2	3.692	5.0	1.555	3.3	0.540	1.9	0.144	75
80							17.1	29.712	12.6	14.033	7.6	4.160	5.4	1.752	3.5	0.609	2.0	0.162	80
85							18.2	33.242	13.4	15.701	8.1	4.655	5.7	1.960	3.7	0.681	2.1	0.182	85
90							19.3	36.954	14.2	17.454	8.6	5.174	6.0	2.179	3.9	0.757	2.3	0.202	90
95									15.0	19.292	9.1	5.719	6.4	2.409	4.1	0.837	2.4	0.223	95
100									15.7	21.215	9.5	6.289	6.7	2.649	4.3	0.920	2.5	0.245	100
110									17.3	25.311	10.5	7.504	7.4	3.160	4.8	1.098	2.8	0.293	110
120									18.9	29.736	11.5	8.816	8.0	3.713	5.2	1.290	3.0	0.344	120
130											12.4	10.224	8.7	4.306	5.6	1.496	3.3	0.399	130
140											13.4	11.728	9.4	4.939	6.1	1.717	3.5	0.457	140
150											14.3	13.327	10.0	5.613	6.5	1.950	3.8	0.520	150
160											15.3	15.019	10.7	6.325	6.9	2.198	4.0	0.586	160
170											16.2	16.804	11.4	7.077	7.4	2.459	4.3	0.655	170
180											17.2	18.680	12.0	7.867	7.8	2.734	4.5	0.729	180
190											18.1	20.647	12.7	8.696	8.2	3.022	4.8	0.805	190
200											19.1	22.705	13.4	9.562	8.7	3.323	5.0	0.886	200
225													15.1	11.893	9.8	4.133	5.7	1.101	225
250													16.7	14.456	10.8	5.023	6.3	1.339	250
275													18.4	17.246	11.9	5.993	6.9	1.597	275
300															13.0	7.041	7.6	1.877	300
325															14.1	8.166	8.2	2.176	325
350															15.2	9.368	8.8	2.497	350
375															16.3	10.644	9.4	2.837	375
400															17.3	11.996	10.1	3.197	400
425															18.4	13.421	10.7	3.577	425
450															19.5	14.920	11.3	3.976	450
475																	12.0	4.395	475
500																	12.6	4.833	500
550																	13.8	5.766	550
600																	15.1	6.774	600

1. Shaded areas indicate velocities greater than 5 FPS
2. Pressure losses based on Hazen-Williams equation

Friction Loss Characteristics
PSI Loss per 100 Feet of Pipe (PSI/100 FT)
Schedule 40 Standard Steel Pipe C = 100

SIZE OD ID WALL THK.	1/2" 0.840 0.622 0.109		3/4" 1.050 0.824 0.113		1" 1.315 1.049 0.133		1-1/4" 1.660 1.380 0.140		1-1/2" 1.900 1.610 0.145		2" 2.375 2.067 0.154		2-1/2" 2.875 2.469 0.203		3" 3.500 3.068 0.216		4" 4.500 4.026 0.237		SIZE OD ID WALL THK.
FLOW (GPM)	V (FPS)	LOSS (PSI per 100 ft.)	V (FPS)	LOSS (PSI per 100 ft.)	V (FPS)	LOSS (PSI per 100 ft.)	V (FPS)	LOSS (PSI per 100 ft.)	V (FPS)	LOSS (PSI per 100 ft.)	V (FPS)	LOSS (PSI per 100 ft.)	V (FPS)	LOSS (PSI per 100 ft.)	V (FPS)	LOSS (PSI per 100 ft.)	V (FPS)	LOSS (PSI per 100 ft.)	FLOW (GPM)
1	1.1	0.909	0.6	0.231	0.4	0.071	0.2	0.019											1
2	2.1	3.282	1.2	0.835	0.7	0.258	0.4	0.068	0.3	0.032									2
3	3.2	6.954	1.8	1.770	1.1	0.547	0.6	0.144	0.5	0.068	0.3	0.020							3
4	4.2	11.847	2.4	3.015	1.5	0.931	0.9	0.245	0.6	0.116	0.4	0.034	0.3	0.014					4
5	5.3	17.910	3.0	4.558	1.9	1.408	1.1	0.371	0.8	0.175	0.5	0.052	0.3	0.022					5
6	6.3	25.103	3.6	6.389	2.2	1.973	1.3	0.520	0.9	0.245	0.6	0.073	0.4	0.031	0.3	0.011			6
7	7.4	33.398	4.2	8.500	2.6	2.625	1.5	0.691	1.1	0.327	0.7	0.097	0.5	0.041	0.3	0.014			7
8	8.4	42.768	4.8	10.884	3.0	3.362	1.7	0.885	1.3	0.418	0.8	0.124	0.5	0.052	0.3	0.018			8
9	9.5	53.192	5.4	13.537	3.3	4.182	1.9	1.101	1.4	0.520	0.9	0.154	0.6	0.065	0.4	0.023			9
10	10.5	64.654	6.0	16.454	3.7	5.083	2.1	1.338	1.6	0.632	1.0	0.187	0.7	0.079	0.4	0.027			10
11	11.6	77.135	6.6	19.631	4.1	6.064	2.4	1.597	1.7	0.754	1.1	0.224	0.7	0.094	0.5	0.033			11
12	12.7	90.623	7.2	23.063	4.4	7.124	2.6	1.876	1.9	0.886	1.1	0.263	0.8	0.111	0.5	0.038	0.3	0.010	12
13	13.7	105.10	7.8	26.748	4.8	8.262	2.8	2.175	2.0	1.028	1.2	0.305	0.9	0.128	0.6	0.045	0.3	0.012	13
14	14.8	120.57	8.4	30.683	5.2	9.478	3.0	2.495	2.2	1.179	1.3	0.349	0.9	0.147	0.6	0.051	0.4	0.014	14
15	15.8	137.00	9.0	34.866	5.6	10.770	3.2	2.836	2.4	1.339	1.4	0.397	1.0	0.167	0.7	0.058	0.4	0.015	15
16	16.9	154.39	9.6	39.292	5.9	12.137	3.4	3.196	2.5	1.509	1.5	0.447	1.1	0.188	0.7	0.065	0.4	0.017	16
17	17.9	172.74	10.2	43.961	6.3	13.579	3.6	3.575	2.7	1.689	1.5	0.501	1.1	0.211	0.7	0.073	0.4	0.020	17
18	19.0	192.03	10.8	48.870	6.7	15.096	3.9	3.975	2.8	1.877	1.7	0.557	1.2	0.234	0.8	0.081	0.5	0.022	18
19			11.4	54.017	7.0	16.685	4.1	4.393	3.0	2.075	1.8	0.615	1.3	0.259	0.8	0.090	0.5	0.024	19
20			12.0	59.400	7.4	18.348	4.3	4.831	3.1	2.282	1.9	0.676	1.3	0.285	0.9	0.099	0.5	0.026	20
22			13.2	70.867	8.2	21.890	4.7	5.764	3.5	2.722	2.1	0.807	1.5	0.340	1.0	0.118	0.6	0.031	22
24			14.4	83.258	8.9	25.718	5.1	6.771	3.8	3.198	2.3	0.948	1.6	0.399	1.0	0.139	0.6	0.037	24
26			15.6	96.562	9.6	29.827	5.6	7.853	4.1	3.709	2.5	1.100	1.7	0.463	1.1	0.161	0.7	0.043	26
28			16.8	110.77	10.4	34.215	6.0	9.009	4.4	4.255	2.7	1.261	1.9	0.531	1.2	0.185	0.7	0.049	28
30			18.0	125.86	11.1	38.879	6.4	10.237	4.7	4.835	2.9	1.433	2.0	0.604	1.3	0.210	0.8	0.056	30
35					13.0	51.725	7.5	13.619	5.5	6.432	3.3	1.907	2.3	0.803	1.5	0.279	0.9	0.074	35
40					14.8	66.237	8.6	17.440	6.3	8.237	3.8	2.442	2.7	1.028	1.7	0.357	1.0	0.095	40
45					16.7	82.382	9.6	21.691	7.1	10.245	4.3	3.037	3.0	1.279	2.0	0.445	1.1	0.118	45
50					18.5	100.13	10.7	26.364	7.9	12.452	4.8	3.692	3.3	1.555	2.2	0.540	1.3	0.144	50
55							11.8	31.454	8.7	14.856	5.3	4.404	3.7	1.855	2.4	0.645	1.4	0.172	55
60							12.9	36.954	9.4	17.454	5.7	5.174	4.0	2.179	2.6	0.757	1.5	0.202	60
65							13.9	42.859	10.2	20.243	6.2	6.001	4.4	2.527	2.8	0.878	1.6	0.234	65
70							15.0	49.164	11.0	23.221	6.7	6.884	4.7	2.899	3.0	1.008	1.8	0.269	70
75							16.1	55.865	11.8	26.386	7.2	7.822	5.0	3.294	3.3	1.145	1.9	0.305	75
80							17.1	62.958	12.6	29.736	7.6	8.816	5.4	3.713	3.5	1.290	2.0	0.344	80
85							18.2	70.438	13.4	33.270	8.1	9.863	5.7	4.154	3.7	1.444	2.1	0.385	85
90							19.3	78.304	14.2	36.984	8.6	10.964	6.0	4.618	3.9	1.605	2.3	0.428	90
95									15.0	40.880	9.1	12.119	6.4	5.104	4.1	1.774	2.4	0.473	95
100									15.7	44.953	9.5	13.327	6.7	5.613	4.3	1.950	2.5	0.520	100
110									17.3	53.632	10.5	15.900	7.4	6.696	4.8	2.327	2.8	0.620	110
120									18.9	63.010	11.5	18.680	8.0	7.867	5.2	2.734	3.0	0.729	120
130											12.4	21.665	8.7	9.124	5.6	3.171	3.3	0.845	130
140											13.4	24.852	9.4	10.466	6.1	3.637	3.5	0.969	140
150											14.3	28.239	10.0	11.893	6.5	4.133	3.8	1.101	150
160											15.3	31.824	10.7	13.403	6.9	4.658	4.0	1.241	160
170											16.2	35.606	11.4	14.996	7.4	5.211	4.3	1.389	170
180											17.2	39.582	12.0	16.670	7.8	5.793	4.5	1.544	180
190											18.1	43.750	12.7	18.426	8.2	6.403	4.8	1.707	190
200											19.1	48.110	13.4	20.262	8.7	7.041	5.0	1.877	200
225													15.1	25.201	9.8	8.758	5.7	2.334	225
250													16.7	30.631	10.8	10.644	6.3	2.837	250
275													18.4	36.544	11.9	12.699	6.9	3.385	275
300															13.0	14.920	7.6	3.976	300
325															14.1	17.304	8.2	4.612	325
350															15.2	19.850	8.8	5.290	350
375															16.3	22.555	9.4	6.011	375
400															17.3	25.419	10.1	6.774	400
425															18.4	28.439	10.7	7.579	425
450															19.5	31.615	11.3	8.426	450
475																	12.0	9.313	475
500																	12.6	10.241	500
550																	13.8	12.218	550
600																	15.1	14.355	600

1. Shaded areas indicate velocities greater than 5 FPS
2. Pressure losses based on Hazen-Williams equation

Friction Loss Characteristics
PSI Loss per 100 Feet of Pipe (PSI/100 FT)
Polyethylene (PE) SDR-Pressure Rated Tube
(2306,3206,3306) SDR 7, 9, 11, 15, 15 C = 140

SIZE	1/2"		3/4"		1"		1-1/4"		1-1/2"		2"		SIZE
ID	0.622		0.824		1.049		1.380		1.610		2.067		ID
FLOW	V	LOSS	V	LOSS	V	LOSS	V	LOSS	V	LOSS	V	LOSS	FLOW
(GPM)	(FPS)	(PSI per 100 ft.)	(FPS)	(PSI per 100 ft.)	(FPS)	(PSI per 100 ft.)	(FPS)	(PSI per 100 ft.)	(FPS)	(PSI per 100 ft.)	(FPS)	(PSI per 100 ft.)	(GPM)
1	1.1	0.487											1
2	2.1	1.760	1.2	0.448									2
3	3.2	3.729	1.8	0.949	1.1	0.293							3
4	4.2	6.353	2.4	1.617	1.5	0.499	0.9	0.132					4
5	5.3	9.604	3.0	2.444	1.9	0.755	1.1	0.199					5
6	6.3	13.462	3.6	3.426	2.2	1.058	1.3	0.279					6
7	7.4	17.910	4.2	4.558	2.6	1.408	1.5	0.371	1.1	0.175			7
8	8.4	22.934	4.8	5.837	3.0	1.803	1.7	0.475	1.3	0.224			8
9	9.5	28.525	5.4	7.259	3.3	2.242	1.9	0.590	1.4	0.279			9
10	10.5	34.671	6.0	8.824	3.7	2.726	2.1	0.718	1.6	0.339			10
11	11.6	41.364	6.6	10.527	4.1	3.252	2.4	0.856	1.7	0.404			11
12	12.7	48.597	7.2	12.368	4.4	3.820	2.6	1.006	1.9	0.475			12
13	13.7	56.362	7.8	14.344	4.8	4.431	2.8	1.167	2.0	0.551	1.2	0.163	13
14	14.8	64.654	8.4	16.454	5.2	5.083	3.0	1.338	2.2	0.632	1.3	0.187	14
15	15.8	73.466	9.0	18.697	5.6	5.775	3.2	1.521	2.4	0.718	1.4	0.213	15
16	16.9	82.793	9.6	21.071	5.9	6.509	3.4	1.714	2.5	0.809	1.5	0.240	16
17	17.9	92.631	10.2	23.574	6.3	7.282	3.6	1.917	2.7	0.906	1.6	0.268	17
18	19.0	102.97	10.8	26.207	6.7	8.095	3.9	2.131	2.8	1.007	1.7	0.298	18
19	20.0	113.82	11.4	28.967	7.0	8.948	4.1	2.356	3.0	1.113	1.8	0.330	19
20			12.0	31.853	7.4	9.839	4.3	2.591	3.1	1.224	1.9	0.363	20
22			13.2	38.003	8.2	11.739	4.7	3.091	3.5	1.460	2.1	0.433	22
24			14.4	44.648	8.9	13.791	5.1	3.631	3.8	1.715	2.3	0.508	24
26			15.6	51.782	9.6	15.995	5.6	4.211	4.1	1.989	2.5	0.590	26
28			16.8	59.400	10.4	18.348	6.0	4.831	4.4	2.282	2.7	0.676	28
30			18.0	67.496	11.1	20.849	6.4	5.489	4.7	2.593	2.9	0.769	30
35					13.0	27.738	7.5	7.303	5.5	3.449	3.3	1.023	35
40					14.8	35.520	8.6	9.352	6.3	4.417	3.8	1.310	40
45					16.7	44.178	9.6	11.632	7.1	5.494	4.3	1.629	45
50					18.5	53.697	10.7	14.138	7.9	6.678	4.8	1.980	50
55							11.8	16.867	8.7	7.967	5.3	2.362	55
60							12.9	19.817	9.4	9.360	5.7	2.775	60
65							13.9	22.983	10.2	10.855	6.2	3.218	65
70							15.0	26.364	11.0	12.452	6.7	3.692	70
75							16.1	29.958	11.8	14.150	7.2	4.195	75
80							17.1	33.761	12.6	15.946	7.6	4.727	80
85							18.2	37.773	13.4	17.841	8.1	5.289	85
90							19.3	41.991	14.2	19.833	8.6	5.880	90
95									15.0	21.922	9.1	6.499	95
100									15.7	24.106	9.5	7.147	100
110									17.3	28.760	10.5	8.526	110
120									18.9	33.789	11.5	10.017	120
130											12.4	11.618	130
140											13.4	13.327	140
150											14.3	15.143	150
160											15.3	17.066	160
170											16.2	19.094	170
180											17.2	21.226	180
190											18.1	23.461	190
200											19.1	25.799	200

1. Shaded areas indicate velocities greater than 5 FPS
2. Pressure losses based on Hazen-Williams equation

Pressure Loss in Valves and Fittings
Equivalent Length in Feet of Standard Steel Pipe

Nominal Pipe Size (Inch)	Globe Valve (Feet)	Angle Valve (Feet)	Gate Valve (Feet)	Side Outlet Std. Tee (Feet)	Straight Run of Std. Tee (Feet)	90° Elbow (Feet)	45° Elbow (Feet)
½	17	9	0.4	4	1	2	1
¾	22	12	0.5	5	2	3	1
1	27	15	0.6	6	2	3	2
1¼	38	18	0.8	8	3	4	2
1½	45	22	1.0	10	3	5	2
2	58	28	1.2	12	4	6	3
2½	70	35	1.4	14	5	7	3
3	90	45	1.8	18	6	8	4
4	120	60	2.3	23	7	11	5
6	170	85	3.3	33	12	17	8

Appendix C

Specifications

This appendix contains example specifications that would accompany irrigation design drawings. The specifications and design drawings, packaged together, constitute a construction document package, per se.

These specifications are intended to be a reference for Construction Specifications Institute style and content only, and are not a base document to be used without specific project editing.

Information on the Construction Specifications Institute publications can be obtained from:

Construction Specifications Institute
601 Madison Street
Alexandria, Virginia 22314-1791
telephone: 703-684-0300

IRRIGATION SPECIFICATIONS
TABLE OF CONTENTS
SECTION 02810-IRRIGATION

DIVISION 2-SITE WORK

SECTION 02810-IRRIGATION

PART 1: GENERAL
1.01 **SCOPE**:

    Furnish all labor, materials, supplies, equipment, tools, and transportation, and perform all operations in connection with and reasonably incidental to the complete installation of the irrigation system, and guarantee/warranty as shown on the drawings, the installation details, and as specified herein. Items of work specifically included are:

    A. Procurement of all applicable licenses, permits, and fees.

    B. Coordination of all utilities.

C. Connection of electrical power supply to the irrigation control system.

D. Maintenance period.

E. Sleeving for irrigation pipe and wire.

1.02 **WORK NOT INCLUDED**: Items of work specifically excluded or covered under other sections are:

    A. Procurement all development, plant investment, or any other fees and permits associated with the purchase and installation of the tap.

    B. Excavation, installation, and backfill of tap into municipal water line.

    C. Excavation, installation, and backfill of water meter and vault.

    D. Provision of electrical power supply to the irrigation control system.

    E. Maintenance period.

1.03 **RELATED WORK**:

    A. **Division 2–Site Work**:

        1. Section 02920 – Fine Grading and Soil Preparation.

        2. Section 02931 – Seeding.

        3. Section 02932 – Sodding.

        4. Section 02950 – Trees, Plants, and Ground Cover.

1.04 **SUBMITTALS**:

    A. Submit samples under provisions of Section 01300–Submittals.

    B. **Materials List**: Include pipe, fittings, mainline components, water emission components, control system components. Quantities of materials need not be included.

    C. **Manufacturers' Data**: Submit manufacturers' catalog cuts, specifications, and operating instructions for equipment shown on the materials list.

    D. **Shop Drawings**: Submit shop drawings called for in the installation details. Show products required for proper installation, their relative locations, and critical dimensions. Note modifications to the installation detail.

1.05 **RULES AND REGULATIONS**:

    A. Work and materials shall be in accordance with the latest edition of the National Electric Code, the Uniform Plumbing Code as published by the Western Plumbing Officials Association, and applicable laws and regulations of the governing authorities.

    B. When the contract documents call for materials or construction of a better quality or larger size than required by the above-mentioned rules and regulations, provide the quality and size required by the contract documents.

    C. If quantities are provided either in these specifications or on the drawings, these quantities are provided **for information only**. It is the contractor's responsibility to determine the actual quantities of all material, equipment, and supplies required by the project and to complete an independent estimate of quantities and wastage.

1.06 **TESTING**:

    A. Notify the engineer/landscape architect/owner's representative three days in advance of testing.

    B. Pipelines jointed with rubber gaskets or threaded connections may be subjected to a pressure test at any time after partial completion of backfill. Pipelines jointed with solvent-welded PVC joints shall be allowed to cure at least 24 hours before testing.

    C. Subsections of mainline pipe may be tested independently, subject to the review of the engineer/landscape architect/owner's representative.

    D. Furnish clean, clear water, pumps, labor, fittings, and equipment necessary to conduct tests or retests.

    E. **Volumetric Leakage Test**:

        1. Cap risers of mainline components for volumetric pressure tests. Backfill to prevent pipe from moving under pressure. Expose couplings and fitting.

        2. Purge all air from the pipeline before test.

        3. Subject mainline pipe to the anticipated operating pressure of 100 PSI for two hours. Maintain constant pressure. The amount of additional

water pumped in during the test shall not exceed 1.24 gallon per 100 joints of 3-inch diameter pipe and 1.6 gallons per 100 joints of 4-inch diameter pipe. Replace defective pipe, fitting, joint, valve, or appurtenance. Repeat the test until the pipe passes test.

4. Cement or caulking to seal leaks is prohibited.

F. **Operational Test**:

1. Activate each remote control valve in sequence from controller. The engineer/landscape architect/owner's representative will visually observe operation, water application patterns, and leakage.

2. Replace defective remote control valve, solenoid, wiring, or appurtenance to correct operational deficiencies.

3. Replace, adjust, or move water emission devices to correct operational or coverage deficiencies.

4. Replace defective pipe, fitting, joint, valve, sprinkler, or appurtenance to correct leakage problems. Cement or caulking to seal leaks is prohibited.

5. Repeat test(s) until each lateral passes all tests. Repeat tests, replace components, and correct deficiencies at no additional cost to the owner.

1.07 **CONSTRUCTION REVIEW**:

The purpose of on-site reviews by the engineer/landscape architect/owner's representative is to periodically observe the work in progress, the contractor's interpretation of the construction documents, and to address questions with regard to the installation.

A. Scheduled reviews such as those for irrigation system layout or testing must be scheduled with the engineer/landscape architect/owner's representative as required by these specifications.

B. Impromptu reviews may occur at any time during the project.

C. A review will occur at the completion of the irrigation system installation and project record (as-built) drawing submittal.

1.08 **GUARANTEE/WARRANTY AND REPLACEMENT**:

The purpose of this guarantee/warranty is to insure that the owner receives irrigation materials of prime quality, installed and maintained in a thorough and careful manner.

A. For a period of one year from commencement of the formal maintenance period, guarantee/warranty irrigation materials, equipment, and workmanship against defects. Fill and repair depressions. Restore landscape or structural features damaged by the settlement of irrigation trenches or excavations. Repair damage to the premises caused by a defective item. Make repairs within seven days of notification from the engineer/landscape architect/owner's representative.

B. Contract documents govern replacements identically as with new work. Make replacements at no additional cost to the contract price.

C. Guarantee/warranty applies to originally installed materials and equipment and replacements made during the guarantee/warranty period.

PART 2: MATERIALS

2.01 **QUALITY**:

Use materials that are new and without flaws or defects of any type, and which are the best of their class and kind.

2.02 **SUBSTITUTIONS**:

Pipe sizes referenced in the construction documents are minimum sizes, and may be increased at the option of the contractor.

2.03 **SLEEVING**:

A. Install separate sleeve beneath paved areas to route each run of irrigation pipe or wiring bundle.

B. Sleeving material beneath pedestrian pavements shall be PVC Class 200 pipe with solvent welded joints.

C. Sleeving beneath drives and streets shall be PVC Class 200 pipe with solvent welded joints.

D. Sleeving diameter: equal to twice that of the pipe or wiring bundle.

2.04 **PIPE AND FITTINGS**:
  A. **Mainline Pipe and Fittings**:
    1. Use rigid, unplasticized polyvinyl chloride (PVC) 1120, 1220 National Sanitation Foundation (NSF) approved pipe, extruded from material meeting the requirements of Cell Classification 12454-A or 12454-B, ASTM Standard D1784, with an integral belled end.
    2. Use Class 200, SDR-21, rated at 200 PSI, conforming to the dimensions and tolerances established by ASTM Standard D2241. Use PVC pipe rated at higher pressures than Class 200 in the case of small nominal diameters that are not manufactured in Class 200.
    3. Use rubber-gasketed pipe equipped with Reiber Gasket System for mainline pipe with a nominal diameter greater than or equal to 3-inches. Use rubber-gasketed deep bell ductile iron fittings conforming to ASTM A-536 and ASTM F-477. Use lubricant approved by the pipe manufacturer.
    4. Use solvent weld pipe for mainline pipe with a nominal diameter less than 3-inches or where a pipe connection occurs in a sleeve. Use Schedule 40, Type 1, PVC solvent weld fittings conforming to ASTM Standards D2466 and D1784. Use primer approved by the pipe manufacturer. Solvent cement to conform to ASTM Standard D2564.
  B. **Lateral Pipe and Fittings**:
    1. Use rigid, unplasticized polyvinyl chloride (PVC) 1120, 1220 National Sanitation Foundation (NSF) approved pipe, extruded from material meeting the requirements of Cell Classification 12454-A or 12454-B, ASTM Standard D1784, with an integral belled end suitable for solvent welding.
    2. Use Class 160, SDR-26, rated at 160 PSI, conforming to the dimensions and tolerances established by ASTM Standard D2241.
    Use solvent weld pipe for lateral pipe. Use Schedule 40, Type 1, PVC solvent weld fittings conforming to ASTM Standards D2466 and D1784 for PVC pipe. Use primer approved by the pipe manufacturer. Solvent cement to conform to ASTM Standard D2564, of a type approved by the pipe manufacturer.
    3. Flexible polyethylene (PE) pipe is an alternate to rigid PVC pipe on spray sprinkler laterals.
    Use SDR-11.5, PE23, rated at 100 PSI, that is National Sanitation Foundation (NSF) approved, conforming to ASTM Standard D2239. Use Type 1, PVC insert fittings conforming to ASTM Standard D2609 designed for use with flexible polyethylene (PE) pipe. Use stainless steel pinch clamps or worm gear clamps (including stainless steel screw) to join pipe and fittings.
    4. For drip irrigation laterals downstream of zone control valves, use UV radiation-resistant polyethylene pipe manufactured from prime Union Carbide G-resin 7510 Natural 7 manufactured by Union Carbide or a Union Carbide licensee with a minimum of 2% carbon black.
    Use PVC/compression line fittings compatible with the drip lateral pipe. Use tubing stakes or landscape fabric staples to hold above-ground pipe in place.
  C. **Specialized Pipe and Fittings**:
    1. Copper pipe: Use Type "K" rigid conforming to ASTM Standard B88. Use wrought copper or cast bronze fittings, soldered or threaded per the installation details. Use a 95% tin and 5% antimony solder.
    2. Galvanized steel pipe: Use Schedule 40 conforming to ASTM Standard A120.
    Use galvanized, threaded, standard weight, malleable iron fittings.
    3. Ductile iron pipe: Use Class 50 conforming to ANSI A21.51 (AWWA C151). Use a minimum of Class 53 thickness pipe for flanged piping. Use mechanical joints conforming to ANSI A 21.10 (AWWA C110)

and ANSI A21.11 (AWWA C111) or flanged fittings conforming to ANSI/AWWA C110 and ANSI B16.1 (125#).

4. Use a dielectric union wherever a copper-based metal (copper, brass, bronze) is joined to an iron-based metal (iron, galvanized steel, stainless steel).

5. Low-Density Polyethylene Hose:
   a. Use pipe specifically intended for use as a flexible swing joint.
      Inside diameter: 0.490 ± 0.010 inch.
      Wall thickness: 0.100 ± 0.010 inch.
      Color: Black.
   b. Use spiral barb fittings supplied by the same manufacturer as the hose.

6. Assemblies calling for threaded pipe connections shall utilize PVC Schedule 80 nipples and PVC Schedule 40 threaded fittings.

7. Joint sealant: Use only Teflon-type tape or Teflon-based paste pipe joint sealant on plastic threads. Use nonhardening, nontoxic pipe joint sealant formulated for use on water-carrying pipes on metal threaded connections.

D. **Thrust Blocks**:
1. Use thrust blocks for fittings on pipe greater than or equal to 3-inch diameter or any diameter rubber gasketed pipe.
2. Use 3,000 PSI concrete.
3. Use 2 mil plastic.
4. Use No. 4 rebar wrapped or painted with asphalt tar based mastic coating.

2.05 **MAINLINE COMPONENTS**:

A. **Main System Shutoff Valve**: per local practice and in compliance with local code.

B. **Winterization Assembly**: per local practice and in compliance with local code.

C. **Backflow Prevention Assembly**: as presented in the installation details.

D. **Master Valve Assembly**: as presented in the installation details.

E. **Flow Sensor Assembly**: as presented in the installation details.

F. **Isolation Gate Valve Assembly**: as presented in the installation details. Install a separate valve box over a 3-inch depth of $\frac{3}{4}$-inch gravel for each assembly.

G. **Pressure Regulator Assembly**: as presented in the installation details. Install a separate valve box over a 3-inch depth of $\frac{3}{4}$-inch gravel for each assembly.

H. **Quick Coupling Valve Assembly**: double swing joint arrangement as presented in the installation details.

I. **Manual Drain Valve Assembly**: as presented in the installation details. Install a separate sump consisting of three cubic feet of $\frac{3}{4}$-inch gravel for each drain valve.

2.06 **SPRINKLER AND BUBBLER IRRIGATION COMPONENTS**:

A. **Remote Control Valve (RCV) Assembly for Sprinkler and Bubbler Laterals**: as presented in the installation details. Use wire connectors and waterproofing sealant to join control wires to solenoid valves. Use standard I.D. tags with hot-stamped black letters on a yellow background. Install a separate valve box over a 3-inch depth of $\frac{3}{4}$-inch gravel for each assembly.

B. **Sprinkler Assembly**: as presented in the drawings and installation details. Use the sprinkler manufacturer's pressure compensating screens (Rain Bird PCS) to achieve 30 PSI operating conditions on each sprinkler and to control excessive operating pressures.

C. **Bubbler Assembly**: as presented in the drawings and installation details.

2.07 **DRIP IRRIGATION COMPONENTS**:

A. **Remote Control Valve (RCV) Assembly for Drip Laterals**: as presented in the installation details. Use wire connectors and waterproofing sealant to join control wires to solenoid valves. Use standard Christy I.D.

tags with hot-stamped black letters on a yellow background. Install a separate valve box over a 3-inch depth of $\frac{3}{4}$-inch gravel for each assembly.

B. **Zone Control Valve Assembly**: as presented in the installation details. Install a separate box over a 3-inch depth of $\frac{3}{4}$-inch gravel for each assembly.

C. **Drip Emitter Assembly**:
   1. Barb-mounted, pressure compensating emitter device as presented in the installation details.
   2. Install emitter types and quantities on the following schedule:
      Ground cover plant: 1 single-outlet emitter each or 1 single-outlet emitter per square foot of planting area, whichever is less
      Shrub: 2 single-outlet emitters each
      Tree: 4 single-outlet emitters each or 1 multi-outlet emitter each (with 4 outlets open)
   3. Use flexible plastic tubing to direct water from emitter outlet to emission point. Length of emitter outlet tubing shall not exceed five feet. Secure emitter outlet tubing with tubing stakes.
   4. Install an access sleeve for each multiple-outlet emitter.

D. **Flush Cap Assembly**: as presented in the installation details. Locate at the end of each drip irrigation lateral pipe. Install a separate valve box over a 3-inch depth of $\frac{3}{4}$-inch gravel for each assembly.

2.08 **CONTROL SYSTEM COMPONENTS**:

A. **Irrigation Controller Unit**:
   1. As presented in the drawings and installation details.
   2. Lightning protection: Provide 8-foot copper-clad grounding rod at controller location.
   3. Wire markers: Prenumbered or labeled with indelible nonfading ink, made of permanent, nonfading material.

B. **Control Wire**:
   1. Use American Wire Gauge (AWG) No. 14 solid copper, Type UF or PE cable, UL approved for direct underground burial from the controller unit to each remote control valve.
   2. Color: Use white for common ground wire. Use easily distinguished colors for other control wires. Spare control wires shall be of a color different from that of the active control wire. Wire color shall be continuous over its entire length.
   3. Splices: Use wire connector with waterproof sealant. Wire connector to be of plastic construction consisting of two (2) pieces, one piece that snap locks into the other. A copper crimp sleeve to be provided with connector.
   4. Warning tape: Inert plastic film highly resistant to alkalis, acids, or other destructive chemical components likely to be encountered in soils. Tape to be three inches wide, colored yellow, and imprinted with "CAUTION: BURIED ELECTRIC LINE BELOW."

C. **Instrumentation**:
   1. As presented in the drawings and installation details.
   2. Provide, install and test an anemometer for irrigation shutdowns at user-preset wind velocity thresholds, soil moisture monitoring to override irrigation in the event of high soil moisture levels, a rain sensor to prevent irrigation during or immediately after rainfall events, and a temperature sensor to prevent irrigation when temperatures drop below a user-preset threshold.
   3. Weather Station:
      a. Use a station that is compatible with the control system specified and that can be used for day-to-day irrigation scheduling.
      b. The weather station is to be interrogated and reports of local reference evapotranspiration (ET_o) rates and rainfall are to be

determined and reported. ET_o rate calculation is to be based on the modified Penman combination equation.

c. System interrogation is to occur from the same microcomputer used for the centralized irrigation control system. Communication to the weather station is to be by dialtone telephone to allow other authorized users to interrogate the weather station. (Ideally, other local users who may or may not have similar control system equipment will be able to interrogate the weather station independently of owner's personnel.)

D. **Power Wire**:

1. Electric wire from the power source to satellite control unit shall be solid or stranded copper, Type UF single-conductor cable, UL approved for direct underground burial. Power wires shall be black, white, and green in color. Size as presented in the drawings. The contractor is responsible for verifying that the power wire sizes shown on the drawings are compatible and adequate for the control system being used.

2. Splices: Use connectors.

3. Conduit: PVC Schedule 40.

4. Warning tape: Inert plastic film highly resistant to alkalis, acids, or other destructive chemical components likely to be encountered in soils. Tape to be three inches wide, colored yellow, and imprinted with "CAUTION: BURIED ELECTRIC LINE BELOW."

2.09 **OTHER COMPONENTS**:

A. **Tools and Spare Parts**: Provide operating keys, servicing tools, test equipment, spare parts and other items indicated in the general notes of the drawings.

B. **Other Materials**: Provide other materials or equipment shown on the drawings or installation details which are part of the irrigation system, even though such items may not have been referenced in these specifications.

PART 3: EXECUTION

3.01 **INSPECTIONS AND REVIEWS**:

A. **Site Inspections**:

1. Verify construction site conditions and note irregularities affecting work of this section. Report irregularities to the engineer/landscape architect/ owner's representative prior to beginning work.

2. Beginning work of this section implies acceptance of existing conditions.

B. **Utility Locations**:

1. Arrange for and coordinate with local authorities the location of all underground utilities.

2. Repair any underground utilities damaged during construction. Make repairs at no additional cost above the contract price.

C. **Irrigation System Layout Review**: Irrigation system layout review will occur after the staking has been completed. Notify the engineer/landscape architect/owner's representative one week in advance of review. Modifications will be identified by the engineer/landscape architect/owner's representative at this review.

3.02 **LAYOUT OF WORK**:

A. Stake out the irrigation system. Items staked include: sprinklers, pipe, control valves, manual drains, quick coupling valves, backflow preventer, controller, and isolation valves.

B. Install all mainline pipe and mainline components inside of project property lines.

3.03 **EXCAVATION, TRENCHING, AND BACKFILLING**:

A. Excavate to permit the pipes to be laid at the intended elevations and to permit work space for installing connections and fittings.

B. Minimum cover (distance from top of pipe or control wire to finish grade):

1. 14-inch over mainline pipe and over electrical conduit.

2. 16-inch over control wire.

3. 10-inch over lateral pipe to sprinklers and bubblers and over manifold pipe to drip system zone control valves.
4. 8-inch over drip lateral pipe in turf or paved areas downstream of drip system zone control valves.
5. 3-inch minimum mulch cover over drip lateral pipe in planting beds downstream of drip system zone control valves.
6. PVC UV radiation-resistant lateral pipe shall be installed directly on the soil surface.

C. PVC or PE lateral pipes may be pulled into the soil using a vibratory plow device specifically manufactured for pipe pulling. Minimum burial depths equals minimum cover listed above.
D. Backfill only after lines have been reviewed and tested.
E. Excavated material is generally satisfactory for backfill. Backfill shall be free from rubbish, vegetable matter, and stones larger than 2 inches in maximum dimension. Remove material not suitable for backfill. Backfill placed next to pipe shall be free of sharp objects which may damage the pipe.
F. Backfill unsleeved pipe by depositing the backfill material equally on both sides of the pipe in 6-inch layers and compacting each layer to 90% Standard Proctor Density, ASTM D698-78. Conduct one compaction test for every 300 feet of trench. Costs for such testing and any necessary retesting shall be borne by the contractor. Use of water for compaction, "puddling," will not be permitted.
G. Enclose pipe and wiring beneath roadways, walks, curbs, etc., in sleeves. Minimum compaction of backfill for sleeves shall be 95% Standard Proctor Density, ASTM D698-78. Conduct one compaction test for each sleeved crossing less than 50 feet long. Conduct two compaction tests for each sleeved crossing greater than 50 feet long. Costs for such testing and any necessary retesting shall be borne by the contractor. Use of water for compaction around sleeves, "puddling," will not be permitted.
H. Dress backfilled areas to original grade. Incorporate excess backfill into existing site grades.
I. Where utilities conflict with irrigation trenching and pipe work, contact the engineer/landscape architect/owner's representative for trench depth adjustments.

3.04 **SLEEVING AND BORING**:
A. Install sleeving at a depth that permits the encased pipe or wiring to remain at the specified burial depth.
B. Extend sleeve ends six inches beyond the edge of the paved surface. Cover pipe ends and mark with stakes. Mark concrete with a chiseled "x" at sleeve end locations.
C. Bore for sleeves under obstructions that cannot be removed. Employ equipment and methods designed for horizontal boring.

3.05 **ASSEMBLING PIPE AND FITTINGS**:
A. **General**:
1. Keep pipe free from dirt and pipe scale. Cut pipe ends square and debur. Clean pipe ends.
2. Keep ends of assembled pipe capped. Remove caps only when necessary to continue assembly.
3. Trenches may be curved to change direction or avoid obstructions within the limits of the curvature of the pipe. Minimum radii of curvature is 25 feet for 2-inch diameter pipe and 100 feet for $2\frac{1}{2}$-, 3-, and 4-inch diameter pipe. All curvature results from the bending of the pipe lengths. No deflection will be allowed at a pipe joint.
B. **Mainline Pipe and Fittings**:
1. Use only strap-type friction wrenches for threaded plastic pipe.
2. PVC Rubber-Gasketed Pipe:
   a. Use pipe lubricant. Join pipe in the manner recommended by manufacturer and in accordance with accepted industry practices.

      b. Epoxy-coated steel fittings shall not be struck with a metallic tool. Cushion blows with a wood block or similar shock absorber.

   3. PVC Solvent Weld Pipe:

      a. Use primer and solvent cement. Join pipe in a manner recommended by the manufacturer and in accordance with accepted industry practices.

      b. Cure for 30 minutes before handling and 24 hours before allowing water in pipe.

      c. Snake pipe from side to side within the trench.

   4. Fittings: The use of cross type fittings is not permitted.

C. **Lateral Pipe and Fittings**:

   1. Use only strap-type friction wrenches for threaded plastic pipe.

   2. PVC Solvent Weld Pipe:

      a. Use primer and solvent cement. Join pipe in the manner recommended by the manufacturer and in accordance with accepted industry practices.

      b. Cure for 30 minutes before handling and 24 hours before allowing water in the pipe.

      c. Snake pipe from side to side within the trench.

   3. Polyethylene (PE) Pipe:

      a. Join pipe in the manner recommended by manufacturer and in accordance with accepted industry practices.

      b. Snake pipe from side to side within the trench.

   4. UV Radiation-Resistant Polyethylene Pipe:

      a. Join pipe in the manner recommended by manufacturer and in accordance with accepted industry practices.

      b. Snake pipe from side to side within the trench, on the soil surface, and hold in place with tubing stakes or landscape fabric staples spaced every five feet. Pipe is not to be compressed or crimped by the stake or staple or other construction activity.

   5. Fittings: The use of cross type fittings is not permitted.

D. **Specialized Pipe and Fittings**:

   1. Copper Pipe:

      a. Buff surfaces to be joined to a bright finish. Coat with solder flux.

      b. Solder so that a continuous bead shows around the joint circumference.

   2. Galvanized Steel Pipe:

      a. Join pipe in the manner recommended by manufacturer and in accordance with accepted industry practices.

      b. Use factory-made threads whenever possible. Field-cut threads will be permitted only where absolutely necessary. Cut threads on axis using clean, sharp dies.

      c. Apply Teflon-type tape or pipe joint compound to the male threads only.

   3. Ductile Iron Pipe:

      a. Join pipe in the manner recommended by manufacturer and in accordance with accepted industry practices.

   4. Insert a dielectric union wherever a copper-based metal (copper, brass, bronze) and an iron-based metal (iron, galvanized steel, stainless steel) are joined.

   5. Low-Density Polyethylene Hose: Install per manufacturer's recommendations.

   6. PVC Threaded Connections:

      a. Use only factory-formed threads. Field-cut threads are not permitted.

      b. Use only Teflon-type tape or Teflon-based paste.

      c. When connection is plastic-to-metal, the plastic component shall have male threads and the metal component shall have female threads.

7. Make metal-to-metal, threaded connections with Teflon-type tape or pipe joint compound applied to the male threads only.

E. **Thrust Blocks**:
1. Use cast-in-place concrete bearing against undisturbed soil.
2. Size, orientation, and placement shall be as shown on the installation details.
3. Wrap fitting with plastic to protect bolts, joint, and fitting from concrete.
4. Install rebar with mastic coating as shown on the installation details.

3.06 **INSTALLATION OF MAINLINE COMPONENTS**:

A. **Main System Shut Off Valve**: Install where indicated on the drawings.
B. **Winterization Assembly**: Install where indicated on the drawings.
C. **Backflow Prevention Assembly**: Install where indicated on the drawings. Install assembly so that its elevation, orientation, access, and drainage conform to the manufacturer's recommendations and applicable health codes.
D. **Master Valve Assembly**: Install where indicated on the drawings.
E. **Flow Sensor Assembly**: Install where indicated on the drawings.
F. **Isolation Gate Valve Assembly**:
1. Install where indicated on the drawings.
2. Locate at least 12 inches from and align with adjacent walls or edges of paved areas.
G. **Pressure Regulator Assembly**:
1. Install where indicated on the drawings.
2. Locate at least 12 inches from and align with adjacent walls or edges of paved areas.
3. Adjust to provide an output pressure of 100 PSI.
H. **Quick Coupling Valve Assembly**: Install where indicated on the drawings.
I. **Manual Drain Valve Assembly**: Install where indicated on the drawings and at other low points in the mainline piping.

3.07 **INSTALLATION OF SPRINKLER AND BUBBLER IRRIGATION COMPONENTS**:

A. **Remote Control Valve (RCV) Assembly for Sprinkler and Bubbler Laterals**:
1. Flush mainline before installation of RCV assembly.
2. Install where indicated on the drawings. Wire connectors and waterproof sealant shall be used to connect control wires to remote control valve wires. Install connectors and sealant per the manufacturer's recommendations.
3. Install only one RCV to a valve box. Locate valve box at least 12 inches from and align with nearby walls or edges of paved areas. Group RCV assemblies together where practical. Arrange grouped valve boxes in rectangular patterns. Allow at least 12 inches between valve boxes.
4. Adjust RCV to regulate the downstream operating pressure.
5. Attach ID tag with controller station number to control wiring.

B. **Sprinkler Assembly**:
1. Flush lateral pipe before installing sprinkler assembly.
2. Install per the installation details at locations shown on the drawings.
3. Locate rotor sprinklers 6 inches from adjacent walls, fences, or edges of paved areas.
4. Locate spray sprinklers 3 inches from adjacent walls, fences, or edges of paved areas.
5. Install sprinklers perpendicular to the finish grade.
6. Supply appropriate nozzle or adjust arc of coverage of each sprinkler for best performance.
7. Adjust the radius of throw of each sprinkler for best performance.

C. **Bubbler Assembly**:
1. Flush lateral pipe before installing bubbler assembly.
2. Install bubbler assembly per the installation details at locations shown on the drawings.
3. Adjust the output flow of each bubbler for best performance.

3.08 **INSTALLATION OF DRIP IRRIGATION COMPONENTS**:

A. **Remote Control Valve (RCV) Assembly for Drip Laterals**:
1. Flush mainline pipe before installing RCV assembly.
2. Locate as shown on the drawings. Wire connectors and waterproof sealant shall be used to connect control wires to remote control valve wires. Connectors and sealant shall be installed per the manufacturer's recommendations.
3. Install only one RCV to valve box. Locate at least 12 inches from and align with nearby walls or edges of paved areas. Group RCV assemblies together where practical.
4. Arrange grouped valve boxes in rectangular patterns.

B. **Zone Control Valve Assembly**: Install at locations shown on the drawings.

C. **Drip Emitter Assembly**:
1. Locate as shown on the drawings and installation details.
2. Flush lateral pipe before installing emitter assembly.
3. Cut emitter outlet distribution tubing square.
4. Install an access sleeve as part of each multiple-outlet emitter assembly for emitters located in turf areas.
5. Use tools and techniques recommended by the manufacturer. Make openings for barb-mounted emitters with the emitter manufacturer's hole-punching tool.

D. **Flush Cap Assembly**: Install at the end of each drip irrigation lateral pipe as shown on the installation details.

E. **Pressure Adjustment Procedure**:
1. Fully open all zone control valves and energize the RCV assembly.
2. Determine which emitter has the least outlet pressure; this is the critical emitter.
3. Identify zone control valve associated with the critical emitter; this is the critical zone control valve.
4. Set discharge pressure of RCV such that the the critical pressure compensating emitter has a pressure of 25 PSI ± 5 PSI. Measure with pressure gauge attached to critical emitter.
5. Identify the critical emitter for remaining zone control valves.
6. Set each zone control valve such that its critical pressure compensating emitter has a pressure of 25 PSI ± 5 PSI.

3.09 **INSTALLATION OF CONTROL SYSTEM COMPONENTS**:

A. **Irrigation Controller Unit**:
1. The location of the controller unit as depicted on the drawings is approximate; the engineer/landscape architect/owner's representative will determine the exact site location during sprinkler layout review.
2. Lightning protection: Drive 8-foot copper-clad grounding rod into the soil. If rock prevents driving, bury at least four feet deep. Use one rod for each controller. Connect controller to grounding rod with AWG No. 10 solid conductor copper wire. Secure wire to grounding rod with brass or bronze clamp. Locate the connection in a separate valve box.
3. Attach wire markers to the ends of control wires inside the controller unit housing. Label wires with the identification number (see drawings) of the remote control valve to which the control wire is connected.
4. Install a 120-volt, 15-amp switched and grounded 3-prong receptacle with GFIC inside the controller unit housing.
5. Connect control wires to the corresponding controller terminal.

B. **Control Wire**:
   1. Bundle control wires where two or more are in the same trench. Bundle with pipe wrapping tape spaced at 10-foot intervals.
   2. Control wiring may be chiseled into the soil utilizing a vibratory plow device specifically manufactured for pipe pulling and wire installation. Appropriate chisel must be used so that wire is fed into a chute on the chisel, and wire is not subject to pulling tension. Minimum burial depth must equal minimum cover previously listed.
   3. Provide a 24-inch excess length of wire in an 8-inch diameter loop at each 90-degree change of direction, at both ends of sleeves, and at 100-foot intervals along continuous runs of wiring. Do not tie wiring loop. Coil 24-inch length of wire within each remote control valve box.
   4. Install common ground wire and one control wire for each remote control valve. Multiple valves on a single control wire are not permitted.
   5. If a control wire must be spliced, make splice with wire connectors and waterproof sealant, installed per the manufacturer's instructions. Locate splice in a valve box which contains an irrigation valve assembly, or in a separate 6-inch round valve box.
      Use same procedure for connection to valves as for in-line splices.
   6. Unless noted on plans, install wire parallel with and below PVC mainline pipe.
   7. Protect wire not installed with PVC mainline pipe with a continuous run of warning tape placed in the backfill six inches above the wiring.
C. **Instrumentation**:
   1. Install sensors per the installation details and manufacturer's recommendations. Install at locations shown on the drawings.
   2. Install electrical connections between central control unit components and sensors per manufacturer's recommendations.
D. **Power Wire**:
   1. Route power wire as directed on plans. Install with a minimum number of field splices. If a power wire must be spliced, make splice with recommended connector, installed per manufacturer's recommendations. Locate all splices in a separate 10-inch round valve box. Coil 2 feet of wire in valve box.
   2. All power wire shall be laid in trenches. The use of a vibratory plow is not permitted.
   3. Green wire shall be used as the common ground wire from power source to all satellites.
   4. Carefully backfill around power wire to avoid damage to wire insulation or wire connectors.
   5. Unless noted on plans, install wire parallel with and below mainline pipe. Install wire 2 inches below top of PVC mainline pipe.
   6. Encase wire not installed with PVC mainline pipe in electrical conduit with a continuous run of warning tape placed in the backfill, 6 inches above the wiring.

3.10 **INSTALLATION OF OTHER COMPONENTS**:
A. **Tools and Spare Parts**:
   1. Prior to the review at completion of construction, supply to the owner operating keys, servicing tools, spare parts, test equipment, and any other items indicated in the general notes on the drawings.
B. **Other Materials**: Install other materials or equipment shown on the drawings or installation details which are part of the irrigation system, even though such items may not have been referenced in these specifications.

3.11 **PROJECT RECORD (AS-BUILT) DRAWINGS**:
A. Submit record drawings under provisions of Section 01700 – Contractor Closeout, Record Documents.
B. Record pipe and wiring network alterations. Record work that is installed differently than shown on the construction drawings. Record accurate

reference dimensions, measured from at least two permanent reference points, of each irrigation system valve, each backflow prevention device, each controller or control unit, each sleeve end, each stub-out for future pipe or wiring connections, and other irrigation components enclosed within a valve box.

C. Prior to construction completion, obtain from the engineer/landscape architect/owner's representative a reproducible Mylar copy of the drawings. Using technical drafting pen or CAD, duplicate information contained on the project drawings maintained on site. Label each sheet "Record Drawing". Completion of the record drawings will be a prerequisite for the review at the completion of the irrigation system installation.

3.12 **WINTERIZATION AND SPRING START-UP**:

A. Winterize the irrigation system in the fall following completion of the project and start up the irrigation system the following spring. Repair any damage caused in improper winterization at no additional cost to the owner. Coordinate the winterization and start-up with the landscape maintenance personnel.

3.13 **MAINTENANCE**:

A. Upon completion of construction and review by the engineer/landscape architect/owner's representative, maintain irrigation system for a duration of 30 calendar days. Make periodic examinations and adjustments to irrigation system components to achieve the most desirable application of water.

B. Following completion of the contractor's maintenance period, the owner will be responsible for maintaining the system in working order during the remainder of the guarantee/warranty period, for performing necessary minor maintenance, for trimming around sprinklers, for protecting against vandalism, and for preventing damage after the landscape maintenance operation.

3.14 **CLEANUP**:

A. Upon completion of work, remove from the site all machinery, tools, excess materials, and rubbish.

Appendix D

Memorandum of Design

February 1, 19XX
To: Whom It May Concern
Re: *project name*
    MEMORANDUM OF DESIGN
    LANDSCAPE IRRIGATION

The purpose of this memorandum is to present the concept for the landscape irrigation system including the anticipated irrigation approach, primary equipment, recommendations, annual water usage, and budgetary construction costs for the above referenced project.

Design Intent and Concept

The goal is to design an irrigation system that will maintain aesthetically pleasing plant material with a reasonable initial construction cost and minimal annual maintenance costs.

The irrigation system anticipated will be a combination sprinkler/drip system using pop-up rotor or pop-up spray sprinklers on turf grasses, pop-up spray sprinklers on perennial beds, and point source drip emitters on non-turf plant materials located outside of turf areas. The primary plant material types will be irrigated on separate laterals.

The water source will be potable water from the point of connection (POC) that is located at northwest corner of the project. The irrigation meter will be 2 inches in size with a capacity of 70 GPM. A main system shut-off valve (manual) will be provided for maintenance. A solenoid-operated master valve will provide for automated shut-downs in the event of a mainline break.

The POC will have a curb stop valve, water meter, backflow prevention device, and an irrigation master valve. The backflow prevention assembly will be housed in an expanded metal cage with steel posts set in concrete at each corner as added protection for the assembly.

Control of the landscape irrigation system will be facilitated by a controller located at the POC. The controller will be pedestal mounted in a stainless steel enclosure. Low-voltage (24 VAC) wiring from the controller to solenoid valves will be single-strand wire suitable for direct burial. It is recommended that controller be located at or near the POC location where 110 VAC power (low amperage) will be required.

Instrumentation will be provided with the control system to include a flow sensor for flow measurement and an anemometer to prevent irrigation under windy conditions.

The mainline will be Class 200 PVC pipe and sprinkler and drip lateral pipe will be Class 160 PVC. Specified pipe burial depths will be 24 inches for mainline pipe and

18 inches for lateral pipe. Control wiring will be adjacent to or below mainline burial depths. Where irrigation mainline and control wire must cross under hard surface, pipe and wire will be routed through separate PVC Class 200 sleeves.

The irrigation system will be designed to be winterized using compressed air injected at a winterization point located at the POC. Gate valves will provide localized isolation of sections of the system to assist in system winterization and maintenance.

Remote control valves will be rated at 200 PSI, having flow control and pressure regulation capabilities. Sprinkler laterals will be designed for 65 to 70 GPM ± and will utilize 2-inch remote control valves whenever possible. Each manual and remote control valve will be housed in a single valve box for valve access.

Quick coupling valves will be located on approximately 200-foot spacings for incidental water needs.

Sprinklers will be spaced not to exceed the manufacturer's recommended maximum spacing and to avoid over-spray onto hard surfaces or unirrigated areas. All sprinklers will be specified to be installed on swing joints or swing pipe.

Drip emitters will be of the pressure-compensating type installed on UV radiation-resistant polyethylene hose at each tree and shrub location.

Landscape Water Requirement

The landscaped area is projected to include approximately _____ acres of irrigated turf. Irrigated turf in the area is estimated to have a peak season daily irrigation water requirement of _____ inches. The daily water requirement during peak season evapo-transpiration for the _____ acre turf area is _____ gallons of water.

Irrigation Equipment Recommendations

Specific irrigation equipment recommendations are as noted in Table 1.

Probable Construction Costs

An opinion of probable construction costs has been prepared based on irrigated areas and an irrigation concept as described previously.

TABLE 1
Landscape Irrigation Equipment Recommendations

EQUIPMENT TYPE	ATTACHMENT NUMBER	PRODUCT DESCRIPTION
Remote control valve	AA	
Pop-up spray sprinkler	BB	
Pop-up rotor sprinkler	CC	
Drip emitter	DD	
Controller	EE	
Quick coupling valve	FF	
Mainline pipe	n/a	Class 200, belled end PVC
Sprinkler lateral pipe	n/a	Class 160, belled end PVC
Drip lateral pipe	n/a	Class 160, belled end PVC and UV radiation resistent polyethylene
Sleeving	n/a	Class 200, belled end PVC

TABLE 2
Landscape Irrigation Opinion of Probable Construction Costs

PROJECT AREA	LANDSCAPE TREATMENT	QUANTITY	UNIT COST	EXTENDED COST
subheading	Shrubs	SF	$x.xx/SF	$xxx,xxx
	Irrigated turf grass	SF	$x.xx/SF	
subheading	Perennials	SF	$x.xx/SF	
	Shrubs	SF	$x.xx/SF	
	Irrigated turf grass	SF	$x.xx/SF	
Total Probable Cost of Landscape Irrigation				$xxx,xxx

1. Costs that may have an impact, such as contractual traffic control, mandatory wage rates, or other extraordinary costs, are not included.
2. Water source plant investment fees, if required, have not been included.

BIBLIOGRAPHY

Bliesner, Ron D., and Jack Keller. *Sprinkle and Trickle Irrigation*. New York: Van Nostrand Reinhold, 1990.

Bucks, D. A., and F. S. Nakayama. *Developments in Agricultural Engineering 9—Trickle Irrigation for Crop Production: Design, Operation and Management*. The Netherlands: Elsevier, 1986.

Frost, Kenneth R., Walter W. Hinz, Claude H. Pair, and Crawford Reid. *Irrigation*, 5th ed. Virginia: The Irrigation Association, 1983.

Goldberg, Dan, Baruch Garnet, and Daniel Raman. *Drip Irrigation—Principles, Design, and Agricultural Practices*. Israel: Drip Irrigation Scientific Publications, 1976.

James, Larry G. *Farm Irrigation System Design*. New York: John Wiley & Sons, Inc., 1988.

Karmeli, David, and Jack Keller. *Trickle Irrigation Design*. California: Rain Bird Sprinkler Manufacturing Corporation, 1975.

Pettygrove, G. S., and T. Asano. *Irrigation with Reclaimed Municipal Wastewater—A Guidance Manual*. Michigan: Lewis Publishers, 1985.

United States Golf Association. *Wastewater Reuse for Golf Course Irrigation*. Michigan: Lewis Publishers, 1994.

Index